FOREIGN POLICY OF TUNISIA

FOREIGN POLICY OF TUNISIA: Transition from Colonial Period to Post Colonial (1946-66)

Anju Bali

GYAN

The publication of this book was financially supported by ICSSR and the responsibility for the facts stated, opinions expressed or conclusions reached are entirely that of the author and ICSSR accepts no responsibility for them.

ICSSR Consultant

Prof. Mansura Haider, Consultant-Ground Floor, Indira Gandhi National Centre for Arts 11, Mansingh Road, 1, C.V. Mess, Janpath, New Delhi-110001.

ISBN : 978-81-212-1234-2

First Published 2014

Published by

Gyan Publishing House
23, Main Ansari Road, Darya Ganj,
New Delhi- 110002
Ph. : 23282060, 23261060, E-mail: books@gyanbooks.com

Laser Typesetting : Sanya Computers, Delhi, *Printed at* : G. Print Process, Delhi

Cataloging in Publication Data—DK

Courtesy: D.K. Agencies (P) Ltd. <docinfo@dkagencies.com>

Pandey, Anju Bali.

Foreign policy of Tunisia : transition from colonial period to post colonial (1946-66) / Anju Bali.

p. cm.

Includes bibliographical references (p.) and index.

ISBN 9788121212342

1. Tunisia—Foreign relations. 2. Tunisia—Foreign economic relations. I. Title.

DDC 327.611 23

Contents

Preface

The foreign policy of any country in the post modern society secures the infrastructural importance. These days Tunisia is crossing the major domestic and foreign challenges but the rational outlook of the people of Tunisia towards this created positive environment in the country. Despite cordial relations between the first President of Tunisia Habib Bourguiba and the French Government, Tunisia often clashed with France. In October 1946, leaders of the Algerian National liberation Front (FLN) were kidnapped by French forces on their way to a meeting in Tunis with President Bourguiba. Demonstrations broke out in Tunis, and relations were strained to the point that Tunisia recalled its ambassador from Paris. Tunisians supported the Algerian rebels openly. This caused widespread French indignation and led to numerous protests and culminated in a suspension of French economic aid to Tunisia in May 1957.

With other Arab countries Tunisia's relations since 1956 have been complicated and troubled. They were distorted from the start by the involvement with France. Relations with Morocco became tense after Morocco failed to support Tunisia in the latter's quarrel with Egypt at the Arab Leaque meeting in 1958. In 1960 relations with Morocco deteriorated when Tunisia cosponsored Mauritaina for admission to the United Nations and became the only Arab country to recognise the new state, whose territory Morocco claimed as part of its own. The Moroccan ambassador left Tunis, and violent attacks were made by Moroccan press and state radio on Tunisia. These were stilled for some time after the funeral of Muhammad V early in 1961, but subsequently they increased again.

Tunisia had good relations with the more moderate African states, notably Nigeria, Togo, Cameroon and the French community. Relations with Libya reached a low ebb in August 1985 after Tunisia expelled a total of 283 Libyan nationals, including most of the Libyan diplomats in retaliation against Col. Gadaffi's decision to expel some 30,000 Tunisian working in Libya. Gadaffi threatened to use of military force. However, Morocco offered to mediate between the two countries. In September 1985, Tunisia severed diplomatic relations with Libya.

Relations between Tunisia and the United States were close. Despite minimal private U.S. investments in Tunisia, the United States had been the largest single provider of aid to the country, providing more than $1billion in the three decades since independence. U.S. assistance was intended to foster economic development and contribute to the stability of a nation whose policies with a few notable exceptions, have generally accorded with those of the United States. Beyond this confluence of views on matters of mutual importance, Tunisia's location beside the narrow sea lanes of the central Mediterranean is of great strategic value to the Western alliance in general and to the U.S. VIth fleet in particular. Initially, development aid constituted the largest portion of U.S. assistance, since the late 1970s however military aid rose in prominence. This contrasts with an annual total aid commitment of roughly $50 million at the end of the 1970s less than half of which was earmarked for the armed forces. The U.S. decision to emphasize military aid came in response to Tunisian government claims that its small armed forces needed more and better equipment to protect the country from neighbours intent in meddling in its domestic politics. Libya's role in orchestrating the attack on Gafsa in 1980 proved that the accusations leveled against Qadhafi had some substances. The United States agreed to Tunisian requests to increase the already expanding military assistance programme by making highly sophisticated weaponry available to the Tunisian military.

This book interprets the conceptual and evolutionary frame work of Tunisian Society. In this context it interprets about the West Asian and North African regional system, the formation of West Asian and North Africa State system, the Arab world, the evolution of regional system, between identity and sovereignty, supra state identity, state formation and foreign policy making, regional stability, decision making in foreign policy, internal setting and external setting. The book deals with Tunisia's relations with the Afro-Asian Arab and Maghreb world. It includes Tunisia's National identity, the Maghreb, emergence of Maghreb concept and Maghreb Nationalism, the conference unity of 1958, Tunisia's relationship with India, Tunisia and NAM etc... It also analyses the relationship between Tunisia and France. In this journey this book focuses on the Tunisian Nationalism, Neo-Destour Nationalism and France, the first Franco-Tunisian experiences and 1938 crisis, Tunisia and Second World War, quest for national self determination in Tunisia, the Bizerte crisis, Arab League support etc... The book also deals with Tunisia and Cold War and goes on to discuss the policy of Tunisia during the Cold War, Tunisia's relations with United States, historical foundations: pre independence relations, Tunisia's relation with the other Western and Eastern countries, Tunisia and United Nations etc... it also discusses economic factors as the determinants of International Relations and emphasises the foreign policy and politico economic agenda, progress towards economic autonomy, the unsolved problems, the end of decolonisation, land Nationalisation, the suspension of French financial assistance, social security law, Neo-Destour socialism: the birth of Economic Planning, the cooperative experiments, the Trade Union Movement and Bourguiba's system, politicisation of cooperation and development etc... the book also synthesises the decision and policy making of planning, foreign policy, socio-economic and political challenges of the country etc....

This work cannot be completed without the constant encouragement and guidance of Prof. A.K. Pasha, former Chairman and Director, Gulf Studies Programme, Centre for West Asian Studies, School of International Studies, Jawaharlal Nehru University, New Delhi who has been a constant source of support and inspiration in my academic pursuits. I am also thankful to A.K. Gupta of ICSSR, Dr. Arshi Khan of AMU, Prof. Kumar Suresh NEPA, Prof. Bulbul Dhar Jamia Millia Islamia, I cannot forget the cooperation and support of His Excellency Ambassador of Tunisia in India Tarek Azouz, Raouff Chatty, and the staff of the Embassy. The constant support of my husband Dr. R.B. Pandey and daughter Sowmya Pandey is unforgettable in this work. I am also thankful to my sisters Rajni, Meenakshi and their family members for their support. Last but not least I would also acknowledge the cooperation my students Sayyid Umer Sameer and Salmanul Farisy.

Acknowledgements

I want to say that at the time of writing this thesis, I have received invaluable guidance and constant encouragement from my Supervisor Prof. A.K. Pasha. He has been a great and constant source of inspiration and encouragement for me. In addition his 'humane' nature with a blend of cooperative attitude has been very helpful to me. He has painstakingly revised and corrected the draft of the thesis till it was made into a coherent, concise and academically contributive one. To him I have no words to express my gratitude and I remain indebted to all he has done for me.

I am also thankful to the staff of our centre who has been generous in helping me out in all possible ways they could.

I can not forget the staff of the Embassy of Tunisia in India for their invaluable support all through the making of this thesis.

Last but not the least, I would also acknowledge the institutional support of different libraries particularly, JNU Library, Indian Council of World Affairs Library, Ministry of External Affairs Library, Parliament Library and Nehru Memorial and Museum Library, Institute of Defence Studies Analysis Library, New Delhi.

The constant inspiration from my husband Dr. R.B. Pandey, sisters Rajni, Meenakshi, and daughter Sowmya all though my life certainly can not be explained in words. Last, the mistakes in this work belong to me only and any kind of suggestions are welcome.

Anju Bali

Introduction

Foreign policy is the link between the internal politics of a state and the international system. It is at the same time a response to domestic needs and an attempt to influence the behaviour of other states. The domestic aspects of foreign policy in new states raises a variety of interesting questions. Does the nature of colonial experience and the nationalist struggle affect foreign policy goals and strategies? Do different degrees of social mobilisation, political participation, and national unity produce different approaches to foreign policy? Are there significant differences between the foreign policies of authoritarian and competitive political systems in new states? From the international point of view, a study of the foreign policy of Tunisia can contribute to an understanding of the effect of various international power configurations on the survival and development of new states. What are the effects of bipolarity, multi-polarity, the Cold War competition, international and regional tensions on the foreign policies of new states? How do the governments of new states like Tunisia perceive and exploit the international environment for their own purposes.

The emergence of the new states from the Western colonial empires since World War II provided rich material for the political-scientists, to study first hand an accelerated and conscious process of nation building, social modernisation, and economic development. It was tempting to use this opportunity to derive scientific theories about the process of development. For the policy-maker, the study of political development was infused with a sense of urgency and purpose because of the potential for political instability, revolutionary change and international involvement in the problems of new states. The experiences of the first two decade, however, demonstrated that the problems of economic and political development are not susceptible to easy generalisation and simple solutions.

Because of the paucity of internal resources and the dependence on external assistance, the governments of the new states have had to use foreign policy to achieve basic domestic goals: decolonisation, national unity, economic and social development. Foreign policy is, therefore, a measure of the capacity of a political system to respond and to manage some of its most pressing problems.

The present inquiry is a study of the foreign policy of Tunisia, in the first two decades of independence. Tunisia shared the problems and goals of the former colonial states. In addition, its policy-makers experimented at one time or another with most of the foreign policy strategies developed by the new states in the post-independence period. Tunisia's approach to the problems of decolonisation, independence, and development may contribute to an understanding of the approaches of similar states to similar problems.

Turning to the effect of domestic politics on foreign policy, one finds that Tunisia presents interesting comparisons with other countries. Tunisia enjoyed a relatively high degree of national unity; it had a long history as a territorial and political unit, a homogeneous population, and a lengthy independence struggle which exposed most of the population to the concept of Tunisian nationalism. Are there significant differences between Tunisia's foreign policy and those of other new states plagued by ethnic, religious, and linguistic diversity? For instance, does Tunisia's high degree of national unity explain its cautious attitudes towards Arab nationalism and other regional integration movements?

The victorious Tunisian nationalists created a single-party system, dominated by a single heroic figure. The system encouraged political consensus and discouraged political competition.

Tunisia, like other states which became independent in the late forties and fifties, entered an international environment characterised by intense Cold War competition. Since then, new power centres have emerged, and the competition for the allegiance of the new states of Africa and Asia has moderated.

All of the Arab states claimed to be non-aligned in the international conflict, but non-alignment had different meanings in different cases. Tunisia numbered among the moderates in intra-Arab politics and with Morocco, Libya, Jordan, Lebanon, Saudi Arabia and Kuwait followed a pro-Western form of non-alignment.

Tunisian foreign policy is not typical of foreign policies of new states in the sense that no foreign policy is typical. In addition, certain aspects of

Tunisian foreign policy are distinctive and should be singled out at this point. Like its Maghrebi neighbours, Tunisia's colonial experience was profound, and its nationalist struggle was long and difficult. Tunisia enjoyed an unusual degree of political stability and continuity which was reflected in a self-conscious and consistent foreign policy. Tunisian foreign policy also reflected the intense ties between France and its colonies before and after independence. The study is based on the hypothesis that the foreign policy of independent Tunisia in the early stages was a continuation of the policies pursued by the French administration and the nationalist movement prior to 1956, with suitable responses generated by the challenges before the new leadership after Tunisia attained its independence. The focus of this study is from the foundation of Tunisia's foreign-policy to its application in world affairs and have been studied under the following chapters.

The first chapter analysed several factors that influenced the making of Tunisia's foreign policy and to generalised with the main characteristics of making of foreign policy.

The second chapter comprises a study of Tunisia's relations with Afro-Asian World. Special emphasis to its relations with the Arab world and its attitude toward the question of Maghrebi Unity.

The third chapter focussed on the policy pursued by Tunisia towards France before and after independence.

The fourth chapter focussed on the policy pursued by Tunisia during the Cold War period. Three factors which focussed are—the role of France, as a protectorate power till 1956, the attitude of the Tunisian nationalists towards the Cold War and the two Super Powers, and finally the attitude of independent Tunisia towards the Cold War.

The fifth chapter analysed the economic challenges, faced by the Tunisians, because of limited resources and failures of economic policies adopted by the government.

The chapter six is the conclusion, based on the above analysis which reflects the overall foreign policy of Tunisia during the first three decades after the independence.

It is within this framework the Tunisia's foreign policy is studied.

1 Conceptual Framework

Given Tunisia's small size, limited resources, and military vulnerability, Tunisia had managed to establish a respectable position in world affairs.[1] Both domestic political and foreign policies have been structured to service requirements for a stable domestic, regional, and international environment which allowed Tunisia to exploit the maximum of economic opportunities with the least political resistance. Its foreign-policy goals have been modest, its techniques eminently practical and realistic, and its results undramatic, though very beneficial to the country in terms of economic assistance.

The impacts of imperialism, above all the imperialist imposition of the regional state system and the indigenous reaction to it, were the first major forces shaping and differentiating regional states and their foreign policies. The most crucial differentiating factor was the level of damage thus inflicted: the more the state system thwarted indigenous interests and identity, the more status quo social forces inside the states were weakened and the more radical, middle-class, or even plebeian forces were mobilised. Where this issued in revolutions, revolutionary coups, or transforming elections that turned states over to these forces, they harnessed state power and policy to their revisionist ambitions. Conversely, the more the new state system satisfied indigenous interests and identity, as in Tunisia, the more relatively status quo elites survived and newly independent states followed policies accommodating their states to the West.

In the Arab world, states' differential experiences with Western imperialism issued in a basic ideological cleavage

The nationalist republics that sought to challenge the Western-sponsored regional disposition were ranged against the conservative monarchies that, created with Western assistance, relied on Western protection against nationalist forces.

Indeed, by the late 1950s, this domestically driven ideological heterogeneity had interlocked with the strategically driven competition of the world's two Superpowers to project their influence into the West Asia and North Africa region. The aid and protection they gave to the opposing regional camps consolidated the polarisation of the regional system in an Arab Cold War that mirrored bipolarity at the global level.[2]

The West Asia and North Africa (WANA) Regional System

West Asia and North Africa (WANA) regional system is taken here to be comprised of the Arab League members, Turkey, Iran, and Israel. The Arab states, with shared identity, intense interactions, and membership in a regional organisation, the Arab League, are judged to make-up the core of the system. None of this means that they necessarily act cohesively in foreign policy; but when the Arab world is divided it is much more vulnerable to penetration from the great powers and to threats from its north Arab neighbours. The non-Arab states Turkey, Iran, and Israel comprise, by virtue of their relative exclusion from the core community, the periphery of the system, but they are, nonetheless, members by virtue of their geographic contiguity and intimate involvement in the region's conflicts. This makes them integral parts of the regional balance of power; in particular, they have tended either to constitute threats to the weaker Arab core or have acted to contain its instability in alliance with external powers.[3]

The Formation of the West Asia and North Africa State System

The WANA marked by high incongruity between the nation (identity) and the territorial state (sovereignty). If, in some respects, the dilemma of the Arab world is "one nation/

many states", there and in the non-Arab West Asia, the multinational state ("one state, plural nations") is also the rule rather than the exception. This is bound to complicate foreign policy-making.

With the end of World War I and the break-up of the Ottoman Empire, what had been previously a largely unified region was fragmented, in the style of the 1878 Congress of Berlin, into bounded territories that had little regard for the idea of nation. This was the enduring European legacy to the region.[4] A partitioned West Asia became a ward of European power.[5] The attitude of the great powers was that the peoples outside the European region were not really in a position to govern themselves.[6] In the case of the Middle East, the mandatory arrangements of the great powers were designed to cloak the wartime agreements that Britain and France had made, regarding the Arab provinces of the Ottoman Empire and where the principle of self-determination of people would not immediately apply.[7] The great powers restructured the region using an Arab 'elite that was divided and unprepared for rule.[8] This set in motion the development of a nationalism, both defensive and negative, that aimed in its various strands at ridding each part of the region of foreign occupation.[9] It also contributed to the destruction of the population's trust in the Western-oriented elite that had cooperated with Europe, destabilising the region's nascent politics.[10] This formative period contributed significantly to the authoritarian character of the emerging regimes as well as the rules and trading structures that circumscribed the relations among the states of the region.

The Arab World

The Arab states, mostly successors of the Ottoman Empire, retain high degree of linguistic and cultural similarity. Similar music and art, food, marriage, and child-rearing practices are recognisable region-wide, extended family ties frequently cross borders. The common Arabic language—the critical ingredient of nationhood-has, owing to a standard newspaper and media Arabic, become more homogeneous, stunting the evolution of national dialects as the linguistic basis of separate nations.

Uniquely in the Arab world, not this or that border, but state boundaries in general, have been regarded by many Arabs as arbitrarily and externally imposed at the expense of Arabism, depriving them of the legitimacy and sanctity they enjoy elsewhere. It is not that most Arabs reject any state boundaries; indeed, most have not insisted on a single Arab state, but the extreme fragmentation of the region is viewed as a divide-and-rule strategy by imperialism and a cause of Arab weakness. At the level of formal ideology, this sentiment was manifest in the doctrines of Arab nationalism, which viewed all Arabic-speakers as forming a nation the states of which, at a minimum, ought to act together for common interests, or be constitutionally confederated, or, in its most ambitious form. Ba'thism be merged into a single state embracing this nation. Arabism is enshrined in state constitutions: Jabbour found thirteen Arab constitutions that defined the nation as the Arab nation, with only Lebanon and Tunisia referring to a Lebanese and Tunisian nationhood.[11]

Nevertheless, there have always been territorial fault lines in the region that could potentially generate identities supportive of territorially-based (as opposed to linguistically or ethnically-based) separate nations. Harik argues that a viable basis of statehood exists in a multitude of geographical entities with distinct historical experiences: where minority sects established autonomous regimes (Yemen, Oman, Lebanon); where tribal or tribal-religious movements founded states (Saudi Arabia); or where Mamluk elites achieved autonomy as Ottoman power declined (Tunisia). The Western imposition of the contemporary state system on these protonations, defining permanent boundaries that protected them from absorption, and endowing them with ruling elites and state apparatuses, crystallised their statehood.[12]

The Evolution of the Regional System

In the years after World War II, the periphery States—Turkey, Iran, and Israel—more advanced in nation building, militarily stronger, and aligned with the West, flanked a weak, fragmented Arab core barely emerging from colonial control. The Arab states were narrowly-based oligarchies or dynasties, highly penetrated by the great power, above all by Great Britain, which retained bases and treaty relations with regimes led by its clients. The main threat to the system was instability within the individual states: the weak popular loyalty to newly-imposed regimes and boundaries, regimes' inability to politically incorporate the rising middle class, gross maldistribution of wealth, still incomplete decolonisation, and the loss of Palestine all soon delegitimised the regimes even as they struggled to consolidate their formal independence. As such, foreign policy as chiefly used to counter domestic threats: either regimes used anti-imperialist rhetoric to shore up their fragile legitimacy or they sought protection from the Western powers against domestic opposition.

The Arab League attempted to institutionalise respect for the sovereignty of individual states while acknowledging shared Arab identities and the need for a collective response to the common threat from Zionism. Its legitimacy was, however, tarnished by its failure to coordinate the defense of Palestine, and the most it, achieved was a consensus against relations with Israel.

Egypt-Centric Pan-Arab System

Oligarchic multipolarity was transformed by congruence between the destabilisation of oligarchic states amidst the political mobilisation of the middle class and the emergence of the radical Nasser regime in Egypt, whose head start in the incorporation of popular support made it the only stable Arab state. Nasser deployed trans-state Pan-Arab ideology to challenge the old regimes, upsetting the oligarchic "balance of weakness." He put Egypt at the centre of the Arab world, giving it a new cohesion, rolling back Western control, and enforcing Arab solidarity against the non-Arab periphery.

The Maghrebi Unity

The Maghrebi dimension overlaps with Tunisia's

membership in the community of Arab states. Powerful Egypt and turbulent Sudan lie to Tunisia's east. Beyond them lie the Mashreq and the Persian Gulf, the conflicts and rivalries of which have a habit of drawing in Arab states further a field. The strategic importance of the WANA region, and the vast hydrocarbon deposits that lie within have also invited international interest that Tunisia has had to take account of in its own foreign policy-making. While Tunisia's African identity and the economic potential of that continent have not incited much international interest and have, therefore, taken a relative back seat in Tunisian foreign policy-making, Islam has in recent years become an important issue in domestic politics with a spill over effect for foreign policy.

Foreign Policy Determinants

The Global Level: Core-periphery Relations

The West Asia and North Africa (WANA) once an independent state, has been turned into a periphery of the Western-dominated world system. According to L. Carl Brown, the West Asia is a penetrated system, one subject to an exceptional level of external intervention and control yet, by virtue of its cultural distinctiveness, stubbornly resistant to subordination.[13] Western penetration has endured in the post-colonial era. Motivated by contiguous location and the exceptional concentration of great power interests—oil, transit routes, Israel. To many Arabs and Muslims, imperialism, far from dead, persists in new forms. As Buzan points out, the Islamic world is the only classical civilisation that has not managed to re-establish itself as a significant world actor since the retreat of Western empires.[14] This defines the parameters within which West Asia states must operate and is a major issue in the politics of the region.

Structuralism, the international-relations theory most concerned with explaining global core-periphery relations, has been widely used by scholars of the West Asia to understand this reality.[15] According to Galtung's influential "Structural Theory of Imperialism," periphery states, including those of the West Asia are subordinated within a global hierarchy, dependent on and tied to the core powers while being only very weakly related to each other.[16] Indeed, many scholars argue that the transformation of the Middle East under imperialism produced an outcome that resembles Galtung's model.

First, where once there was a universal trading empire, imperialism fragmented the region into a multitude of relatively weak and, to an extent, artificial states. As Brown shows, these states, at odds with each other and insecure, sought external patrons and resources for the regional power struggle set in motion by this fragmentation. Especially where the new states emerged as Western protectorates against indigenous opposition, they have remained dependent for their security on the Western global powers long after formal independence. Unlike India and China, the post-colonial state system nullifies rather than restores the pre-colonial universal state.

Second, the parallel incorporation of the regional economy into the world capitalist system shattered regional economic interdependence and restructured the region into a classic dependent economy marked by the production and export of primary products (e.g., cotton and oil) and dependence on imports of manufactures and technology. Oil may be thought to be fundamentally different from other primary products, given the high-level of revenues it generates and the dependence of core economies on it, but in fact the recycling of petro dollars has perpetuated overall regional dependency on the import of capital (foreign aid, loans, and investment), and hence high-levels of debt, in a way not significantly different from the export of other primary products.[17]

Economic dependency means a major function of foreign policy must be to secure and maximise resource flows from external sources. Because states' revenue bases are exceptionally dependent on external resources—whether foreign aid, taxes on foreign trade, or oil revenues and not on 'domestically raised taxes, they may be more responsive to the demands of global powers than to domestic opinion in designing their policies.[18] Indeed, some West Asia states explicitly design their foreign policies to serve economic ends; from trading policies favourable to great power patrons in return for aid to merely subordinating nationalism in policy-making to ensuring a favourable investment climate.

Third, according to Galtung, the "bridgehead" that the "core" establishes in "the centre of the periphery nation 'for the joint benefit of both" is equally important to sustaining the region's subordination to the "core"[19] Specifically, imperialism, in implanting "client elites" and fostering "compradors"—traders and exporters has created shared economic interests between the core and dominant local classes while retarding national bourgeoisies with an interest in autonomous national and regional development. Arguably, the current dominant form of this relation is manifested in the way the overwhelming investment of surplus petro dollars by Arab oil monarchies in the West gives their ruling families a much greater stake in the core economics than in that of the region. According to Bruce Moon, such relations tend to generate a "constrained consensus" that results in significant congruence between the foreign policies of regional states and those of the core. This is a function of the overlap of local elites' economic interests, world views (through Western education), and threat perceptions (fear of radical movements) with those of core elites.[20]

Fourth, while such manipulation of interests is far more important than crude power in sustaining regional subordination, where there is insufficient overlap of interest's, the core powers use economic punishments withdrawal of aid, economic sanctions, and the like-against economically vulnerable regional states.[21] As a last resort, military force is periodically used by Western powers to prevent in Brown's words, any 'regional power trying to "organise the system" against them. Such intervention by the hegemonic powers is consistent with Wallerstein's argument that the maintenance and expansion of the world capitalist system depends on a hegemon a dominant state that defends the system, breaks down barriers to core-periphery economic links (e.g., promoting economic liberalisation), and assures reliable access to raw materials, especially the cheap energy concentrated in the West Asia.[22] The core periphery struggle over oil has been a dominant theme in the region's politics from the overthrow of Iran's Mossadeq to the formation of the Organisation of Petroleum Exporting Countries (OPEC) and continued till date.

The structuralist view of world capitalist dominance over the region is contested by more realist-centred views and, even in the structuralist view, core-periphery relations are not static. Global penetration does not mean the region lacks all autonomy in the conduct of foreign policy. First, as Oran Young argues, there is always a certain discontinuity between the possession of global power and its exercise in regional arenas: to the extent great powers are unable or uninterested in fully controlling a regional sub-system, the potential for regional autonomy increases.[23]

This has been facilitated when, as during the Cold War, global bipolarity "split the core," so to speak. The superpower rivalry that made local clients valuable actually gave regional states leverage over their patrons, even allowing the "tail to wag the dog" over regional issues where the client's vital interests were more at stake than those of the global patron. It also allowed them to extract enhanced military capabilities that would, ironically, make external intervention more costly. Bipolarity arguably gave local states a crucial three-decade window of opportunity to consolidate their autonomy.[24]

Additionally, as Thompson has observed, the lack of horizontal ties among periphery states in Galtung's model applies in the West Asia chiefly at the economic level and has not prevented the survival in the region of dense trans-state cultural and political ties; these provide potential vehicles for the mobilisation of region-wide anti-imperialism by nationalist regimes seeking a collective challenge to the dependency-system.[25] Thus, in the 1950s superpower competition, in limiting the ability of the Western great powers to use military force in the region, cleared space for Nasser's attempt to use Pan-Arab ideology to organise the Arab states, albeit briefly, against Western intrusion.

Also, at the economic level, local states made efforts to reduce the asymmetry of their relation to the core. The limits of such strategies were, however, underlined by the fate of poorer states such as Egypt, where statist failure ended in a post-Nasser dependency on donors who expected and got an end to Egypt's radical nationalism.

In addition, the globalisation of capitalism is drawing regional states into ever denser webs of economic dependency—or interdependency. While globalisation continues to meet more resistance in the West Asia than elsewhere, notably in the region's evasion of full economic liberalisation, increasing numbers of states, such as Tunisia and Egypt, see it as an opportunity for increased investment and markets. They have seemingly made the decision to be players rather than victims, even if this means the sacrifice of some autonomy. But to the extent external penetration of the region tends to generate popular local resistance—recently in the form of political Islam—elites may have to temper such ambitions.[26]

In summation, the impact of the region's position in the world system on the foreign policies of local states is by no means straightforward, (1) Where the interests of local regimes overlap, with those of core patrons, reason of state and alliance with a great power coincide and states tend to "bandwagon" with their global patron to contain local threats, (2) On the other hand, penetration generates resistance and where nationalist movements come to 'power, nationalist regimes have sought to organise a regional coalition to balance against external powers, (3) However, this is only possible under favourable conditions: 'when the great powers are divided (as in the Cold War)—and hegemonic intervention is thus deterred, and when the region is relatively united against the outside', the conditions for regional autonomy may be better than in the reverse case.

Between Identity and Sovereignty

The unique features of the WANA state system specifically the uneasy relation of identity and state sovereignty, immensely complicate foreign policy-making in the West Asia. The realist model, in which elites represent loyal populations insulated from external influence in the conduct of foreign policy, must be substantially modified in analysis of the region. Many West Asia states lack the full features—impermeability, secure national identity—that realism assumes. The Arab world, in particular, is less well-represented by realism's impenetrable "billiard balls" than (in Paul Noble's words) a set of interconnected organisms separated only by porous membranes.[27]

Indeed, the consolidation of a system of nation-states in the region is obstructed by the profound flaws originating in its largely external imposition: the resulting often arbitrary borders and ill-fit between states and national identities mean that loyalty to the individual states is contested by substate and suprastate identities. The resultant embedding of the state system in a matrix of fluid multiple identities means that the "national interest" that realism assumes underlies foreign policy is problematic and contested.

Suprastate Identity. While irredentism is a feature of much of the Third World, what makes the WANA region, or more specifically its Arab core, unique is its history of exceptional suprastate identities. Because the state system was imposed on a pre-existing cultural and linguistic unity that more or less persists, the mass loyalty to the state typical where it corresponds to a definite nation is, in the Arab world, diluted and limited by strong popular identifications with larger communities the Arab nation and the Islamic *umma*.[28] The result, according to Kienle, is a system of territorial states, not-so far at least-nation-states.[29] This is most striking in the most artificial state (Syria, Jordan), but even in those such as Egypt, which have their own viable separate identities, suprastate identities sufficiently persist to prevent the consolidation of distinct nation-states.

The result, according to Bahgat Korany, is a duality where ruling elites are caught between *raison de la nation (Pan-Arabism) and raison d'etat* (sovereignty) in foreign policy-making. On the one hand, as Kienle observed, state elites have treated the Arab world as a single arena at political competition and mass publics have believed that shared Arab interests—the Palestine cause, autonomy from the West—should limit the sovereign right to put particular state interests first: on the other hand, leaders have tenaciously defended state against suprastate constraints.[30] However, as Michael Barnett's constructivist study argues, identity is "constructed" not given or constant, and the interaction of Arab leaders has determined the evolution of identity over time between Korany's Pan-Arab and sovereignty poles.[31] Arab leaders' behaviour helped to establish Pan-Arabism. They sought all-Arab leadership by competing to win over public opinion through the "outbidding" of rivals in promotion of Arab causes. The conduct of the game involved "symbolic-politics" not military force, that is, pressuring or threatening rival state elites by making Pan-Arab ideological appeals to their populations. This would be, in a consolidated nation-state system, be seen as interference in domestic affairs and have had little chance of success; it was natural and successful in the Arab world precisely because of the power of suprastate identity.

The "outbidding" of rival leaders established Pan-Arab norms of behaviour: states sought Pan-Arab leadership by raising the standards, states seeking to maintain such leadership had to be seen to live up to Pan-Arabism and states perceived to violate its norms became more vulnerable to subversion. Even Nasser felt constrained to satisfy the expectations of his Pan-Arab constituency, which "entrapped" him and his rivals in a dynamic of nationalist outbidding against Israel and led to the disastrous 1967 war, at great cost to state interests.

The interactions of leaders also "deconstructed" Pan-Arabism, so to speak: interstate disagreements over its meaning and the failures of Arab unity projects and of Arab collective institutions disillusioned and demobilised Arab publics, reducing Pan-Arab constraints on state leaders. Ironically, the use of Arabisrn by ambitious leaders to subvert rivals only heightened the sense of threat from Arab states, reinforced the differentiation between the individual states, and led state elites to promote distinctive state identities and the norm of state sovereignty to legitimise their self-defense. The outcome was, according to Barnett, "normative fragmentation." Identities remain contested, but have become too complex and multiple to sharply or uniformly constrain state elites in their conduct of foreign policy.[32]

This account of the decline of Pan-Arabism must be qualified in two respects. First, contructivism's neglect of power leads it to ignore the extent to which the decline of Pan-Arabism was ultimately rooted in the power struggles unleashed. Second, however, Pan-Arabism continues to have a residual affect on foreign policy-making. Because state identities are still no good substitute for Arab identity in most, if not all, the Arab states, the legitimacy of regimes continues to be contingent on being seen to act for Arab or Islamic interests, and political Islam, in some respects, has become a surrogate for Pan-Arabism. Foreign policy-makers must therefore still disguise, justify, or even modify the pure pursuit of reason of state. As Sela showed, 'moreover, "dualism" also led to the emergence of the Arab summit system, which institutionalised a version of Arab solidarity more compatible with state sovereignty.[33]

In summary, the Arab world retains some features of an "international society," a community hound by rules and norms; but it is sliding toward merger with the wider West Asia, a mere "system of states" mostly linked by power and interest.[34]

State Formation and Foreign Policy-making

The capacity of WANA states to cope with the pressures from their multi-level environment depends on a degree of internal cohesion. This is a junction of their level of state formation. If, they are to conduct foreign policies that rationally cope with external exigencies, state elites must command the legitimacy and institutions to establish a certain autonomy of domestic demands while sustaining some minimum-level of public support. While realism tends to take such capacity for granted, in the WANA state formation remains problematic and a matter of considerable controversy.

According to advocates of what might be called the "domestic vulnerability model" of foreign policy-making, the main threat to unstable Third World regimes is domestic, and foreign policy is a key instrument of survival at home, whether used to build domestic legitimacy through nationalism or to secure external support against domestic opposition.[35] This model is relevant in so far as Middle Eastern states, lacking secure national identity and democratic accountability, suffer legitimacy deficits; but it ignores the crucial importance of external threats' in foreign policy-making.

The most popular alternative, what might be called the "leadership dominant model," assumes that leaders, facing few institutional constraints at home, are able to translate their idiosyncratic personal values, styles and pathologies—into foreign policy.[36] However, this imagine a domestic vacuum that is questionable even in authoritarian regimes, where leaders may face informal 'domestic constraints, such as the need to protect regime legitimacy. Legitimacy in states where imperialism remains a perceived threat and where little welfare and few political rights are typically delivered tends to be exceptionally dependent on foreign-policy performance.

In the first model, leaders are "too weak," in the second "too strong," but both assume an absence of the institutions (enabling leaders to mediate between domestic demands and external constraints) that are arguably needed for the effective conduct of foreign policy. This, can, however, be misleading if taken too far. As compared to the decade after independence, there is evidence of an increasing durability and stability of West Asia states.[37]

How far this is so an empirical question and, in reality, levels of MENA state formation are very uneven. As such, the domestic politics and leadership-dominant models can be retained as ideal types reflective of more under and "overdeveloped" regime types at opposite ends of a continuum; while states with more balanced institutional profiles can be located on either side of its mid-point. Individual states are, moreover, likely to *move over time* through several different phases in state formation that are arguably associated with differences in foreign policy. The broad lines of these phases the most relevant for the Arab world are:

1. The post-independence period (roughly 1945-1960) in the Arab core was an era of weak states' governed by externally imposed or narrowly-based elites chiefly driven by fear of domestic instability from masses inflamed by nationalism. In foreign policy, they opted either to rely on external protection against such threats embedding themselves deeper into the dependency web or sought legitimacy by anti-imperialist anti-Zionist rhetoric. Each strategy had costs: the first risked domestic subversion, the second, foreign defeat or economic loss, in either case resulting in more unstable and vulnerable regimes. By contrast, in Turkey and Israel, where states' were more consolidated and institutionalisation combined with democratisation gave leaders substantial legitimacy and hence autonomy in foreign policy-making, classic reason of state prevailed.

2. By the 1960s (after 1956 in Egypt), state building was under way in the Arab world, a function of the need to master domestic instability and trans-state penetration and or to dilute international dependency. The different origins and initial social bases of regimes, however, dictated quite different state-building strategies that biased foreign policy in conflicting radical and conservative direction.[38]

In the opposite strategy, that of the authoritarian-nationalist republics, regimes originating in middle-class overthrow of Western client elites sought to consolidate their power through the mobilisation of countervailing popular support and dilution of dependency on the West. Wealth redistribution (e.g., land reform, nationalisations) and public sector-led development bolstered autonomy of the dominant classes and enabled regimes to access aid, markets, and protection from the Eastern bloc. While these regimes attempted to incorporate the middle and lower classes through party building, because the military remained a vehicle of factional politics and because they lacked a secure social base in a dominant class, they remained unstable, Hence, legitimacy was sought through radical nationalist foreign policies.

3. A third stage was apparent by the mid-1970s, namely the increased consolidation of both kinds of states.[39] The main incentive was now the high threat of war while booming oil revenues and continued superpower patronage provided the means. Successful state building shared certain commonalties across the region.

Regional Stability and Foreign Policy-making

To the degree a state system is consolidated, geo-politics becomes, as realism expects, an increasingly important determinant of foreign policy. A state's capabilities, and the strategic importance or vulnerability of its location, shapes the main threats it faces and its likely ambitions: hence, small powers are more likely to seek the protection of greater ones and stronger powers are more likely to seek spheres of regional influence. Once ideological revisionism is replaced by geo-politics, the balance of power is more likely to be stable. This tendency is apparent across the West Asia, and is, so far, the main source of regional stability.

Realist solutions to the problem of order remain more relevant in the West Asia and North Africa than elsewhere because, as Yaniv argues, transnational norms restraining inter state conduct are the least-institutionalised there.[40] This, in turn, is arguably because the conditions that pluralists expect to generate the norms that tame the power struggle-democratic cultures and economic interdependence are absent or weak in the region. Economic dependence on the core states and autarky-seeking neo-mercantilist reactions against dependence have both stunted the regional economic interdependence that pluralism expects to generate shared interests in the peaceful resolution of conflicts. Moreover, not only do most regimes remain authoritarian but, against pluralist expectations, relative democratisation does not necessarily lead to less risky or more status quo foreign policies because populations have remained mobilisable by trans-state and irredentist ideology. This is consistent with the findings of Mansfield and Snyder that established democratic regimes may be more pacific, but fragile democratising regimes are actually more inclined to war than stable authoritarian ones since winning elections encourages resort to the nationalist card.[41]

Decision-making in Foreign Policy

State decision are not made by states but on their behalf, by individuals and by groups of individuals. The central task of foreign policy analyst is to find the locus of foreign policy decision-making power. In small and developing nations, this power is usually vested in the hands of one man. This man is not difficult to identify. He is always the strongman of the country, in a non-revolutionary period, he is invariably the head of the government, and also the supreme leader of the dominant party in his country. He wields total power and is the main architect of his country's foreign policy. The reason for this is that during the struggle for independence, the clandestine nature of the liberation movement requires secrecy, stern party discipline, and complete obedience of the rank and file to the incontestable decisions of the party leader. This pattern tends to carry over into the post-independence period with the hero of the fight for independence now installed as the head of the government. The political careers of Nehru Nkrumah, Bourguiba, etc., are illustrious examples of this pattern.

Furthermore, due to his dominant personality and his acquired experiences, the reliance of the decision-maker of a small and developing nation on the advices of the experts is, in most cases, very little, and their influence upon him in matters of external policy depends upon their informal relationship with him rather than on their institutional roles. Thus, regarding the formulation of general lines of foreign policy, the role of the foreign office in small and developing countries is of tangential importance.

The decision-maker's choice of ends and means in foreign policy is determined by, among other things, his personality. Here, we do not bother ourselves with the biological construction of the decision-maker, but classify his personality according to inference drawn from his past actions. His statements, although designed for public consumption, should also be taken into consideration. In international politics explanation plays a particularly important part because much of the behaviour is verbal in form; purposes are made articulate and policies are carried out with due regard to the "announcements of other states". Besides, "it would be extremely difficult for a statesman to deceive systematically since he is himself influenced by the motives he claims and by the explanation he proffers. The motives avowed are generally deduced systems and soon become accepted as part from the prevailing values and parcel of it".[42]

This much can be said by way of generalisation about foreign policy decision-making in small and developing nations:

1. The power of foreign policy decision-making usually resides in the hands of one man. He is the undisputed leader of the country and his action is not significantly hampered by constitutional limitations; especially when his country is confronted with problems of exceptional magnitude, he usually takes full charge of foreign policy.

2. His choice of ends and means will be determined by, among other things, his personality. His motivations (inferred) are not determined as much by his association with any particular group, but by his role as a national leader.

3. The influence of others upon his action will be determined by their informal rather than their institutional relationship with him.

4. One does not have to pay serious attention to the role of the legislature as far as foreign policy-making is concerned. Because, as a rule, "legislatures confirm rather than initiate foreign policy",[43] and in small and developing countries, the legislature largely tends to act as a rubber stamp for executive programmes.

Internal Setting

The internal setting is comprised of all relevant factors and conditions prevalent within the national boundaries which may affect foreign policy.

First of all, the degree of influence and the scope of international activities of a state tends to be proportional to its national strength, the principal component of which are military power, the quantity and quality of its popularity, geographic location and its natural resources and technology, the degree of political stability within the country, and its international prestige which is largely a reflection of the quality of leadership of its decision-maker.

Secondly, the geographic position of a country also influences the direction of its foreign policy and its feasibility. Geographic setting has made for example the break away from Russia easier for Yugoslavia than for Hungary.

Thirdly, cultural orientation gives foreign policy a distinct national colour. The decision-maker in small and developing countries is relatively free from the requirements of his institutional role, but not of his social role as a cultural-bearer. Therefore, foreign policy made by him is "a manifestation of a community's values, attitudes, ways of thinking, and other aspects of culture which differentiate it from every other community."[44]

In small and developing countries, the effect of cultural environment may give rise to conflicting results. On the one hand, the values system, the national history, the wish of the people, to a certain extent, act as a general limiting factor upon the choice of a nation's ideological affiliation and allies. On the other hand, the cult of personality prevalent in these countries and the character of political loyalty in non-western societies give to the leadership... a high degree of freedom in determining matters of strategy and tactics....

So long as harmonious relations exist within the group, it is generally possible for the leaders to make drastic changes in strategy. Indeed, it is not in common for the membership to feel that matters relating to external policy should be left solely to the leadership and it may not disturb them that such decisions reflect mainly the idiosyncrasies of their leaders.[45]

Within the context of cultural orientation, past political experience including colonial domination or lack of it also dictates foreign policy of newly-independent nations *vis-a-vis* their former colonisers and the latter's allies.

Fourthly, the need for political as well as economic-modernisation has made it necessary for small and developing countries to be dependent upon developed nations for economic assistance and political guidance. Their choice of benefactors or allies would define the direction of their nation's foreign policy (pro-western, pro-communist, or uncommitted).

Fifthly, the economic or political conditions in some small and developing countries may induce their leaders to embark upon an aggressive foreign policy in order to divert the attention of their nationals from domestic failures.

External Setting

In the final analysis, foreign policy is a question of "adjusting the actions of states to each other,"[46] the external setting which reflects the foreign policies of their external community is of primary importance to decision-makers.

Foremost in their minds is the policy of the super-powers. Although the power stalemate of our time provides small and developing nations with unprecedented opportunities to bargain with both sides while rejecting the dictation from either, in questions of war and peace, it is the voice of the super-powers that is decisive. It would be inconceivable that a war can be fought and won against their wish. The termination of the Anglo-French-Israeli in vision of Egypt over the Suez crisis in 1956, constituted a clear illustration of the 'limitation of small states' power to affect war and peace.

Foreign policy of small and developing nations is made within the framework of a divided world. The degree of their freedom in foreign policy-making tends to vary in inverse proportion with the degree of tension between the two super-powers the degree of involvement and of their vital interests.

Furthermore, the foreign policy of small and developing nations, due to their limited power, tend to be regional rather than world-wide. In any case, they have to take into consideration the foreign policies of their neighbouring states. Military and economic weakness as well as the need to concentrate on internal development have induced them to develop friendly relations with their neighbours, except under exceptional circumstances (such as the case of Israel *vis-a-vis* its Arab neighbours).

If the neighbour is a big country, the latter's position would impose a severe limitation upon the choice of foreign policy of small nations as evidenced in the relationship between Russia and Finland, between Communist China and the countries surrounding it. Prevailing trends in international politics at a given time also exerts a great influence upon the foreign policy of small states.

Regionalism, for one is a new force in international politics. Willy-nilly, small and developing nations have to take a stand *vis-a-vis* the pull of regionalism, or the "pan" movement. Usually, they guarantee a pronounced support to cultivate favourable sentiments of neighbouring countries. In this case, the attitude of the dominant power-or powers, in the region (who would inevitably vie for the role of leadership) is of primary significance to the decision-makers of small and developing countries.

Anti-colonialism and non-alignment are familiar features of small and developing nations/foreign policy/ Kenneth T. 'Young summarises this trend as follows:

> In diplomacy, the new professionals (in the small and developing nations) incline towards regional associations and avoidance of too close a political identification with East or West. In seeking to achieve an independent, or at least a complementary, diplomacy, they will try to strengthen, bilateral relations with their neighbours, explore economic and cultural cooperation on a regional basis as the Magreb in North Africa or the Mekong Commission in South East Asia, and take common positions on issues before the United Nations.[47]

Sometimes, foreign policy of small and developing nations is not only a concern of those located in the same, region, but of others as well. These countries tend to be the former colonial powers which have developed a traditional interest in those countries. As such, their position should also be taken into account.

Attitudes of international and regional organisations, such as the United Nations, the South East Asia Trades Organisation, etc... are also, part of the external setting. Developments at the UN, for example, have permitted the small states to rely heavily on it to speed up the process of decolonisation throughout the world. In another case, SEATO's incapacity to take positive action has not allowed the small states which it was designed to protect to count on it as a reliable ally.

Finally, foreign policy is policy towards some thing (issue) or some state. In deciding the ends and means of foreign policy, the sizing up of the position and power of the target state is essential. This assessment is purely subjective and largely reflects the decision-maker's knowledge and experience. In case the target state is familiar to the decision-maker's community (for example, a colonial power or a neighbouring state), his assessment is also, to a large extent, influenced by his community's sentiment toward the target state. Generally, the relationship between the newly-independent countries and the former colonial powers varies within the gamut of conflict or suspicion and co-operation depending on past behaviour and present policy of the colonial powers, the impact they leave on the cultural orientation of the small and developing countries, the advantages and disadvantages of their co-operation, and on the decision of the latter's leaders. As such the foreign policy of a small state like Tunisia is identified with personality of President Habib Bourguiba.

Decision-making in Tunisia's Foreign Policy

Tunisia is a Presidential Republic, although the National Assembly has the power of legislating, legislative proposals of the President take precedence over those of legislators. He can also exert the power delegated by the Legislature to make decrees "for a limited period and for special reasons" (Article 28 of the Tunisian Constitution). Article 30 of the Tunisian Constitution provides that Permanent Committees will be elected from among the Deputies which will remain constantly in session, even during the recess of the National Assembly, to share with the President, the governing power. But so long as they have not been formed, the President's constitutional powers remain unchecked during Assembly's recess.

In exceptional times when the safety and independence of the nation is endangered, and if the "ordinary machine of state is unable to function," the President is vested with the power to take "exceptional measures." (Article 32)

In normal time, it is the President who shall "draw up the general policy of the country and control its execution." His sole obligation is "to keep" the National Assembly informed of the development of this policy." He alone shall[1] choose the members of his government, who are responsible to him (Article 43). He will make both the civil and military appointments (Article 45), and is the Commander-in-Chief of the army (Article 46). He appoints and receives diplomatic representatives (Article 47) and, with the "agreement" of the Assembly, he ratifies treaties, declares war, and makes peace (Article 49).[48]

This broad decision-making power granted to the Tunisian President is further, enhanced by the election of

Habib Bourguiba to the Presidency and by the political realities of Tunisia. Constitutionally speaking, the National Assembly represents the only check on Presidential decision-making power. However, in the first election of November 1959, all the ninty seats of the Assembly were won by the Neo-Destour party and its allies. Considering the stern discipline of the party, it is unlikely that Bourguiba would find any effective opposition in the Assembly against his foreign policy. *Vis-a-vis* his close advisers, the Ministers, Bourguiba's expertise in foreign affairs and his dominant personality are such that "no minister dares to take a dccision of any importance without consulting him"[49]

To the masses, Bourguiba's public image as a father, a brother, a friend, his prestige as the first founder of the Neo-Destour, the first organiser of "Tunisia's independence, and the first President of the Republic earns him confidence, respect, and unconditional support, and gives him great freedom, in making decisions". The power of Bourguiba and the rationale behind it may be summed up in those candid words of Habib Bourguiba, Jr. the former Tunisian Ambassador to the United States:

> "Although he was not always unanimously followed, he was the only policy-maker of the Neo-Destour during the pre-independence period.... Presently, he enjoys such great prestige among the people and the members of the Government, because his ideas have so often proved accurate and convincing, that his decisions are always executed entirely, and faithfully".
>
> "The result is that, owing to his legendary past, and to the power granted him by the laws and the people. President Bourguiba happens to be roughly speaking, the only policy-maker in the Tunisian Government, although he may follow the advice, given to him in Government sittings or party meetings".[50]

To a certain extent, Bourguiba was an idealist. He cherished a love for the liberty of the individual and dislikes any kind of political domination, doctrine based on oppression.

During the war, he refused to the Axis who freed him. During his political agitation, his slogan was "human dignity." Bourguiba's early writings show him passionately engaged in the issues of the day, castigating the arrogance of the protectorate authorities, and blaming them for the misery of the people. But he also explained that the solution of such problems must first be sought by the Tunisian people themselves. They must be made aware of their true destiny and their potential power. Nothing had happened to be ashamed of, he argued, Tunisian people were as good as any in the world. All that was needed was to shake off the apathy, get rid of the complex of inferiority, and recapture pride and dignity while at the same time mastering modern, European techniques. He said in an article:

> "Is this country without vitality, a degenerate people which is declining, reduced to nothing more than... I dustbin of individuals, a lump of people? Or is it, on the other hand, a sound and vigorous people which international competition or a momentary crisis has forced to accept the tutorship of a strong state? Contact with a more advanced civilisation has led to a healthy reaction. A true generation is being produced. Thanks to a judicious assimilation of the principles and methods of this civilisation. Tunisia will inevitably attain by degrees its definitive emancipation".[51]

Although Bourguiba always holds a prejudice favourable for his opponent, and compromising in tactics, he is absolutely firm on principles. The essential characteristics of Bourguiba's strategy is the constancy of objective and flexibility of means of achieving it. In the struggle against France, he had never hidden his aim, which was the independence of his country. He candidly admitted that independence would not be absolute, and it should reconcile with interdependence, but he wanted to get for Tunisia gradually and persistently all the sovereign attributes of independence. In working toward his uncompromising aim, Bourguiba prefers negotiation, tactical compromise, to fighting.

> When too big a cupboard has to be taken through too narrow a door, it is absurd to smash the furniture, or to break down the wall; it is far better to dismantle the cupboard and reassemble it on the other side.[52]

He possesses an extra-ordinary personality of a man composed of two separate individuals:

> The first, M. Bourguiba is a southern politician, subtle, sly, quick to fit his aims to his means, one of those men who become the strategists of Congress in Washington and Radical-Socialist Cabinet Ministers in France. He is a man who learned his sciences at French universities, acquiring a taste for clear reasoning and the great works of the French classicists and romantics; then, during his stays in France, Britain and the United States, learning at least a theoretical respect for democracy and developing a passion for the political life and the parliaments of the West.
>
> The second, M. Bourguiba is a speaker endowed with a fantastic power of electrifying the masses, feeding on popular fervour, an Arab *zaim* drunk with the sound of his own words, an oriental chieftain hard put to resist the temptations of ancient Turkish autocracy. He is a man surrounded only by pliant subordinates, those who would have resisted him having been broken, sent away or won over.
>
> For the past five years, he has wielded practically unlimited power, setting up a relatively gentle dictatorship, without terror and imbued with a controlled paternalism. It is the government of a "father of his people", in a country where, as in all the Mediterranean region, the father who loves greatly also punishes greatly, and the children speak to him without raising their voices. To understand fully the personality of M. Bourguiba, one would have to imagine a character made up of parts of Harry Truman and Father Divine, Adlai Stevenson and Billy Graham, Harold MacMillan and Sir Oswald Mosley.[53]

In International politics, Bourguiba is known for his intellectual attachment to France and the Western world, his dislike of repressive political doctrines, his paternalistic attitude towards the African states, his suspicion of Egyptian ambition, his pride in his people and his country, and his desire to serve as a link between the West and the African world.

To achieve his aims, Bourguiba patiently and skillfully applied all his trump cards to appeal to "international morality", to the people of the world, and to the mind and conscience solidarity of other statesmen.

In sum, this, together with its specific location and history, have combined to make Tunisians constantly aware of their own vulnerability to the ambitions of external powers and foreign policy is therefore inevitably geared toward minimising this vulnerability. Since ancient times, Tunisia has been subject to one invasion after another. The Carthaginians, Romans, Vandals, Byzantines, Arabs, Ottomans, and French all coveted Tunisia as a strategically valuable vehicle for their own ambitions. The country sits reaching out into the Mediterranean, far enough westward to be accessible to Europe, but close enough to the Middle East to identify with the peoples and issues of western Asia. It has historically also been a gateway from Africa to these two arenas. The central location is not matched, however, by geographic or resource strength. Beyond the sea lies the European continent, from whence came the most recent wave of occupiers. Today, more than ever, Tunisians are aware of the economic might of that continent, and its continuing ability to assert itself over Tunisia to the latter's disadvantage. As Europe develops and asserts its own collective foreign policies, backed by military capabilities in the Mediterranean. Tunisia must keep one eye always to the north. The other eye must inevitably be focussed primarily on the more immediate neighbourhood. Algeria, Morocco, and Libya all have regional, if deeply varying, ambitions and all are actually or potentially more powerful than Tunisia. The rivalry between them, and particularly between Morocco and Algeria, is a constant factor in

Tunisia's perceptions of its own interests and policy requirements.

The Maghrebi dimension overlaps with Tunisia's membership in the community of Arab states. Powerful Egypt and turbulent Sudan lie to Tunisia's east. Beyond them lie the Mashreq and the Persian Gulf, the conflicts and rivalries of which have a habit of drawing in Arab states further a field. The strategic importance of the WANA region, and the vast hydrocarbon deposits that lie within it, have also invited international interest that Tunisia has had to take account of in its own foreign policy-making. While Tunisia's African identity and the economic potential of that continent have not incited much international interest and have, therefore, taken a relative back seat in Tunisian foreign policy-making, Islam has in recent years become more of an issue in domestic politics with a spill over effect for foreign policy. Geography makes Tunisia vulnerable to the interests of both regional, intra-continental, and international powers. One may ask, however, what particular resources are located in Tunisia that either stimulate those interests, or enable Tunisia to withstand them. Thus, the making of foreign policy in Tunisia is similar to that of new liberated states from the colonial power. In addition, its policy-makers experimented at one time or another with most of the foreign policy strategies developed by the new states in the post-independences period, to use foreign policy to achieve basic domestic goals; national unity, economic and social development.

Bourguiba's Early Life, His Policy of Gradualism and Neo-Destour Party

Habib Bourguiba was born in 1903. He showed interest in political life since his high school days. He was educated in Tunis and Paris. He married a French woman. He began to practice law in Tunis in 1927, and became an active member of the Destour party and began to publish a radical journal (L'Action Tunisienne) in 1932, less than a year later, the paper was banned by the authorities but the name of editor had become well-known.[54]

Bourguiba addressed at the Ksar Hellal Congress of March 1934. The main thrust of his speech was that the new team had greater credibility among the French authorities. He also made the point that it was precisely the ability of the new team to have ear of the government in France that led the executive commission of the Destour party to fear them.[55] At the end of the day, a resolution was passed, dissolving the executive Commission. Another resolution passed a new charter of internal by-laws which called for a 'Bureau politique'—composed of president (Mahamoud Materi), Secretary-General (Habib Bourguiba), Assistant secretary-General (Taharsfar), Treasurer (M'Hamed Bourguiba) and Assistant Treasurer (Bahri Guiga). A 'National Council' was also instituted, composed of the Bureau politique and thirty members elected from the party cells. Finally, party Congress was to be held annually in order to elect a new Bureau politique and National Council and to oversee the finances and activities of the party.[56]

The new Destour believed that it had solved the question of political survival by the new organisational plan which it had adopted. That called for a double-tiered leadership, the Bureau politique and the National Council.[57]

The Neo-Destour party announced that the platform adopted at the Qism-al-Qabal conferences of 1933 that is the achievement of an independent and sovereign Tunisia remained the basic policy of the party. At the same time, the party decided to proceed to its realisation in stages. An initial step it pressed for a return to the spirit and the latter of the occupation statutes, which either had not been mutilated in a manner contrary to its original purport. Under the treaty of protectorate French trusteeship over Tunisia was not intended to be permanent. In pursuance of its aim, the party urged the speedy implementation of the following reforms : abolition of the "colonial allowance" (this is an allowance amounting to one-third of the basic salary paid to French employees in Algeria, Tunisia and Morocco), cessation of official colonisation of the land, compulsory education for all, the setting up of elected municipal councils, appointment of Tunisians to various government jobs, including a greater share in pivotal posts, a more effective relief programme, anti-usury legislation, abolition of the Grand Council and its replacement by a duly-elected Tunisian parliament and a government responsible to it.[58]

Thus, gradualism was seen as an intrinsic part of the policy of Neo-Dastour party's programme. The Tunisian Trade Union (UCTT) took shape in 1945. This Tunisian Labour Organisation was perhaps the strongest arm of the Neo-Destour. Through it, the Neo-Destour was able to effect political strikes.[59] The Tunisian Artisan and Commercial Union (UTAC) was founded in 1946, the National Union of Tunisian Agriculture (UNAT) in 1946, General Union of the Students of Tunisia (UGFT) in 1953, and the National Union of the Tunisian Women (UNFT) was founded in 1957.[60]

The Neo-Destour party launched a programme of mass education or re-education, a programme whereby the intellectuals went to tiny, backward villages, taught people who had been idle, simply to read and write and to learn a new interpretation of their Moslem heritage. Citing the Koran and the life of the Prophet Muhammad, they took the approach that the Moslem religion was really not one of asceticism and renunciation, but one which upheld the dignity of man, held him alone responsible for his actions and made it a sacred duty to try to improve his life on earth.[61]

Soon after its appearance on the scene, the Neo-Destour became the leading nationalist party. Its activities sparked by the exuberance of youth, eclipsed those of the old Destour. In the ensuing years, several attempts were made to bring the factions together but to no avail. The most important hopeful attempt was in 1937, when Thaalbi tried to effect reconciliation but he too failed. His sympathies were with the older-group and the Neo-Destour refused to buckle under his pressure.[62] In 1946 another unsuccessful attempt was made to heal the breach. A national front was formed but it did not last. Besides differences between the two groups, there seemed to be an irreconcilable clash in temperament and personality of the respective leaders.

The fundamental difference between the New and the old Destour was, however, a matter of tactics as at particular moment in history, the first called for action while the second rested on quiescence for the sake of survival.[63] Unlike the old Destour, the Neo Destourians were secular nationalists. Yet, they too were not averse to using religion as a political weapon occasionally. They also turned to the masses for support. The Neo-Destour was committed to the national independence as well as to the modernisation of the country via extensive grassroots, organisations, and political education and mobilisation.[64]

Thus, we see that the Neo-Destour achieved its superiority over the old-Destour through an intensified campaign of mass education, organising youth groups, holding demonstrations and establishing party organisations throughout the country.[65]

Neo-Destour's greatest triumph was the launching of a strictly Tunisian labour movement, which was to become not only its most important striking arm within Tunisia, but also one of its most effective means for obtaining outside help. Moreover, the early period of the Neo-Destour Party leaves no doubt as to the popularity of Bourguiba among the masses, which continued even after the establishment of the Republic of Tunisia. His charisma also operated on a person to person level as his penetrating blue eyes bore into his interlocutor.

The Neo-Destour Party employed methods of widespread political agitation as a result of which Bourguiba was exiled. With the victory of the Popular Front in France in 1936, Bourguiba returned to Tunisia but little was achieved in direct negotiations with the new French Government of Leon Blum, from which much had been expected in the way of reforms. Neo-Destour was built up as a powerful organisation and its strength was proved in a successful general strike in 1938. Following widespread clashes with the police, martial law was proclaimed. Some 200 nationalists were arrested and both the Destour and Neo-Destour parties were dissolved. Bourguiba remained in detention in Europe until the Axis Powers freed him in 1943.

After renewed difficulties with the French, he went into exile from 1945 to 1949.[66] Some of his time was spent in

Cairo at the Maghreb Bureau there. He also travelled to the USA and sought support for the Tunisian cause at the UN. But he achieved limited success. In the meanwhile, events were moving fast in North Africa and an atmosphere was being created for a negotiated settlement. That brought Bourguiba back to Tunisia.

In April 1950, Neo-Destour's proposals were put forward for the transfer of sovereignty and executive control to Tunisian hands, under a responsible government with a Prime Minister appointed by the Bey and an elected national assembly which would draw up a democratic constitution. These proposals were met with a reasonable response in France and a new Tunisian government was formed in August 1950.[67] Further reforms were affected in September 1950, and February 1951, when French advises to the Tunisian ministers were removed and the resident general's control over the Council of Ministers was reduced. The essence of the reforms was to grant the Tunisians a greater measure of self-rule by increasing the participation of Tunisians at all levels of government administration.

The Colon lobby, however, saw a long-term threat to its privileged position in these moves and put pressure for a strong-arm measure. Bourguiba was arrested once more, in February 1952, on the order of a new resident-general, Jean de Hauteclocque. A wave of violence spread throughout the country, culminating in the arrest and removal from office of the Chief Minister and the imposition of French military control. Mendes-France permitted Bourguiba to live under surveillance in France and a year later in 1954, he returned finally and in triumph to Tunis.[68]

By this time, Bourguiba was a national hero but he was not yet in power. In July 1954, the French accepted the principle of internal autonomy for Tunisia. Negotiations began between the two sides. Bourguiba advocated moderation and a willingness to meet the French more than half-way. The final agreement was signed in June 1955. Series of conventions were signed to implement this agreement. The main items of the agreement were Tunisian foreign policy would remain under French supervision, three-seventh of membership of municipal councils, where a large French population exists, should be French; Tunisia would remain within the French bloc and the French union, for the next ten years, police officers should continue to be French, during a period of twenty years affairs of justice would be gradually transferred to the Tunisians, Arabic would become the official language of the country, but French should continue to be taught in all schools.[69]

The Tunisian State in 1955, was apart from the French pressure, an absolute monarchy. There was no constitution nor did they have full power, at least in theory, to appoint Ministers of his own choosing and to enact any law. For Burguiba and the Neo-Destour it was necessary to fight against the French as well as the 'legal' Tunisian state. They had to appeal for the transformation from the "pays legal" to the "pays reel". Pressure had to be applied to be court but not so much as to drive it irrevocably into the hands of the French.

The apprenticeship of the Neo-Destour was not an apprenticeship in democracy. Through most of its history, the Neo-Destour was illegal, and its leaders were in detention or in exile. Bourguiba's leadership while acknowledged by public opinion had inevitably suffered by his inability to exercise continuous and detailed control.[70]

Bourguiba, at that time had to confront three dangers. Firstly, he had to avoid giving the French an excuse for coercive action. Secondly, he was to transform the Beylical regime without violence. Thirdly, he was to guard against dissidence within his own party particularly from those, who accused him of showing too much restraint toward the French. This radical group within the Neo-Destour Party was led by his close associate, Salah Ben Yousseuf. Bourguiba's steps to complete control were rapid. Ben Yoursseuf was expelled from the party for opposition to the recent agreement (1955) and for dividing the party. A Neo-Destour Party Congress at Sfax in November 1955, confirmed the expulsion and re-elected Bourguiba as the party president.[71]

The Congress accepted the agreement but at the same time reaffirmed that it would be satisfied only with complete independence and demanded the election of a constituent assembly. Clashes between 'Bourgouibist' and 'Yousseufist' factions followed and in December, a conspiracy to set-up a terrorist organisation to prevent the implementation of the agreement was discovered. Salah Ben Yusseuf fled to Tripoli in January 1956. Many suspected Yousseufists were placed in detention. At the same time, Fellaghas (armed bands) which had been active in 1952-54 against the French were revived.[72] These armed bands became active in the remote parts of the country and acts of terrorism were being committed against the Frenchmen and also members of the Neo-Destour.

Final independence to Tunisia was accelerated due to events in Morocco where the French and king Mohammad V were negotiating for full independence for Morocco. French opted for full independence for Tunisia also. Both these developments were also influenced by the Algerian war of independence which had started in 1954.

Against this background, a Tunisian delegation, led by Bourguiba began negotiations for Tunisian independence with the French government in Paris on 27th February, 1956. On 20th March, 1956, a protocol was signed by Tunisian Prime Minister, Taher Bin Ammar, and French Foreign Minister, M. Pinay, which recognised the independence of Tunisia in foreign and defence matters. It sought for the abolition of the treaty of Bardo (1881), and arranged for further negotiations between the two countries on all issues.[73] A transitional period was envisaged during which French forces would gradually be withdrawn from Tunisia including from the major base at Bizerta.[74] Set was not ready for Bourguiba to create institution that would enable him to assume power.

Elections for a constituent assembly were immediately held on 25th March, 1958. They resulted in all the 98 seats being won by candidates of the National Front. All of whom acknowledged allegiance to the Neo-Destour. The election was, however boycotted by the 'Youssefist' opposition. Habib Bourguiba became Prime Minister on 11th April, 1956, leading a government in which 16 of the 17 Ministers belonged to the Neo-Destour. He was now legally in power and there was no opposition in the assembly and very little in the country. Salah Ben Yousseuf was in exile and his group was under pressure in Tunisia. Bourguiba's political objectives were to unify the party on the broadest possible base and to secure a virtual monopoly over it. The institution of monarchy under the Bey of Tunis stood in his way to absolute power. Accordingly, in July 1957, the Assembly declared Tunisia to be a Republic and Bourguiba became President. He succeeded to the absolute executive and legislative power of the Bey. The Assembly had only the function of framing the Constitution. It did not control the government and did not pass ordinary laws. This period of legal absolutism came to an end with the proclamation of the new Constitution on 1st June, 1959.

Bourguiba cannot be discussed as a simpleton or as a man who ruled his country by whim and fancy rather than foresight and meticulous planning. His survival is the often troublesome political climate of Tunisia attests to the latter.

Thus, in brief we can say that the success of Neo-Destour Party and Bourgubia was due to the mass support enjoyed by them due to the various affiliates like labour union, etc., by organising youth groups, and by active party activities like leading demonstrations, establishing party organisations, as well as the gradualist approach both towards France and Tunisian elite. Moreover, the charismatic and authoritative leadership of Bourguiba was also vital causes.

References

1. David Long and Bernard Reich, *The Government and Politics of the Middle East and North Africa,* Boulder, CO: Westview Press, 1995, p. 444.
2. Malcolm Kerr, *The Arab Cold War: Gamal Abd-al-Nasir and His Rivals, 1958-1970,* London: Oxford University Press, 1971.

3. Louis J. Cantori and Steven L. Spiegel, *The International Politics of Regions: A Comparative Approach,* (Englewood Cliffs, NJ: Prentice Hall, 1970), pp. 192-207; Tareq Y. Ismael, *International Relations of the Contemporary Middle East: A Study in World Politics,* (Syracuse, NY: Syracuse University Press), pp. 5-13.
4. B.A., Roberson, *Ed., the Middle East and Europe. The Power Deficit.* (London: Routledge, 1988), pp. 4-5.
5. Ronger Adelson, *London and the Invention of the Middle East: Money, Power, and War, 1902-1922,* (London : Yale University Press, 1995), p. 117.
6. B.A., Roberson, "The Superpowers and the Middle East", *in Global Politics.* (Milton Keynes: Open University, 1988), p. 11.
7. James Gelvin, "The Ironic Legacy of the King-Crane Commission", in David W. Lesch, ed., *Te Middle East and the United States: A Historical and Political Reassessment,* (Boulder, CO: Westview Press, 1996), pp. 11-16.
8. For detail see Rashid Khalidi et al., eds., *The Origins of Arab Nationalism,* (New York: Columbia University Press, 1991; Zeme N. Zeine, *The Emergence of Arab Nationalism, with a Background? Study of Arab-Turkish Relations in the Arab Nationalism, with a Background Study of Arab-Turkish Relations in the Near East,* 3rd ed. (Delmar, NY: Caravan Books, 1976).
9. Bassam Tibi, *Arab Nationalism, A Critial Enquiry,* edited and translated by Marion Farouk-Sluglett and Peter Sluglett (London: MacMillan, 1990), pp. 116-122.
10. Abbas Alnasrawi, *Arab Nationalism, Oil, and the Political Economy of Dependency* (London: Greenwood, 1991), p. 30.
11. Cited in Nazih Ayubi, *Overstating the Arab State: Politics and Society in the Middle East,* (London; I.B. Tauris, 1995), p. 146.
12. Iliya Harik, "The Origins of the Arab State System", in Ghassan Salame, ed., *The Foundations of the Arab State,* (London: Croom Helm, 1987), pp. 19-46.
13. L. Carl Brown, *International Politics and the Middle East: Old Rules. Dangerous Game,* (Princeton, NJ: Princeton University Press, 1984), pp. 3-5.

14. Barry Buzan, "New Patterns of Global Security in the Twenty-First Century", *International Affairs,* Vol. 67, No. 3, July 1991, pp. 246-47.
15. For details see Samir Amin, *The Arab Nation: Nationalism and Class Struggles, (London:* Zed Press, 1978); Abbas Alnasrawi, *Arab Nationalism, Oil and the Political Economy of Dependency,* (New York and London: Greenwood Press, 1991).
16. Johan Galtung, "A Structural Theory *of Imperialism",* *Journal of Peace Research* Vol. 8, No. 2, 1971, pp. 81-98.
17. Roger Owen, *The Middle East in the World Economy, 1800-1945* (London: Methuen, 1981) Alnasrawi, *Arab Nationalism, op.cit.,* No. 15, pp. 1-23.
18. Bruce Moon, "The State in Foreign and Domestic Policy", in L. Neack, J. Hey and P. Haney, eds., *Foreign-Pottcy Analysis: Continuity and Change in its Second Generation,* (Englewood Cliffs, JN: Prentice Hall, 1995), pp. 197-98.
19. Galtung, *"A Sructural Theory of Imperalism", op.cit.,* No. 16.
20. Bruce Moon, "Consensus or Compliance? Foreign-Policy Change and External Dependence", *International Organisation,* Vol. 39, No. 2, Spring 1995, pp. 297-330.
21. Jeanne A.K. Hey, "Foreign Policy in Dependent States," in L. Neack, J. Hey, and P. Haney, eds., *Foreign Policy Analysis: Continuity and Change in its Second Generation,* (Englewood Cliffs, NJ: Prentice Hail, 1995), pp. 201-213; Adrienne Armstrong, "The Political Consequences of Economic Dependence," *Journal of Conflict Resolution,* No. 25, 1981, pp. 401-428.
22. Immanuel Wallerstein, "The Rise and Future Demise of the World Capitalist System: Concepts for Comparative Analysis", *Comparative Studies in History and Society,* Vol. 6, No. 4, 1974, pp. 387-415; Wallerstein, *The Modern World System,* (New York: Academic Press, 1974.)
23. Oran Young, "Political Disontinuities in the International System", *World Politics,* Vol. 20, No. 3, April 1968.
24. Fawaz Gerges, *The Superpowers and the Middle East: Regional and International Politics,* (Boulder, CO: Westview Press, 1994), pp. 1-17, 245-251. L. Carl Brown, *International Politics and the Middle East,* pp. 197-232; see also Alan Taylor, *The Superpowers and the Middle East,*

(Syracuse, (NY: Syracuse University Press, 1991); Yezid Sayigh and Avi Shlaim, The Cold War and the Middle East, (Oxford: Claredon Press, 1997); Yair evron, *Nations, Superpowers and Wars,* (London: Elek Books, 1973); David Lesch, *The Middle East and the United States,* Boulder, CO: Westview Press, 1996).

25. Wiliam R. Thompson, "The Arab Sub-system and the Feudal Pattern of Interaction: 1965", *Journal of Peace Research,* No. 7, 1970, pp. 151-167.

26. Paul Aarts, "The Middle East: A Region Without Regionalism or the End of Exceptionalism?" *Third World Quarterly,* Vol. 20, No. 5, October 1999, pp. 911-925.

27. Paul Noble, "The Arab System: Pressures, Constraints, and Opportunities", in Bahgat Korany and Ali E. Hillal Dessouki, *The Foreign Policies of Arab States: The Challenge of Change,* (Boulder, CO: Westview Press, 1991), p. 57.

28. Michael Hudson, *Arab Politics: The Search for Legitimacy,* (New Haven, CT: Yale University Press, 1977), pp. 33-55; Bahgat Korany, "The Dialectics of Inter-Arab Relations, 1967-1987", in Abdullah Battah and Yehuda Lukas, eds., *The Arab-Israeli Conflict: Two Decades of Change,* (Boulder, CO: Westview Press, 1988) pp. 164-178.

29. Eberhard Kienle, *Ba'th Versus Ba'th: The Conflict between Syria and Iraq,* (London: I.B. Tauris, 1990), pp. 1-30.

30. Bahgat Korany, "Alien and Besieged Yet Here to Stay: The Contradictions of the Arab Territorial State", in Ghassan Salame, ed., *The Foundations of the Arab State,* (London: Groom Helm, 1987), pp. 47-74; Kienle, *Ba'th Yersus Ba'th,* pp. 9, 27.

31. Michael Barnett, *Dialogues in Arab Politics: Negotiations in Regional Order:* (New York: Columbia University Press, 1999), Constructivism is explicated in Alexander Wendt, *Social Theory of International Politics,* (Cambridge: Cambridge University Press, 1999).

32. For other similar explorations of this dynamic, see Noble, "The Arab System", pp. 55-60; Gregory Gause, "Systemic Approaches to Middle East International Relations", *International Studies Review,* Vol. 1, No. 1, Spring 1999, pp. 11-31; Michael N. Barnett, "Sovereighty, Nationalism, and Regional Order in the Arab States System",

International Organisation, Vol. 49, No. 3, Summer 1995; *Michael N. Barnett, "Institutions, Roles and Disorder: The Case of the Arab States System",* International Studies Quarterly, Vol. 37, No. 3, September 1993; Roger Owen, "Arab Nationalism, Arab Unity and the Practice of Intra-Arab State Relations", in Roger Owen, ed., *State, Power and Politics in the Making of the Modern Middle East,* (London: Routledge, 1992), Chapter 4, pp. 81-107.

33. Avraham Sela, *The End of the Arab-Israeli Conflict: Middle East Politics and the Quest for Regional Order,* Albany: State University of New York Press, 1998), p. 15.

34. Hedley Bull, *The Anarchical Society,* (London: MacMillan, 1977), p. 77.

35. For detail see Robert Goode, "State Building as a Determinant of Foreign Policies in the New States", in Laurence W. Martin, ed., *Neutralism and Non-Alignment,* (New York: Praeger, 1962); Peter Calvert, *The Foreign Policies of New States, (Sussex:* Wheatsheaf Books, 1986); Ali E. Hilal Dessouki, "Dilemmas of Security and Development in the Arab World: Aspects of Linkage", in Bahgat Korany, Paul Noble, and Rex Brynen, eds., *The Many Faces of National Security in the Middle East,* (New York; MacMillan, 1993), pp. 76-90).

36. For an assessment of this approach, see Bahgat Korany, *How Foreign Policy Decisions Are Made in the Third World,* (Boulder, CO: Westview Press, 1986).

37. Adeed Dawisha and I. William Zartman, *Beyond Coercion: The Durability of the Arab State,* (London: Croom Helm, 1988), pp. 15-25; Malik Mufti, *Sovereignty Creations: Pan-Arabism and Political Order in Syria and Iraq,* (Ithaca and London: Cornell University Press, 1996), pp. 9-16.

38. Nazih Ayubi, *Overstating the Arab State: Politics and Society in the Middle East, London: I.B. Tauris, 1995),* pp. 196-255: James Bill and Robert Springborg, *Politics in the Middle East,* (Glenville, IL: Little, Brown, 1990) pp. 177-299.

39. Dawisha and Zartman, *Beyond Coercion;* Mufti, *Sovereign Creations, op.cit.,* No. 37.

40. Avner Yaniv, "Alliance Politics in the Middle East: A Security Dilemma Perspective", in Auriel Braun, ed., *The Middle East in Global Strategy* (Boulder, CO: Westview Press, 1987), pp. 115-35.

41. Edward Mansfield and Jack Snyder, "The Dangers of Democratisation", *International Security,* Vol. 20, No. 1, summer 1995, pp. 5-38.
42. Joseph Frankel, *The Making of Foreign Policy,* London: Oxford University Press, 1963, pp. 216-217.
43. *Ibid.,* p. 23.
44. Harold and Margaret Srout, *Foundations of International Politics,* New York: D. Van Nostrand Co., 1962), p. 132.
45. Lucian W. Pye, "The Non-Western Political Process," in James N. Rosenau, ed., International Politic and Foreign Policy, (New York; The Free Press of Glencoe, 1961 p. 288.
46. George Modelski, *A Theory of Foreign Policy,* (New York: Frederick A. Praeger, 1962), p. 3.
47. Kenneth T. Young. New Politics in New States. *Foreign Affairs,* Vol. 39, No. 3, April 1961, p. 503.
48. *Constitution of the Tunisian Republic,* Tunis: Secretariat of State for Information, 1959.
49. Keith Gallard, "The Republic of Bourguiba" *International Journal.* Vol. XVI. Winter 1960-61, p. 35
50. Habib Bourguiba. Jr., The Foreign Policy of Tunisia in Joseph E. Black and K.W. Thompson eds., *Foreign Policies in a world of Change* (New York, Harper and Row, 1963), p. 356.
51. As quoted in Charles F. Gallapher, Tunisia in Gavendolen M. Carter ed. *African One Party States.* (New York Cornell University Press, 1962), p. 30.
52. Jean Lacouture, "Dilemma of the Two Bourguibas," *The New York Times, Magazine,* August 20, 1961, p. 13.
53. Jean Lacouture, "Dilemma of the Two Bourguibas," *The New York Times Magazine,* August 20, 1961, p. 13.
54. Keith Callard. "The Republic of Bourguiba", International Journal, Vol. 16, No. l, 1960-61, p. 18.
55. Norma Salem, Habib Bourguiba Islam and the creation of Tunisia (London, 1984), pp. 95-96.
56. Salem, No. 54, p. 96.
57. *Ibid.,* p. 96
58. Fais, No. 14.
59. Clement Henry Moore, "The Neo-Destour party of Tunisia:

A Structure for Democracy", World Politics, Vol. 14, No. 3, April 1962, p. 462.

60. Zertman, No. 1, pp. 77-78.
61. Hahn, No. 24, p. 19.
62. Rivlin, B, No. 41, p. 171-72.
63. Rivlin, B, No. 41, p. 172.
64. David E. Long and Bernard Reich, ed. Government and politics of the Middle East and North Africa (Colorado, 1980), p. 440.
65. Rivlin, B, No. 41, p. 172.
66. K. Callard, No. 53, p. 18.
67. The Middle East and North Africa, No. 5, p. 815.
68. Middle East and North Africa, No. 5, p. 779.
69. Nicola A. Ziadeh, whither North Africa (Institute of Islamic Studies, Muslim University, Aligarh, 1957).
70. Keith Caltard, No. 53, pp. 19-20.
71. *Ibid.*
72. *Ibid.*
73. Ziadeh, No. 68, p. 41.
74. The Middle East and North Africa, No. 5, p. 780.

2 Tunisia's Relations with the Afro-Asian, Arab and the Maghrib World

Tunisia's foreign policy towards the Afro-Asian countries is, to a very large extent, a function of its decision-makers' attitude with respect to the problems of national identity which focusses on Maghrebian unity, Arab unity, and African unity. In the Tunisian Constitution of 1959, where the Tunisian people proclaimed their determination to remain "true to the coachings of Islam, to the ideal of a Union of the Great Maghreb, to their membership in the Arab family, the co-operation with the African people in building a better future....", it was apparent that, of the three problems, the problem of Maghrebian unity occupied top priority. Hence, the efforts are being made to analyse the Tunisia's relations with Afro-Asian World, with special emphasis to its relations with the Arab world and its attitude towards the question of Maghrebi unity.

Tunisia's National Identity

Tunisia is the home of an old-established people, probably in essence of the same Berber and Carthaginian population as inhabited the country in the time of the Romans. This population was Arabised as the result of the Arab invasions of the seventh and subsequent centuries, while the Arab invaders themselves were eventually fused into the general mass. There must also be an appreciable intermixture of Europeans of Mediterranean origin, who became Muslims after entering Tunisia individually, or who arrived as refugees from Muslim Sicily and Spain. By the fusion of all these elements a distinct state came into being during the rule of the Hafsid dynasty from the thirteenth to the sixteenth centuries, though it was only under subsequent Turkish rule that Tunisia acquired her present frontiers. The continuity of settlement, the long tradition of sedentary and urban life, and the response to western and northern invasions have given Tunisia its distinctive national identity.

Historically, the Jewish minority in Tunisia has played an important role. The Jewish minority came to Tunisia in a series of emigrations, the earliest, it is supposed, at the time of the first diaspora, in the sixth century B.C. Some Berbers were converted to Judaism in Roman times and in the eleventh century, there was all influx of Jewish refugees from Muslim and Christian Spain.

The French protectorate witnessed two changes in the population of the country. The first was the immigration of Italians, Maltese, and French - the French being, at first, in the minority among the Europeans. Other North Africans also entered the country from Algeria, Morocco, and Libya as miners, watch-keepers, or in pursuit of their traditional crafts. At the same time, the Muslim (and Jewish) population began to grow rapidly.[1]

The importance of the past to modern Tunisia is not therefore, that of continuous history as a nation state, of slow constitutional development or the prolonged defence of established frontiers. For most of its history, Tunisia has been part of a larger empire or, in times of weakness, has enjoyed central government only over the more established coastal regions. But there is nothing in the past which Tunisians renounced as alien, and much that they accept with pride. Lacking'the exclusiveness of severe Arab nationalists and the intolerance of puritanical Muslims they do not exclude a pre-Arab past from their national heritage as some West Asian Arabs have done.[2]

The Maghrib

The modern concept of Maghrib was born as part of an aspiration for an Arab "renaissance". Admittedly, one finds in the records of earlier times many manifestations of solidarity and vague feelings of unity (such as the protest by Moroccan Sultan Muhammad Ibn 'Abdallah against France in 1771 over the bombardment of Bizerta and Sousse in Tunisia). Rather, such reactions merely reflected the historical unity of North Africa, a unity that was one of the main historical foundations of modern thought about a regional political entity but was not an integral part of today's Maghrib concept.

Equally irrelevant to the development of the Maghrib concept are the projects and ideas that were circulating in French colonialist circles about "unifying" North Africa in a colonial setting, such as the schemes concerning the Protectorate in Tunisia, its integration into "French Algeria," and the merging of both countries with Morocco into a so-called "French North Africa" (which would, of course, be integrated into the French economy). A related trend was the notion among some European settlers during the 1950s of a kind of integration under which the settlers would be the dominant group in North Africa under the Maghrib itself would become a state similar to South Africa.

The concept of the Maghrib that emerged early in this century was and is based upon three key elements: (1) the notion of the Umma or Islamic community, which holds an enduring appeal for Muslims and, a *fortiori*, for Arabs; this is the socio-political counterpart of the Islamic dogma of *al-tawhid* (the oneness of God); (2) the nationalist reaction against French colonialism and the latter's attempts to undermine the Arab-Islamic identity of the peoples of the area and to separate them from the Arab-Islamic world, the source of their aspirations to freedom and progress; (3) the aspirations of the Maghrib's people for a modern and progressive renewal, which are shared by brethren people of the Arab world and by the Third World as a whole.[3]

The Maghrib or the Arab West covers a territory of 1,749,000 square miles with a total population of approximately thirty million. It is composed of four politically different states: traditional monarchical Libya, constitutional monarchical Morocco, bourgeois republican Tunisia, and proletarian republican (or socialistic) Algeria. Except for

Libya which is politically the least developed of all and whose history follows a somewhat different course, the other three countries have much in common.

For over two centuries, the peoples of these areas were included within the Empires of Almoravids and Almohades. Islam is their common religion, Arabic their common language. History, geography and ethnic factors have bound them together, but set them apart from the Arab East. Although there has been much intermingling of races, the peoples of the Maghrib are basically of Berber origin. Together they share the Mediterranean coast with its common climate and cultivation and the same colonial experience. The period of French colonisation has strengthened the difference between the Eastern Arabs and the North Africans, while tied the latter together by new economic, political and cultural bonds. These bonds have been responsible for the aspiration to Maghrebian unity.

The concept of the Maghrib generally refers to the inhabitants of Algeria, Libya, Morocco, and Tunisia as constituting the people of one nation, but most often understood as the symbol of potential unity of the people of Algeria, Morocco, and Tunisia.[4]

Emergence of the Maghrib Concept

According to some historical sources, Ali Bach Hamba, one of the inspirers of the Tunisian nationalist movement, was "the first leader who thought it was necessary to unify the Arab Maghrib in its struggle for independence. Hamba helped the Algerian patriots; his brother founded in Berlin a committee called The Tunisian-Algerian Committee, and at the same time established contacts with members of the liberation movement in Marrakesh (Morocco) when this country was defending its own existence; later, he worked hand in hand, in Istanbul, with El-Atabi, the Moroccan Mujahid.[5]

Within the ranks of the nationalist vanguard of North Africa, and specially among the members of a movement called "Young Tunisia" founded in 1908 with Ali Bach Hamba as one of the main leaders, there was considerable interest in seeking the help of the Ottoman state, and in establishing connections with it within the framework of the Islamic League. The followers of Turkey's Sultan 'Abd al-Hamid, and their friends among the Salafiyyin in the Arab and Islamic world, were encouraging the Maghrib's nationalists to join with the Islamic League to combat French occupation. But the defeat of Turkey in World War I, and the abrogation of the Caliphate by Mustafa Kemal Ataturk in 1924, compelled the nationalist movements of the Maghrib to rely upon themselves in co-ordinating their propaganda efforts, defending their claims and defining their objectives.

In the mid-1920s, members of the Tunisian, Algerian, and Moroccan nationalist movements began to use Paris as a meeting place. Many organisations were established to defend the interests of workers from the Maghrib.[6] In 1923, for instance, a group calling itself L'Etoile Nord-Africaine was established in Paris to help those workers; in 1926, it became political association which worked to defend the Arab Maghrib and published the French-language newspaper *Al Oumma*. The president of this association, Messali El Hadi, was one of the main leaders of the Algerian nationalist movement.[7]

The Association of North African Muslim Students (ANAMS) which was clearly and consistently-oriented toward the idea of an Arab Maghrib trying to achieve unity through a common struggle for freedom. In fact, the ANAMS played a crucial role in the establishment of personal ties among those students living in France, who later became the backbone of the ruling elites in Morocco, Algeria, and Tunisia, before and after independence. As they advocated the concept of a unified Arab Maghrib, North African students transformed the simple co-ordination of political actions of the moment into an elaborate theory. Thus, the fifth convention of the ANAMS held in 1935 in Tlemcen, Algeria, asserted that "the unification of education" in the Maghrib was a driving force "making possible the awareness of our national unity in North Africa, a unity-based on a common mentality, a common religion, common feelings." The resolution adopted by the same convention states:

"Let no one say we want to create an artificial unity. Absolutely not! We are merely restoring a unity that existed in the past, a unity testified to and warranted by history itself.[8]

During the 1930s, the Maghrib concept became prevalent in North African countries; this idea underlay the thrust of their nationalist movements. For instance, the programme adopted at a convention of the nationalist movement of Spanish-occupied North Morocco held in Tetouan in 1936, included a paragraph recommending "the restoration of ties between the Maghrib's countries—Tunisia, Algeria, and Morocco, and also between them and the Arabo-Islamic countries." In addition, the programme called for "the unification of the various levels of education, and the writing of a common history book to be studied in each of the three countries.[9]

During the same year, a young Tunisian patriot established an association called North African Youth. A condition of membership in this group was adherence to the belief that North Africa is one and indivisible, a single homeland to be defended by its people in a united front.[10]

In Algeria, the Association of the 'Ulama" established in 1928 by the famous Salafist 'Abd al-Hamid Ibn Badis, contributed, through its periodical *Ashihab* and other publications, to the 'emergence of national (Arab-Islamic) awareness not only in Algeria but also in Tunisia and Morocco.

In 1937, L'Etoile Nord-Africaine was succeeded by the Party of the Algerian People. Its programme called for: "the constitution of a common front in which Tunisians, Algerians, and Moroccans should be united for struggling against the imperialistic front." The concept of Maghrebi unity remained alive within the ranks of North African students, workers, and political exiles in Paris.[11] At a convention of the Association of Islamic Culture on February 4, 1939, the organisation's founder, Shaykh al Hadi Senoussi, emphasised that the peoples of North Africa were one people and that the borders separating them were but artificial obstacles.[12]

With the establishment of the Arab League after World War II, Cairo became the hub of the activities of Maghribi nationalist movements, The leaders of many of these movements met there at the Convention of the Arab Maghrib (February 15-22, 1947), which was attended by the secretary of the Arab League and other Arab notables. The main purpose of the convention was to study "the most efficient means of coordinating various activities, unifying representative offices abroad, and fostering the solidarity of the Maghrib, in order to serve the cause of liberation and define its targets."[13]

In fact, the convention succeeded in defining the common goal on which the liberation movements of North Africa would focus. The convention publicly declared "that the Protectorate Treaty imposed upon Tunisia and Morocco is null and void, that France has no rights whatsoever in Algeria, and that Algeria refuses any form of integration into the French Union." Furthermore, the convention announced "the establishment of a permanent committee composed of Maghribi nationalists, with the purpose of coordinating and unifying their plans of common action and struggle." Moreover, the convention committed itself "to work for the orientation of labour, social, cultural, and economic organisations in the three Maghribi countries in a nationalist direction." It decided to establish in Cairo an Office of the Arab Maghrib, which did much to aid the cause of North African independence through it, informational work at the Arab and international levels.

On December 9 of the same year, the Committee or Liberation of the Arab Maghrib was established, upon the recommendation of the Cairo convention. The chairmanship of this committee was offered to the chief of the Moroccan Rif revolution, 'Abd al-rim al-Khaltabi, who had taken refuge in Egypt that June.[14]

Maghribi Nationalism

The period of colonial rule witnessed the rise of nationalism in Maghrib. In fact, Maghribi nationalism began in part as a direct reaction to Western colonial rule. Although influenced by the revival of Arab political consciousness, which made itself felt in the mid-nineteenth century, the form of this nationalist expression was largely European in ideology, terminology, and structural organisation with French leftist political thought particularly influential. Because of this origin, Maghribi has continued to display tendencies that sometimes conflict. That is, traditionalist, religious, and purely Arab components vie with modernist, secular, and bilingual elements, resulting in an ideological cleavage that has yet to be resolved in a manner satisfactory to both masses and elites.[15]

The nationalist response to colonialism was relatively similar throughout the Maghrib. Three distinct ideological tendencies are discernible, and by independence, each was present in all three Maghrib countries, although their functional weight and the timing of their emergence were not identical in Algeria, Tunisia, and Morocco. First, there were the liberal assimilationists—sons of the old, traditional elite who admired and imitated the colonial rulers, assimilated some of their styles and values, accepted their rules of the game, and attempted to engage in a dialogue. Liberals were particularly influential during the early and middle years of colonialism in Algeria and Tunisia.

A second elite group was composed of traditionalists, who assumed a nationalistic-scripturalist orientation. This perspective was advocated by the learned, scholarly, and urban families, which had historically constituted a distinctive high-status group. They called for a reaffirmation of national, cultural, and religious integrity in the face of Western colonial domination. During the period of colonialism, this group was also the first to call for the maintenance of a national personality, usually by stressing the use, revision, and celebration of the Islamic heritage (scripturalism) and by emphasising Arabism as a language, culture, and common history (nationalism).

A third group was composed of populists. Trained in European schools and environments, these individuals sought to generate in their own societies the liberal trends formed in Europe through bourgeois revolutions. At the same time, they rebelled against the colonial status quo and appealed for mass mobilisation against foreign domination. Unlike the traditionalists, the populists had a broader base of support, higher levels of education, and a more cosmopolitan outlook. And unlike the assimilationists, they were determined to attack and oppose colonial domination. In essence, the populists were secularists with a modernising view of political change, who, while profoundly marked by a nationalist ideology and political activism, were influenced by Europe, which represented a model for their own growth. Thus, although they were militant in their struggle against France, they tended to be somewhat reconciliatory once in power.

A fourth category of elite types has emerged in the post-independence period. Emanating essentially from the radical intelligentsia and workers, this most recent nationalistic group calls for mass mobilisation and the radical restructuring of indigenous society. Its members have tended to view the infrastructure of dependency of their societies much more seriously than their predecessors had done. This orientation has only recently appeared, however, and even today its in influence is indirect.[16]

Islam, Arab and Maghribi Nationalism

The Maghrib is religiously more unified, with the Malikite school of orthodox or Sunni Islam predominating. There are no indigenous Christian minorities and, except for the Kharijites of Jerba and the Mzabites of Algeria, no major Islamic sects. Indigenous Jews, once numerous, now constitute an insignificant and steadily diminishing minority. Because of this religious uniformity, Islam is an important common denominator throughout North Africa, mitigating differences of tribe, language, and life-style. Notwithstanding different policies toward religion and religious practice, adopted by the various political leaders of the Maghrib,[17] Islam is designated as the state religion in each of the three constitutions. The Algerian and Tunisian presidents must be Muslims, and in the Moroccan constitution the king is given the title "commander of the faithful."

Despite the predominance of Islam as a social, cultural, and ideological force, traditional Islamic institutions have declined significantly in importance, especially in Tunisia and Algeria. This decline can be attributed to modernisation and the increased power of the central state apparatus. It is also in part the result of Islamic reformist movements that influenced the Maghrib in the late nineteenth century.[18]

Linkage to Islam and Arab nationalism, recognition of unity of objectives, and permanent coordination of actions: this is the content of the Maghrib concept as it evolved through a common struggle against French occupation. Thus, the Maghrib concept was used to ignite the enthusiasm of the struggling masses, and to thwart the colonialists and fanatics of the French administration, who could never accept the possibility of liquidating French domination in North Africa.[19]

Obviously, while the liberation war was raging in Algeria it was impossible for either Morocco or Tunisia to claim their respective historical borders or that part of the Sahara which belonged to them. All were convinced that it was necessary to lower the tone of all territorial claims and give highest priority to the immediate task of supporting the Algerian people, by all means and with no conditions, in their struggle for national liberation. The border problem, it was widely agreed, could be solved after the independence of Algeria, in the spirit of Maghribi unity. This was the thrust of a joint declaration (1961) by the Moroccan government and the provisional government of the Algerian Republic.[20]

Inevitably, the border problem soon became impossible to ignore. In fact, war erupted between Morocco and Algeria just one year after the independence of the latter. Border disputes continue to cloud the relationships between the Maghrib's countries; such disputes are the main factor in the so-called "problem of the Western Sahara," which threatens at any moment to rekindle the armed struggle between Algeria, Morocco, and Mauritania, despite the relative decrease of tension between Tunisia, on one side, and Algeria and Libya, on the other side. In any case, the clearing of the atmosphere could not be other than temporary, for the absence of democracy in the countries of the Maghrib can only lead to political regimes of the same kind, in spite of the various masks under which they may hide. In order to make up for their inability to liquidate the colonial heritage or start a real process of development, these regimes resort, from time to time, to distracting their people from domestic problems by focussing on some "external" danger beyond the borders.[21]

Mass solidarity among the Maghribi people was something deep and continuing and sometimes its manifestations were concrete and even violent: examples include the 1937 strike in Tunisia organised by the Neo-Destour Party to protest the incarceration of certain Moroccan nationalist leaders; the unrest in Morocco and Tunisia caused by the Setif (Algeria) massacre in 1945; the violent demonstrations in Casablanca protesting the December 1952 assassination of Ferhat J.H. had a Tunisian labour union leader; and the violent demonstrations that took place in Algerian cities during August 1955 as an expression of solidarity with the Moroccan people, on the occasion of the second anniversary of the deportation of Mohammed V, the King of Morocco.

Nevertheless, the colonialist barriers separating the countries of the Maghrib did impose a sort of duality on the perception held by both the masses and the elites of the idea of Maghribi unity. As Julien observes, "Despite their will for union, the Algerian, Tunisian, and Moroccan parties and groups were led to organise themselves on a local basis and to formulate particular claims. Nationalism, pan-Maghribism, and pan-Arabism overlapped without contradiction, but with different expressions that depended on country and period. Those trends represent three facets of one problem which each nation is trying to solve in relation to local conditions.[22] While nationalism, pan-Maghribism, and pan-Arabism co-existed without conflict before independence, circumstances determined the extent of the influence of each of these three facets of the Maghrib collective ego. The colonial heritage played a role in magnifying the narrow, sometimes chauvinistic, "national ego," to the detriment of the Maghrib concept and pan-Arabism.[23]

Tunisia adopted the cause because she was basically sympathetic to the concept or Maghrebian solidarity and welcomed any alliance which would strengthen her posture in the struggle for independence. A sever blow was dealt to the incipient effort when Tunisia accepted in 1955, France's offer of internal autonomy, and Bourguiba urged the Tunisian *fellaghas* to lay down their arms and stop their campaign against the French troops. This move enraged the Algerians and Moroccans, who maintained that the Tunisians had broken their common pledge to lay down their arms only when all three countries became independent and complained that even if Bourguiba wanted to stop the fighting in Tunisia he could at least have let the fellaghas go over the Aures to help the FLN.

For those who are familiar with Bourguiba's tactic of "stages" and his politics of national interest, 'the Tunisian move was logical and comprehensible. The following period was devoted to the manoeuvering for complete independence and the consolidation of governmental power in Tunisia. Little was said and less was done about Maghribian unity.

Complaint about Tunisian betrayal persisted. Even in 1961, after the Bizerte affair Bourguiba still had to justify his action by saying that:

> People have criticised us for not engaging in a war side by side with our Algerian brothers. But logically there had to be a base for the Algerians, and this base, Tunisia could not assure them while directly participating in the fighting.[24]

At the same time, he loudly supported the Algerian nationalists to dissipate their suspicion of Tunisia. Immediately after gaining their independence in 1956, both Morocco and Tunisia pronounced in support of Algerian independence and offered their mediation to help settle the Algerian war and to bring about a fruitful co-operation between France and the Maghrib.

The guiding principle of Tunisian foreign policy then was to help the Algerian nationalists within the framework of Maghribian solidarity, but without; jeopardising Tunisia's, immediate interest which was to prevent the Algerian war from spilling over into Tunisia which, in turn, meant the adoption of a "correct attitude" with respect to the Algerian dispute.

On October 22, 1956, the Sultan of Morocco, accompanied by his principal assistants, flew to Tunis to discuss with Bourguiba and other Tunisian leaders on the Algerian situation and other matters of North African interest. Their joint communique' mentioned the "complete agreement" of the two governments on the Algerian question, their "entire solidarity with the Algerian people in their efforts to obtain their freedom and their pledge to concert appropriate measures which will serve the interests of the brother-countries of the Maghrib pending the signing of a treaty of alliance and co-operation which the two Governments have agreed to conclude.[25]

The Tunisian-Moroccan discussions of October 1956, were designed to pave the way for further talks on Maghribian co-operation which were expected to take place in Tunis between the two Governments and the Algerian leaders who were to join them from Rabat. En route to Tunis the latter were arrested by the French authorities; the projected conference of North African leaders never met. The first official attempt at laying a foundation for Maghribian co-operation was nipped in the bud.

Enthusiasm waned, only to be revived with full fanfare and rising expectation during the short period between the bombing of Sakiet in February 1958, and the coming in power of de Gaulle as a result of the Algerian settlers' uprising in May 1958. Political turmoil, common danger and unknown opportunities provided the background for the Tangier conference in April 1958, between the leaders of the political parties of the three countries.[26]

The Conference of Unity 1958

The Maghrib concept has been a driving force in the

nationalist struggle of North African peoples since the beginning of the century. However, it was not officially endorsed until 1958; the Tangiers Conference, often called "the Conference of Unity" (April 27-30, 1958) was the first public event in which the Maghrib, concept was given a clear definition. It was no longer construed as a simple "co-ordination of activities" but rather as an organised activity leading to the establishment of a federal union that would group together the three countries of the Maghrib.[27]

The Tangiers Conference was attended by the leaders of Morocco's Istiqlal party, the leaders of Tunisia's Neo-Destour Party, and some leaders of the Algerian National Liberation Front. (Libya, then still a monarchy, was invited to attend the Tangiers Conference but declined to attend). The meeting ended with the adoption of several resolutions and recommendations; among other things it was decided to increase the support given to the Algerian Revolution, with a recommendation that a provisional government of revolutionary Algeria be established "to denounce the help given by some Western countries to France in the war it is waging against the Algerian people" and "to liquidate the after-effects of colonialism in the Maghrib."[28]

The most important resolution however, was that concerning "the unification of the Arab Maghrib." It stated "that the people of the Maghrib are unanimous in seeking to unify their destinies on the basis of an unfailing solidarity of common interests"; it declared "that it is high time to put that will of unification in concrete form, through common projects enabling the people of the region to have the place they deserve in a world of nations"; it decided "to undertake the necessary action to carry out this unity, considering the federative formula as the most adapted to the real situation of the countries participating in the conference"; it proposed, in consequence, "the formation, as a temporary stage, of a consultative council of the Maghrib, stemming from the National Assemblies of Morocco and Tunisia and from the National Council of the Algerian Revolution, with the task of reviewing the issues of common interest, and of submitting recommendations to local governments."

Also, the conference recommended "to the governments of the Maghrib's countries to refrain from committing themselves individually to external and defensive alliances before establishing federal institutions".[29]

Some observers have conjectured about a possible link between the announcement of a project of "federal union" of the Maghrib's countries, on the one hand, and the formation of the Egyptian-Syrian union and the Hashemite federal union of Iraq and Jordan, on the other hand (both of the latter unions were proclaimed in February 1958, several months before the Tangiers Conference). Jean Lacouture, a French Journalist, speculated that the emergence of the two bilateral unions might have pushed the leaders in Rabat and Tunis into proclaiming quickly their "decision of unifying the Maghrib" as a means of placating domestic populations, who found attractive the Mashriq's steps toward unity.[30]

So far, the Tangiers resolutions regarding the unification of the Maghrib have remained a mere project for the future. Indeed, as we have noted earlier, the Maghrib concept, which had an exceptionally strong practical impact before independence, has come to a standstill, losing all operational efficacy, because of (1) the lack of democracy in the three countries of the Maghrib, and (2) the inability of their rulers to liquidate the colonial heritage.

A six-man Maghrib Secretariat came into being as a result of the Tangier Conference to assure the realisation of the resolutions adopted until a split in the Istiqlal party in January 1959, caused it to lapse.[31]

In June 1958, and official meeting between the Governments of Morocco and Tunisia and the representatives of the FLN was held in Tunis whereupon the participants pledged to conduct "common action on the diplomatic plane in view of arriving at a peaceful solution for the Algerian problem." The three parties rejected de Gaulle's plan for "integration", upheld the right of the Algerian people to sovereignty and independence, and took note of the effort of the Moroccan and Tunisian Governments to find means to put an end to the Algerian war.

Meanwhile, steps were agreed upon between Tunisia and Morocco to create "permanent mixed commissions" to promote economic, cultural, technical and social co-operation between the two countries. They also pledged to hold "continuing consultations" to reinforce their co-operation and coordinate their efforts on the diplomatic plane and to "help realise the Union of the Arab Maghrib".[32]

When working for Meghribian unity, Bourguiba was motivated by the desire to satisfy popular aspiration to a Greater Meghrib and by his determination to use the appeal of Maghribian unity to prevent a drift of the FLN toward Nasser, to press the Algerian leaders to adopt a moderate stand in order to facilitate an early settlement of the Algerian crisis, and to orient North Africa toward the West by working for a fruitful Franco-Maghribian co-operation.

But the success of Bourguiba's policy depended heavily upon the French-attitude in Algeria. When De Gaulle, "the man of the Algerian solution" as they called him in North Africa, came to power in France, hope was high and Maghribian leaders were hopefully, waiting for his favourable response to their plea. They waited in vain. De Gaulle offered no magic solution to the Algerian problem. Effort towards unity lost its dynamic and friction began to develop between the brother countries.

In October 1958, both Tunisia and Morocco were admitted to the Arab League whereupon Tunisia immediately engaged itself in a bitter quarrel with the United Arab Republic. The first sign of basic disagreement between Tunisia and Morocco appeared when the League voted unanimously to condemn Tunisian position. Morocco failed to come to the defense of Tunisia. Critical of the League and disappointed over the attitude of its Maghribian ally, the Tunisian delegate left the 1958, meeting and boycotted the League.

Political gap between Morocco and Tunisia was formalised in 1959, when Tunisia promulgated its first Constitution and became a Republic while Morocco remained a "defensive" monarchy. Tension mounted again when in

1960, Tunisia, together with France, recognised Mauritania whose territory was claimed by Morocco, and sponsored its admission to the United Nations. The year of 1960, also marked the beginning of the United Nations operation in the Congo. Disagreement over United Nations policy in the Congo divided the African countries.

Throughout the revolutionary period, when all their efforts were directed toward their own struggle, the leaders of the Algerian Revolution avoided considering the problem of the colonial heritage as it affected Morocco and Tunisia. This was quite understandable, because they wanted to maintain fraternal relations with all sides. But the relations between Tunisia and Morocco deteriorated rapidly, due to the opposition of Tunisia to the Moroccan claim on the "province of Chenguit" (in Mauritania). The Moroccan and Tunisian governments broke off diplomatic relations and engaged in sharp polemics on the radio and in other information media. Both protagonists were obviously trying to win support from the Algerian Revolution's leaders by exploiting the Maghrib concept in their quarrel.

In December 1960, President Bourguiba declared with much enthusiasm that Tunisia had decided to link its destiny to that of Algeria and that both countries would, therefore, merge in one republic, with Tunisia renouncing its independence. This declaration of faith was presented "as the only way to get the Algerian question out of the deadlock." Nevertheless, the declaration could be construed as an attempt to push Morocco aside and evade the Tangiers resolutions.[33]

Turning to the possibility of the unification of the Arab States of North Africa, Bourguiba said that these countries, which were united by links of languages, religion, and history, had all been dominated by the same colonialsim, had struggled for the same ideal of independence, and had helped one another. He was convinced that their union would increase their influence in the world, and that economic and social development would come about more easily in a North African framework. Unity, however, should not be imposed but should come from the will of the people. Tunisia hoped that the eastern Arabs would engage in a similar process of unification with the same methods, so that later they could realise the union of all the Arabs in a form decided by the peoples themselves.[34]

In January 1961, Morocco played host to the Casablanca Conference which supported Moroccan claim to Mauritania, adopted a militant stand on the question of colonialism, and a critical attitude towards the United Nations operation in the Congo. Being left out by the Casablanca powers, Tunisia later decided to join the moderate Monrovia group which was comprised mainly of former French colonies: the two countries of the Maghrib now found themselves belonging to two opposite groups in Africa.

Tunisian-Algerian relations did not fare any better. In 1959, Tunisia enraged the Algerian leaders by allowing the oil pipeline from the Edjele to pass through its territory after Libya had refused to permit its installment at Tripoli to express its solidarity with Algeria. Bourguiba maintained that though he supported the Algerians in their war with France, he had no right to reject any proposal which would help to improve the economic position of his country which was too poor to afford a purely sentimental gesture that could do no possible good to the Algerians.[35] But the Algerians did not agree with him, they lashed out as agreement that "jeoparside(d) the highest principles of our struggle... the total liberation of Algeria, including the Sahara, and the unity of the Maghrib.[36]

In addition, French intransigence in Algeria and fierce fighting undermined Bourguibist techniques and his infallibility. As the Algerian war grew in intensity, the Algerians became more militant and more uncompromising, and the gap between Algerian attitude and Tunisian policy widened. Suspicion and friction developed between the Algerian leaders who distrusted Tunisia's intention and the Tunisian leaders who disagreed with Algeria's militant stand. The participation of the FLN in the Casablanca group and its growing alignment with Nasser strained further the relations between the two countries. Up to the eve of the Bizerte crisis their leaders still kept exchanging heated arguments over Tunisia's claim over part of the Sahara.[37]

Only the magnitude of the Bizerte crisis in July the three Maghribian countries together. But this superficial unity against a common enemy did not seem strong enough to outweigh their basic differences. Tunisia had become a Republic and remained a faithful supporter of the United Nations and its Secretary-General, whereas Morocco and Algeria had joined a militant political group in Africa opposing to the United Nations operation in the Congo and aligned themselves with Tunisia's erstwhile rival, the UAR.

Less than a year later in July 1961, the Moroccan government reacted in a similar way. In a joint declaration released in Rabat, it was announced that the Moroccan government and the provisional government of the Algerian Revolution had reached an agreement about "the measures to be taken for building the Maghrib"; but Tunisia was totally ignored. Later, on January 23, 1962, the highest Moroccan authorities announced the decision taken by both governments to set up a joint ministerial committee "for studying the path to be followed for building the Maghrib." Two 'weeks later, this committee came into existence; Tunisia' and the Tangiers resolutions were once more ignored. However, just two years after this, "unity" declaration (Algeria having become-independent in the meantime): the two countries were fighting each other over, the border post at Hassi Beida.[38]

In 1962, Algeria became independent. But a struggle for power developed between the Algerian Provisional Government (GPRA) headed by Ben Khedda on the one hand and Ben Bella, his supporters and the External Algerian Liberation Army based in Tunisia on the other. At the beginning, Bourguiba seemed to have backed the wrong horse. Undoubtedly, recalling the first moment of Tunisian independence, he threw his support to Ben Khedaa whom he sympathised and respected for his gift of compromise as opposed to the aggressive Ben Bella. Although Bourguiba thought of Ben Bella as an "honest man who (was) sincerely mistaken", he tended to liken, Ben Bella's detachment from the GPRA to the ill-fated Youssefist movement.[39] As the factional conflict deepened, Tunisia prudently avoided diplomatic recognition of the Ben Khedda Government and attempted to establish informal diplomatic contacts with the Ben Bella's faction as well. In October 1962, after Ben Bella had established himself the victor in the internal conflict in Algeria, Tunisia tendered its recognition to the new government,[40] but a diplomatic faux-pas had been made which was mostly responsible for the uneasy relations between Tunisia and Algeria. Tunisia had hoped for an independent Algeria grateful for her support and counsel, and moderate in outlook. But the long, bloody war in Algeria and the initial miscalculation or Bourguiba had given Tunisia a strong, but suspicious, bitter, and militant neighbour.

There had been serious hope that Algerian independence would be achieved peacefully and within the framework of Maghribian unity and Franco-Maghribian co-operation. Expectation rose to its peak in 1958, with the Tangier and Tunis conferences when the Maghribian leaders met to lay the foundation for Maghribian unity and appealed to France to lend a helping hand. In this period, the keystone of Tunisia's strategy was to have been

> ...an independent Algeria, closely tied to Tunisia by bonds of sympathy, gratitude and similarity of outlook and socio-economic patterns, reinforced by an Algerian need for and deference to Tunisian diplomatic leadership. Morocco would presumably have been drawn into this body politics as a republic rather than a monarchy, and Libya would have been fatally attracted by the gravity of the federation. And in the whole, Tunisia had certainly hoped to play the same geographical, cultural, and synthesising role it had performed in its earlier history.[41]

Once more, the North African students were those who took the initiative. In fact, from April 17 to 19, 1962, while the Evian negotiations which led to the independence of Algeria were entering a crucial stage, the General Federation of the Students of the Maghrib held a seminar in Tunis on the subject of "The Economic Foundations of the Maghrib." One of the most important participants, Abderrahim Bouabid, lawyer, former Moroccan minister of economic affairs, and member of the General Secretariat of the National Union of Popular Forces (first secretary of the Socialist Union of Popular Forces), stated: "A content must be given to the idea of unity of the Maghrib, and the means to reach this target must be defined." As regards the economic unity of the Maghrib, he made some practical and clear proposals which can be summarised as follows: (1) the co-ordination of economic planning in the countries of the Maghrib as a first step toward the development of a regional economic plan; (2) the establishment of a regional administration for agricultural and mining resources, in order to promote co-operation in export activities; (3) the exploitation of common energy resources and the formulation of unified oil and natural gas policy; (4) the establishment of a regional iron and steel complex; (5) the establishment of a regional chemical industrial complex; (6) the creation of a custom union and the co-ordination of financial and monetary policies.[42]

The Tunisian delegate, Ahmed Ben Salah, then minister of planning, discussed the ideological content of Bouabid's proposals. He stated that the economic foundations of the Maghrib could not rest on "liberalism"; in his view, "liberalism" would mean the continuation of colonialist bonds, while the Maghrib's unity should shatter those bonds and curb the social classes that had inherited the interests and the mentality of colonialism. In his view, this did not imply the adoption of a "foreign" ideology, since the unity of the Maghrib must be built on "a sound economic basis, with total independence from all kinds of foreign ideology," in the context of a choice "to achieve economic development instead of mere growth that can be statistically expressed but is far from meeting the real needs of the people," Moreover, "the necessity of an economic balance between the industrial, agricultural, and other sectors" was to be taken into account.[43]

Less than a month after the Tunis seminar, from May 25 to 27, 1962, the National Union of Popular Forces held its second convention in Casablanca.[44] Here, the Maghrib concept was interpreted as in the Tunis seminar, but with a clearer political formulation and a broader content. The ideological report adopted by this convention stated the: following: "The Maghrib is one homeland": "the independence of Morocco and Tunisia, its complex and well-known circumstances ... were but an awful colonialist manoeuver aimed at dismantling the revolutionary front of the Maghrib and dangerously isolating our Algerian brothers." But is it possible "to refuse independence?" Further on the report read:

> to maintain the territorial and political partition of the Maghrib will inexorably lead to neo-colonialism as well as to political regimes that are subservient to foreigners and domestically repressive, because the schemes of concerned foreign states, aiming usually at reaching a certain balance, will exacerbate the rivalries, conflicts, and artificial antagonisms that exist between the interests and respective personalities of the countries of the Maghrib. [Moreover, the report stated] that the so-called conflict between Algeria and Morocco, concerning their borders and their sovereignty over certain parts of the Sahara, is artificial and dangerous; it is a conflict that cannot be solved by negotiation on the basis of documents resulting from various foreign interventions on the contrary, it will represent an exorbitant price for the division of the Maghrib and will weaken the warring parties.
>
> "that it is only within the frame of the Maghrib that a true policy of economic planning can be worked out; it is also within the same frame that a land reform programme would have the best chances of success." Thus, the unity of the Maghrib "will be realised by the masses and not by a 'generous' gift of politicians whose only concern is to seek opportunities to show their

> diplomatic courtesy and their ability to conclude bartering deals ... As an organised and conscious force, the masses will be not only an efficient tool of unity but also, once this unity is realised, a guarantee of its success, its right orientation, and its potential to carry out the great mission of building, on a scientific basis, a democratic and prosperous society."

The report stated as to the geographic setting of the Maghrib's unity, it stretches:

> "from the Senegal river, on the Atlantic coast, to the Egyptian-Libyan border." This is why' "the unity of the Maghrib is an integral part of the revolutionary mass movement of the African continent." It is also in direct osmosis with the unity trend of the Arab world and is one of its most important stages." In itself, Arab unity "cannot secure the objective conditions necessary to its success if it does not rest on popular awareness, based on responsibility, political development, and scientific organisation. Therefore, it is presently impossible to separate the struggle for unity from the struggle for democracy; it is equally impossible to separate the battle for unity from its progressive foundations and revolutionary perspectives.[45]

At the official level, some practical initiatives were taken "in order to build the Maghrib's unity." In the wake of the "war of sands" between Algeria and Morocco (fall 1963), contacts were established between the governments of Algeria, Morocco, and Tunisia and specialised commissions were set up. Then periodical interministerial meetings were organised, including the historic meetings of the three ministers of economic affairs that took place in Tunis during September 29, October 1, 1964, and at which it was decided "to establish a well-defined economic' and commercial framework for the realisation of the economic unity of the Maghrib." The ministers decided to set up for this purpose a permanent consultative commission on the Maghrib with the task of preparing studies and projects relating to "the economic integration of the Maghrib.[46] The commission held several meetings; the ministers met from time to time; and modest practical steps were taken, while studies, projects, and agreements piled up. It might have seemed that the Maghrib concept was at last on its way to realisation, if only in small steps.

The June 19, 1965 Algerian coup *d'etat,* however, led to the emergence of another viewpoint within the ambitious, "revolutionary" bureaucracy. It gradually became apparent that the Algerians were "manoeuvering and hesitating" in connection with the inter-ministerial meetings and those of the permanent consultative commission.

French policy in Algeria had written the epitaph to such hope. And at the wake of Algerian independence, no firm foundation for Maghribian unity had been built, the three brother countries of the Maghrib were far from ready for good neighbourly relations, let alone for Maghribian unity.

There were cleavages between the homogeneous, open, republican, and disciplined society of Tunisia, and the diversified, withdrawn, autocratic atmosphere of Morocco, and the self-reliant, harsh Algerian leadership who distrusted the moderation 'and elasticity of Tunisian tactics and did not share the generally friendly feelings shown by Tunisia to the West and its ideals. Furthermore, being jealous of her newly won independence, proud of her war achievement, and eager to carry the torch of revolution throughout Africa, Algeria was in no mood to relinquish any part of her sovereignty and revolutionary fervour in favour of co-operation.' And the participation of oil-rich Algeria was an indispensable condition for the viability of Maghribian unity.

While newly-found friends in Africa and elsewhere soothed the need for Maghribian unity, the unsolved frontiers problem, untamed by the hope for joint exploitation of the Sahara resources, threatened to erupt into open conflict. Thus, in the post Algerian independence period, between Morocco and Algeria there were several armed clashed in the Tindouf area over the border problem. 'Between Tunisia and Algeria, diplomatic relations were severed and vituperations were exchanged over Tunisian charge that

Algeria had aided the plot to assassinate President Bourguiba in December 1962, and harboured Tunisian exiles.[47]

But beneath all these political differences and personal rivalries, a case could still be made for Maghribian co-operation. History, geography, and ethnic factors have created special bonds between the three North African nations and produced food for popular sentiment and habit to think of the Maghrib as an indivisible whole, different from the Arab East and Black Africa. Economic necessity and national interest also advocate for co-operation.

A report released in May, 1964, by the UNESCO's "Industrial Co-ordination Mission" in North Africa warned that because of the lack of regional co-operation, the economies of the four Arab nations (including Libya) of North Africa might be headed toward "disintegration" rather than money-saving integration. The report further suggested that co-ordination of iron and steel production and marketing was "imperative". It specifically pointed out that Tunisia's recent steel plant project near Bizerte was "too small to be economical and that a Maghrib-wide market was needed to attract investment. As far as energy was concerned, the mission recommended that Algeria with abundant cheap power-based on its natural gas, could supply electricity to neighbouring Morocco and Tunisia where power costs were high. Such link-ups would save up to $30 million in power plant outlays and up to $1 million a year in power costs in all three countries. Also, the three subsidised national airlines—Royal Air Maroc, Air Algerie, and Tunis Air—could be easily integrated to cut costs and eliminate competition. In short, the team suggested that the region develop big economical one-of-a-kind plants notably in flat grass, ammonia, and rayon-instead of small duplicating national plants.[48]

There is little doubt that the Tunisian leaders-and others-have been aware of these facts. Bourguiba, when introducing the visiting Libyan Prime Minister to the Tunisian National Assembly in January 1957, assessed the political strength of a united Maghrib as follows: "These four countries will constitute a material and above all a moral force which other countries will have to take into account.[49] Later, he added: "all our economic and social problems will be easier to solve at the level of the Maghrib.[50]

In the earlier years of the Tunisian Republic, efforts at Maghrib building were partly motivated by deep-seated popular desire, partly by the wish on the part of the Tunisian leaders to make up for the guilt complex caused by the acceptance of internal autonomy and "desertion" of the common armed struggle, and partly by their desire to orient the Maghrib toward the West. At that time, the link (political and sentimental) with France was rather strong, and Bourguiba once had wanted to include France into his Maghribian "ensemble": he had urged for the creation of a "French-North African community" in which Algeria would acquire an independent status like that of Tunisia and Morocco.[51]

But the concept of Algerian independence, then, was anathema to the French; Bourguiba's plea was not heeded. Hope was aroused in 1958, when De Gaulle, who had been reported to favour autonomy for Algeria within a federal system embracing France, Algeria, Tunisia, and Morocco, came to power in France.[52] But events soon bore out that was vain hope. Tunisia now was prepared for a long war in Algeria. Efforts at Maghribian unity building as such were somewhat slowed down in favour of the concentration in helping the Algerians to achieve their independence so that Algeria, once obtained independence, would be grateful to Tunisia's assistance and leadership, and would be willing to cooperate with Tunisia. But uncontrollable events, especially the development of the Algerian war, had destroyed Bourguiba's design.

Recent discovery of Algerian and Libyan oil pointed up to the economic advantages of Maghribian co-operation and added incentive to the undertaking (at least, as far as the Tunisians were concerned), but it also caused serious disagreement among the Maghribian brothers over the use of the Sahara resources. The bitter quarrel between the FLN and the Tunisian Government shortly before the Bizerte crisis over Tunisian claim over part of the Sahara, and the armed clashes between newly independent Algeria and Morocco in 1962-1963, showed that, at times, the consideration of national interest had prevailed over purely sentimental aspiration to Maghrib unity.

Tunisia's effort at Maghrib building was paralysed for a moment, after the Bizerte episode and during the first year of Algerian independence. It was resumed slowly in 1963, when the two neighbours decided to patch-up their differences.

Bourguiba now was set for a long-term planning toward Maghribian unity. The talk of the day was not much on Maghribian unity, but on Maghribian co-operation. And it was not so much motivated by sentimental links as by economic interests and by the fact that it would constitute a convenient alibi to the pull of Arab unity and African unity. In a speech on the occasion of the festivities in celebration of the evacuation of Bizerte, attended by Nasser and Ben Bella, Bourguiba declared that:

> ... it is our duty to try sincerely and honestly to unite ourselves even more closely with those nearest to us, that is to say, with our Arab and Moslem neighbours, starting with the Algerians and Libyans. In the subsequent stage, this action will extend to the Great Arab Maghrib, then to the entire Arab nation and, finally, to the whole continent of Africa."[53]

The Tunisian President resorted to his famous "strategy of stages" to say, in effect, that building Arab unity or African unity was a long process and that, for the time being, he would prefer to concentrate in cultivating effective co-operation with his immediate Maghribian neighbours, especially with Algeria.

For, except for the Treaty of friendship signed in 1957, between Tunisia and Libya, there has been little concrete co-operation between the two countries. Libya is composed of three very dissimilar, uncomplementary regions flung out over a vast space (Tripolitania, Cyrenaica, and Fezzan), its sense of national being is still rudimentary, its personality still unformed.[54] Rich in oil resources, Libya is attractive as a potential economic partner, but little co-operation with it could be possible so long as it does not overcome the fundamental problems of nation-building.

Towards Morocco, Tunisia's policy has been correct and warm. Their conflict over Mauritania died down somewhat after the disbandment of the two opposing Casablanca and Monrovia groups to which they had belonged, and their participation in the Organisation for African Unity in 1963. Yet basic differences between a republic and a monarchy remained. Although a series of conventions-cultural, economic and judicial had been concluded by representatives of the two countries in 1959, up until July 1964, only a very few of their provisions had been carried out.[55]

Besides, Morocco was not as rich as Algeria and was not linked to Tunisia by geographic proximity. Tripartite co-operation (i.e., the inclusion of Algeria) was preferable to bipartite relationship.

It is, therefore, mainly with Algeria that Tunisia sought to cultivate economic relations. Economic necessity, among other things, has brought the pragmatist Ben Bella and the realist Bourguiba together. They have met several times since Algeria became independent and apparently have decided to overcome their personal disagreement. Tunisia's subtle offer in the Spring of 1963, to help ease Algeria's economic difficulties as deeply appreciated by Algeria and has done much to restore confidence and mutual understanding between the two countries.

This led to a series of agreements signed in the Fall, 1963, providing for the linking of telephone and telegraph lines, the sharing of natural gas and oil resources, co-ordination of production and marketing or many products, and co-operation in several other spheres.[56] Steps were also taken to integrate certain of their industrial projects such as the Renault-Berlier assembly line, glass industry, and the production of superphosphates at Gabes (Tunisia) from ammonia provided by Algeria.[57]

Parallelly, there were also encouraging signs with respect to co-operation on a wider basis, the highlight of which came-in October 1964, when the economic ministers of Morocco, Tunisia, Algeria, and Libya met in Tunis to conclude a protocol under which a permanent consultative committee would be formed to draft measures for economic co-operation, namely the establishment of freer trade and harmonisation of customs policies, to consider means for unifying the industrialisation of four countries, and to study the adaptation of the Maghrib policies to those of the European Common Market.[58] A month later, a source of friction between Morocco and her Maghribian allies seemed to have finally been removed when it was reported that Mauritania was also included in some discussions on Maghribian unity.[59]

These are preliminary but important steps toward close economic co-operation which is perhaps the surest foundation for the creation of a Greater Maghrib, the future political orientation of which would to a certain extent, be determined by the response of the Common Market to their individual and collective bids for associate membership.

With time, patience, perseverance, and encouragement and assistance from the Common Market countries, especially France, there is a good possibility that a modified version of Bourguiba's old dream of a Greater Maghrib attached to the West might be realised.

Tunisia and the Arab World

(A) The problem of Arab Nationalism: Arab nationalism can be tentatively defined as "the consciousness of belonging to the Arab people and sharing in the common history, traditions, culture and aspirations of the community. Its grand goal is the political, economic, and cultural unification of all the Arab states.[60] The idea of Arab nationalism has a powerful hold on the imagination of the peoples of the Arab East and North Africa, and few Arab leaders are strong enough to ignore its appeal.

Centuries of Arab history, beginning in the early part of the seventh century when the Arabs were, for the first time, united under the leadership of the Prophet and his successors have developed between the Arab people everlasting linguistic and cultural ties. The Arabic language and the religion of Islam are living proofs of Arab unity; and the shared memories of past glories and resentment against Western material superiority induce the aspiration to receive the golden age of Arab greatness through the strength of unity.

Yet Arab national consciousness had remained dormant until the catalyst of European nationalist ideology caused the awakening of Arab nationalism. One of the early manifestations of Arab nationalism appeared in Syria just before and during World War I, when a clandestine group there issued the first call for the rejection of Turkish rule. Initial Arab unity movement was strictly regional in character and was restricted to only a few Arab areas the manifestoes of the *Ligue de la Patrie Arabe* in 1905, advocating the replacement of the Ottoman Caliphate by an Arab Caliphate centred in the Hijaz, referred only to Hijaz, Syria, and Iraq (two satellites ruled by Sharif Husayn Ibn Ali's two sons, Faysal and Abdallah). The idea of Arab unity then did not include Egypt or North African countries which were developing their own nationalisms and had different interests than the Asian Arab world. It was not until the 1940's that Egypt decided to embrace the Arab cause, and not until the Palestinian question had presented the Arab states with a common threat that they gathered together in the Arab League established in March 1945, to further the cause of Arab unity.[61]

The League began to come increasingly under Egyptian leadership, especially after the Egyptian Revolution of July 23, 1952, and after Nasser, having settled the canal Zone and the Sudanese problems, turned his attention to the struggle for Arab unity, along with his attempt to play a role as one of the "big three" of the neutralist bloc, besides Nehru and Tito.[62]

The common hatred toward Israel, the inspiration of past glories, the unity of language and religion, envy and an emotional reaction to the overwhelming power and progress of the West in the modern world with its implicit imputation of inferiority to the East, the alleged advantages of regional co-operation (as shown by the European Common Market), and the desire to play a major role in world affairs have drawn the Arabs together. But there have been divisive factors at work to undermine this effort toward Arab unity.

A careful reading of Islamic history may reveal a golden age of Arab greatness, but hardly a continuing tradition of political unity. Before the advent of the Abbasid Caliphate, the building of the Arab empire was "an expression of the Arab nation, not of Islam." There was no sense of unity and purpose between the Arab ruling class and the conquered peoples. They fused into the great Muslim community only with the end of the Umayyad empire and the advent of the Abbasids. But the empire was racked with political conflict and division. It began with the establishment of a separate state, and eventually a separate Caliphate in Spain by a member of the deposed Umayyad family in 756. North Africa, because of its geographical separation from the centre of the empire (Baghdad), developed an independent existence soon after the initial Arab conquest. In 868, a Turkish soldier, Ahmad Ibn Tulun, assumed the independent rulership of Egypt, Palestine and Syria. In 874, Transoxiana (in Central Asia) and the greater part of Persia became independent under the Persian Samanid dynasty. In the early part of the tenth century, the independent Fatimid dynasty was established in Tunisia, and it quickly spread its rule to include Egypt, Western Arabia, Palestine, and Syria. A seemingly normal unity was established under the Ottoman empire in the sixteenth century.

But only Iraq and Syria were under effective Ottoman control. Lebanon, Egypt, Morocco, Algeria, Tunisia, and Libya were ruled by virtually independent dynasties.[63]

Growing up under these historical circumstances, each of the Arab countries have developed, beneath the overriding unity of Arabic language, religion, and institutions, its own personality with all the peculiarities of its own social structure, its special economic interests, and its particular relations with the outer world.

While, as stated above, Western colonialism awoke Arab nationalism, it also consolidated existing differences in the Arab world. Moreover, the cultural diversity of the colonial powers—France, Spain, Italy, England, introduced new elements of diversity. The implicit acceptance of European ideas of national sovereignty by the Arab nationalist leaders educated in Western culture when they fought for their nation's independence and later built their community accordingly also put a brake on the drive toward Arab unity.

And when the Arab League was established, it was nothing but "an association of people, who (were) vividly conscious of a network of traditions, interests, feelings, and sympathies that unite(c) them with one another, but who Iive(d) in communities each with its separate social, economic and political structures, its local loyalties, its attention to particular interests.[64]

The history of the Arab League characterised by periods of high hopes intervened by personal rivalries and internecine quarrels is merely a reflection of this conflict between popular aspiration to Arab unity and the political realities of the Arab world.

(B) Tunisian Policy: There is no question that the Tunisian leaders feel the weight of popular aspiration to Arab unity, but they are also aware and wary of Arab quarrels. Besides, due to the fact that North Africa has led a historical experience different from the Arab East, the appeal of Arab nationalism in Tunisia has not been as strong as in the Arab East, and it has been often overshadowed by the appeal of Maghribian unity and Tunisian nationalism.

The nationalist movement in the Arab world inspired Tunisian nationalism but did not absorb it. Tunisian leaders sought and enjoyed the support of the Arab League but they conduct their own struggle with their own method and earned their own success. From his exile days in Cairo,

Bourguiba had been aware of Egyptian ambitions, and had learned that the League plagued by dissension among its members possessed no material strength and was in no position to help Tunisia.

When Tunisia gained independence in 1956, it was under no moral obligation to join the League in return for any political debt. Furthermore, Tunisia liked to consider itself the foremost intellectual centre of the Arab West" more progressive and further emancipated than many brother countries in the East who had preceded it to independence by as much as a generation.[65] On the other hand, Tunisia did not really share with the other Arab nations those ideological concerns that cemented the League countries together, such as the burning Palestinian question and emotional anti-colonialism. (Bourguiba used to criticise the Arab practice of mobilising all the vital energy of the people for an all-out struggle against "exagerated colonialism.")[66]

These deep-rooted feelings and the political distrust of Egypt and the policies of Nasserite regime explained the lukewarm attitude of Tunisia toward the Egypt—dominated League. As a matter of fact, Tunisia's relations with the Arab League could be largely considered as a corollary of its relations with the dominant country in the region: Egypt.

Egypt's president Gamal Abdel Nasser was by far the most prominent figure in the Arab world when Tunisia gained its independence. Bourguiba and the Egyptian leader strongly disagreed over many fundamental issues and never worked well together. Bourguiba did not share Nasser's enthusiasm for Arab unity, preferring to focus on less broadly defined 'questions more susceptible to immediate resolution, nor did he approve of Nasser's confrontation politics with Israel.

Bourguiba endeavoured to distance his country from the turbulent politics of the Arab east[67] because of Nasser he said. "The desire for supremacy, is the worm in the bud. When one partner wishes to dominate the group, sooner or later that group will fall apart."[68] As a protest of Nasser's domination of the Arab League, Tunisia did not join the organisation until 1958; for several years thereafter it participated only minimally in its affairs.[69] Tunisia joined the United nations immediately, however. By thus distancing himself from his fellow Arabs while maintaining close ties with France, Bourguiba left himself open to the charge that he was more anxious to remain in the good graces of the West than to do battle with the most critical issues facing the Arab-Islamic world.

Bourguiba was eager that he should be seen as a committed and competent Arab nationalist. He was unable to reconcile himself, however, to Nasser's geopolitical visions for the region, especially when it came to Arab policies toward Israel and Nasserist conceptions of Pan-Arab unity. In February 1965, he proclaimed that, while Israel was a danger, even a catastrophe for the Arabs, "the negative attitude of the Arab leaders has no effect but that, of strengthening the status quo.[70] He criticised Nasser's aggressive rhetoric, arguing that negotiating with Israel would be more productive for the Arabs, managing thereby to endear himself to the West while engendering hostility toward his government in the Arab world. What he argued was his realism was also reflected in his attitude toward Arab unity. Again he rejected Nasser's grandiose visions, arguing that:

> The only justification we find for unity is that of facilitating economic and social advancement in countries that have attained different stages of development but which, by their solidarity and their co-operation, might become mutually complementary and back each other up... We think the only way of initiating co-operation between us is that of free discussion on the basis of the mutual respect of national sovereignties.[71]

At the very outset, foundations were not made for a smooth relationship between Tunisia and Egypt. The two countries were governed by two leaders of strong personalities whose political convictions were diametrically different: Nasser as the Arab high-priest of positive neutrality and anti-Western policy, while Bourguiba posed himself as the chief advocate of an anti-communist and pro-Western stand.

The uneasy relationship between two countries began in 1955, when Egypt appeared to favour Ben Youssefs in the power struggle for the control of the Neo-Destour party be between him and Bourguiba.[72] To add fuel to the fire, the Egyptian delegate, Minister of Religious Foundations, Bakhouri, who attended the Neo-Destour Congress at Sfax where Ben Youssefs exclusion from the party was formally sanctioned, angered the Sfax leaders by attending Ben Youssefs opposition rally in Tunis and making a speech complimenting him.[73] Relations between Egypt and Tunisia continued to deteriorate, especially after Ben Youssef was granted political asylum in Cairo from where he agitated against Bourguiba. Their conflict also deepened as a result of the struggle for influence over the conduct of the war in Algeria.

In the first period of Tunisian independence, distrust of Egypt was too deep, pro-Western sentiment and the aspiration and hope to orient the Maghrib toward the West were too strong for the lure of Arab unity.

Thus, at the Sfax Congress in 1955, although Bourguiba repeatedly emphasised that Tunisia was an Arab Moslem nation with links of solidarity with the Middle East countries of the same racial and religious origin (a concession to population sentiment), his main plea was for co-operation with France (official policy).[74] The rationale of Tunisian policy toward the Arab world was laid in 1956:

> Tunisia must display sympathy with other Moslem nations, but may agree or disagree, because each has its own problems Tunisia must follow a realistic course with no automatic unity with the other Arab nations on all their plans. The fact that these people share a language and a religion is no reason why all should follow the same politics.[75]

To Bourguiba, the consideration of national interest took precedence over the call for Arab unity. And Tunisia's "economic needs and political convictions", conceived by him, dictated a close co-operation with the free world, and disengagement from Arab politics if this should become necessary to achieve the former objective, because the policy of co-operating only with other Arab states was fruitless since the Arab nations were "united in poverty" and could not help each other effectively.[76]

Bourguiba pledged to keep hands-off from Arab disputes, but in return, asked his "brothers in the Orient" to do the same for Tunisia and to understand her "position and reasoning", because "every country has its own needs.[77]

Tunisia's pro-Western policy caused suspicion in the Arab world; Bourguiba was criticised as a "vassal" of the West. The pressure for a return to the Arab world and away from the West was particularly strong in the aftermath of the Sakiet incident when French airplanes staged an attack on a Tunisian frontier village, allegedly a shelter of FLN fighters. And when Morocco decided to join the Arab League in October 1958, Tunisia reluctantly followed suit.

The Tunisian delegate, Habib el Shatti, chose the first Council meeting of the League on October 11, 1958, to clarify Tunisia's position. In an obvious reference to the United Arab Republic, he explained that Tunisia had held aloof from the Arab League in the past because "certain member-states have sought to impose their domination on other delegations", and that the League was "working in favour of one faction only and was receiving order from one member." The Tunisian delegate, in effect, demanded a formal commitment of non-intervention in Tunisian affairs as well as the rejection of UAR's domination of the League.[78]

Tunisia's attack caused the walkout of the UAR and a subsequent unanimous vote of the League Council condemning the Tunisian statement which was ordered to be expunged from the minutes of the meeting.[79] On its part, Tunisia broke off diplomatic relations with the UAR and shortly afterward made public the arrest of several UAR officers who were said to be plotting with Ben Youssef against

Bourguiba.[80] Tension between the two countries rose to a peak when Nasser called Bourguiba "a liar" and indirectly urged Tunisians to treat their President as the Iraqis treated their former Premier Nuri as-Said (the assassinated pro-Western Premier)[81].

Tunisia also boycotted the League meeting and asked, as the prize of its return, for a formal apology and disavowal of Tunisian political refugees in Cairo. The League refused to make such concession and Tunisia stayed away from the Arab League for two years. Meanwhile, the conditions of international politics changed radically which posed a serious challenge to the desirability of Tunisia's pro-Western policy.

The year of 1960, introduced to the international scene several newly-independent African nations and shifted the focus of world's attention to Africa. There was fear in Tunisia that her unequivocal pro-Western stand might serve as a ready scape-goat for emotional African reaction to the colonial question, and that such a policy might put Tunisia out of tune with other African countries. The desire to align herself with the rising force of small nations and the fear of too great a political isolation with the Afro-Arab world, especially after Tunisia had been left out of the Casablanca Conference in January 1961, revealed the need for a reorientation of foreign policy.

One Tunisian official wryly told his western friends: "we may soon be left with only America and France as friends; we have nothing against you at all, but it's not altogether respectable to be seen exclusively in your company.[82]

At the end of January 1961, Tunisia decided to return to the Arab League after two years of absence. The move was partly motivated by the fear of being isolated in the Afro-Arab world, partly prompted by the persuasion of Iraq and Jordan (Jordan had charged that Cairo fomented the assassination of its Premier Hazza Massali in September I960) seeking a counterbalance to the predominance of the UAR.[83]

With this decision, Tunisia seemed to have changed from a policy of complete disengagement from Arab affairs to a policy of staying aloof from Arab quarrels, but not from Arab affairs.

Tunisia's main concern was still the attitude of Cairo. Speaking of Tunisia's return to the Baghdad Congress of the League, Bourguiba expressed his hope that the occasion "would be the starting point of a new tendency towards union and fraternity", but cautioned that "the unity of the Arab world can only be based on mutual respect and consideration", not on the means of "domination, insults, or terrorism.[84]

The Bizerte crisis in July 1961, however, provided Tunisia with an opportune moment to get off dead centre of its diplomatic isolation. Being a victim of colonialism itself, Tunisia now requested an emergency meeting of the Arab League Council which unanimously decided to send military volunteers and a medical mission to Tunisia, and co set up a committee consisting of delegates of the UAR, Tunisia, Morocco and Libya to cany out its decisions. Offers of military assistance from the Governments of the UAR, Jordan, and the Sudan, and messages of support from Morocco, Iraq, Saudi Arabia, and Lebanon simultaneously poured into Tunisia.[85] As a result of this renewed friendship, and the desire to seek allies in its struggle against France, Tunisia announced the resumption of its diplomatic relations with the UAR on August 3. The assassination of Ben Youssef, Bourguiba's rival, in Frankfurt, Germany on August 12, finally removed a serious obstacle to the rapprochement between the two countries. Bitterness toward the UAR and Nasser seemed to have disappeared. In an interview on August 21, with the Cairo newspaper *Al Goumhouria,* President Bourguiba said: "I recognise now that President Nasser's intentions were good, and that he desires only the interests of the Arab nation." He added, perhaps in a moment of excitement. "Now we have no objection to the establishment of an Arab nation, because it would be the best protection that we could have to defend our interests, and especially now that we have the same objectives."[86]

The rapprochement between the UAR and Tunisia was further facilitated by a slight departure from the original positions taken by both sides, mostly by the UAR. Tunisia abandoned its fiery pro-Western policy to adopt the "fashionable" non-alignment stand. The UAR, after several years of waving the revolutionary flag and weary of being charged by several Arab countries of interfering in their internal affairs, tended to move toward a more moderate approach. Nasser had cracked on Egyptian communists. At Belgrade he moved away from communist-leaning "positive neutralism" toward true non-engagement.[87] Switching from a "unity of purpose" policy (Arab Socialism) to a "unity of ranks" policy, Nasser went out of his way to make peace with the Arab monarchs, from King Hassan of Morocco to Sheikh Abdullah al-Salim al-Sabah of Kuwait.[88] As regards the leader of "bourgeois" Tunisia, he swallowed his Nuri as-Said curse and said on his visit to Tunisia on the occasion of celebrations marking the Bizerte evacuation in December 1963: "I pray that God will allow President Bourguiba to continue to lead the Tunisian people, as he has done hitherto on the road to independence.[89]

Elated, Bourguiba declared: "All our past differences are the result of misunderstandings... This meeting... has contributed to eliminate finally everything which might have divided us in the past".[90]

Since her return to the Arab League, Tunisia was doing her best to cultivate friendly relations with all Arab nations on a country-to-country basis. With respect to Arab unity, she adopted a cautious, if not cool, attitude. Bourguiba maintained that there were many obstacles to Arab unity, such as the actual partitions between the Arab states imposed by history. Unity, therefore, should not be taken for granted; it should be built "prudently and carefully" by eliminating obstacles "one after the other", because unity "will never be achieved solely by professions of faith, even if they are supported by acclamations. Nothing is to be gained by forgetting that the Islamic and African Arab states have been separated from each other for "centuries.[91] Applying his "strategy of stages" to the concept of Arab unity,

Bourguiba suggested that, as far as the Tunisians were concerned, effort at building an Arab nation should be preceded by effort at building a Greater Maghrib. To create favourable conditions for the realisation this objective, he recommended that direct contacts between the Arab people should be encouraged, minds and hearts be opened to get rid of prejudices and erroneous judgements.[92]

Thus, from a policy of remaining aloof from Arab affairs in 1956, the changing conditions of international politics has forced Tunisia to adopt a policy of closer identification with the Arab world. The direction of Tunisian policy has changed somewhat. But the hallmark of Tunisian tactic remained the same: its moderate and gradual approach to Arab unity, devoid of extreme measures and over jealous actions, has enabled Tunisia to maintain sound relations with both the aggressively republican states of the Arab League (the UAR, Syria, Iraq, Algeria, and in part, Yemen) each considered itself more socialist and progressive than the others and, on the other hand, with the suspiciously defensive monarchies (Saudi Arabia, Libya, Jordan, and Morocco). Aside from tactic, the internal setting of Tunisia was also responsible for this success: although Destourian socialism was not fully approved or understood by the more radical socialist states, but it could not be openly attacked as reactionary. To the monarchies, Tunisia's pattern of reform rather than revolution, and its scrupulous attention to its own affairs, offered no threat.[93]

The official Tunisian position on Palestine perfectly reflected Bourguibist principles. It acknowledged the justice of the Palestinian cause but questioned the tactics Arab leaders used to assist the Palestinians. In the course of a visit to the Middle East in 1965, Bourguiba urged the Palestinians to adopt the same step-by-step method that the Neo-Destour had successfully used in its independence struggle. As a specific opening manouver, he suggested that their leaders accept the provisions of the 1947 UN partition plan for Palestine. Israel would almost certainly reject this overture, he went on, thereby assuming an obstructionist role and winning international sympathy for the Palestinians' willingness to compromise. The newly created Palestine Liberation Organisation (PLO), then very much under Egyptian control, ridiculed Bourguiba's ideas, accused him of defeatism, and began a steady propaganda barrage in which Nasser joined. So, vehement were the attacks on Bourguiba in the Palestinian and Egyptian media that Tunisia severed relations with Egypt in the following year.[94]

Israel's stunning defeat of Egypt, Syria, and Jordan in June 1967, seemed to bear out Bourguiba's criticisms of Arab policy on Palestine. But events in Tunisia in the weeks surrounding the war revealed a significant gap between the thinking of the ruling elite and the rest of the populace on this emotionally charged issue. In common with Arabs everywhere, Tunisians saw the June War as both a humiliating disaster and a positive proof of the expansionist aims of Zionism. In their anger, they rejected moderating as an appropriate response. A wave of demonstrations in support of Nasser and pan-Arabism swept the country, as did acts of anti-Semitism against Tunisia's small Jewish community, which had traditionally enjoyed good relations with its Muslim neighbours. The spontaneity and vigour of this support for the Palestinians prompted Bourguiba to act more in harmony with popular opinion, in a show of Arab fraternity, a few Tunisian military units were even dispatched to the front, but, owing to the shortness of the war," never saw action.[95]

Bourguiba's independent views on the Palestine problem won him much admiration in the rest of the world, because they appeared to many to be both eminently sensible and very brave. Yet this did not signify any lack of sympathy on, his part for the common Arab cause. Where the Arabs had gone wrong, he was arguing openly by 1965, and has done ever since, was that they refused to see reality as it was. If they had recognised the State of Israel as a fact, and showed willingness to cooperate with it in the vital matter of the social and economic development of the area, then if such co-operation could not have been achieved and conflicts arose, the world would have put the blame for it on Israel and not on the Arabs. As it was, Bourguiba often said, the

Arabs had all the time appeared as aggressors, although the truth was that Israel, whose establishment on Arab soil itself constitute an 'enormous international injustice', was constantly expanding at the cost of its neighbours. It was not so much that the Arabs erred in their hostility, to Israel, but that they employed wrong tactics in their struggle against the Jewish State.[96]

Tunisian diplomacy worked hard towards a fair settlement of the Middle East problem. Plans such as that suggested by president Tito of Yugoslavia, or the one put forward by General de Gaulle, found complete agreement in Tunis. What mattered, from the Tunisian point of view was that Israel should withdraw from occupied territories, that the problem of Palestinian refugees should be settled and that Israel should be' recognised and have her frontiers guaranteed. But in 1968, neither side seemed anxious to reach a compromise, and Tunisia's voice of reason seemed to have been making little impact.[97]

The restoration of diplomatic ties with Egypt symbolised the improvement of Tunisian relations with the Arab East after the war. Bourguiba stressed the dangers of renewed full-scale war in the Middle East, but even he agreed with the widespread sentiment that, under the circumstances, armed struggle was the only option available to the Palestinians. The upswing in guerrilla activities after the June War created new tensions between the revitalised PLO and the governments from whose territory its commandos operated. Jordan's King Hussain particularly worried about the implications for himself and his country of nourishing the Palestinian revolution. After the war, the king launched a war to drive the PLO from Jordan. Characteristically, Bourguiba urged moderation on both sides. Tunisian Prime Minister Badi Ladgham played an important role in mediations that helped end the fighting, although not before it had badly scarred all the parties.

Tunisia has been and is identifying itself more and more with the Arab world. But so long as Maghribian unity remains an unfinish business, he could but expect anything more than a half-hearted effort from the Tunisians with respect to Arab unity, because, as Ambassador Bourguiba, Jr. Said: "We believe more strongly in the Maghrib than in a huge Arab state that would stretch from Morocco to Iraq."[98]

Tunisia and Africa

The significance of Africa came to the attention of Tunisian foreign policy-makers rather late. Thus, the place of the African continent was not mentioned in the early statement on the tripartite base of Tunisia's foreign policy which read:

> Tunisia policy is determined both by its history and by its geography. Because Tunisia is part of Africa, it tends to identify itself firmly with other African nations, whose interests it shares. As a member of the Arab community, it has brotherly relations with the Arab countries to the East. And because it is situated in the "West", and is a neighbour to Europe, and in particular to France, it looks for security and economic progress in a close alliance with the free nations of the west. It is along these three lines that our foreign policy must develop.[99]

Not until 1957, when Bourguiba went to Accra to take part in Ghana's independence ceremonies that Tunisia's policy toward Africa began to take form.

Although there had been extensive trade contacts across the Saharan oases with Black Africa in both the Carthaginian and medieval periods, contacts between Tunisia and the African states south of the Sahara was non-existent both before and during the period of Western domination.

When Tunisia gained independence in 1956, there was little knowledge about Black Africa and Tunisia was too busy with her internal problems, with the Algerian war, and with her relations with France to pay attention to the not yet independent countries of Africa.

Yet to the African countries struggling for independence, Tunisia represented a modern nation and Bourguiba was widely regarded as the most successful African statesmen who, with the least bloodshed, brought to his country independence and respect. It was with great pride and paternalism of an elder brother that Bourguiba went to Ghana when it became the first tropical African country to gain independence.

The objectives of his trip were: (1) to assert the maturity of Tunisia and, hopefully, its leading role in African politics; (2) to emphasise the importance of a "decisive event for the African continent;" (3) "to get acquainted with this country (Ghana) where Tunisia (enjoyed) the best reputation thanks to the wisdom of its policies, which (were) both firm and flexible;" and (4) "to make useful contacts with the numerous guests there."[100] Bourguiba's longer-range objective seemed to impress the Africans with Tunisia's peaceful evolution toward independence through methods of "free negotiations" and "cooperation" in view of encouraging them to turn, once liberated, "towards the Western European countries and the United States, which (were) more advanced both technically and industrially and (would) be able to help them exploit the wealth of their continent."[101]

On his return, Bourguiba confessed that the trip had been "a true discovery, the discovery of a vast African continent from which we have been separated for so long and with which we hope to establish new relations," and maintained that "the presence of Tunisia in this important region of the African continent (was) essential." Stopping over Nigeria on his way back, he also sensed its imminent independence and the awakening of Africa. Tunisia now decided to involve itself in African politics, because, Bourguiba explained: "Though the Tunisians are concerned with immediate problems they are also interested in the immense development effort of the African continent. It is important that we should keep pace with events.[102]

In April 1958, Tunisia was one of the seven independent African nations (others: Ethiopia, Ghana, Libya, Morocco, Sudan the UAR) to take part in the Pan-African Conference. The participating countries declared their, intention to project a "distinctive African personality" into the field of foreign policy, and to support the United Nations Charter; urged a definite date for colonial territories to attain independence; and agreed to establish a permanent machinery of the Conference at the United Nation by the delegations of the participating countries for the purpose of co-operating their efforts at the world's organisation.[103]

In June, Prime Minister Nkrumah of Ghana visited Tunisia to discuss with President Bourguiba on "questions of common interests" which resulted in "complete agreement" between the two leaders. Solidarity, mutual support, and the development of diplomatic relations, trade, and cultural ties were pledged.[104]

Six months later, the First All-African Peoples Conference met in Accra (Ghana), Tunisian influence became apparent when the Conference urged the adoption of non-violence in the struggle for independence of African nations.[105]

In the early period of African awakening (1957-1958), Bourguiba was perhaps the first African statesman who commanded the most respect of the Western countries. He was the man who could negotiate effectively with General de Gaulle, and his prestige was mostly responsible for Anglo-American defiance of France to ship arms to Tunisia. Consequently, the leaders of other African nations which freshly gained their independence or were struggling for it, wanted to identify with Bourguiba, or at least to seek close relations with him, to secure fame by association and to benefit from his influence in any dealing with the West. Up to a point, the pattern of Tunisian development from a protectorate to an independent nation was attractive, Bourguiba's urge for co-operation with the West desirable. The tactic had been partly successful in Tunisia, but further testing was required to prove the possibility of a peaceful evolution in Africa and a happy co-operation between it and the West whereby Tunisia would play, if not the role of leadership, at least that of a prominent middleman.

Unfortunately, there was Sakiet, there was Bizerte, there was the Algerian war, colonialism, the vacillating policy of the United States, the agitation of the Arab world, the courtship of the communist nations, and the emotional reaction of Africa. Together these uncontrollable events and factors helped discredit Bourguiba's peaceful and moderate approach to African politics and reduce Tunisia's initial influence in Africa.

The year of 1960, introduced a new dimension to international politics; the boom of African independent nations and their admission to the United Nations which greatly increased the importance of Africa, enhanced its prestige, and opened new opportunities for the nations of Africa to make themselves heard. Meanwhile, an ominous sign appeared at the horizon of African politics when the delegate of Communist China was first seen attending the meet at Conakry (Guinea) to discuss their common problems Conference problems.[106] Then came the Congo crisis doubling itself as a test of the new power acquired by the African nations and their maturity.

As the beginning, the African nations were unanimous in their desire to keep the Congo out of the power struggle between the two blocs and in their support of United Nations intervention to keep the peace in their brother nation. But later, when the United Nations had to chart a course of action with regard to the dispute between President Kasavubu and Premier Lumumba, conflict broke into the open between the African nations resulting in the formation of two rival groups (Monrovia and Casablanca) which differed sharply over the questions of United Nations operation in the Congo, of Mauritania, of Algeria, and the approach to African unity.

The Casablanca group formed in January 1961, was consisted of Ghana, Guinea, Mali, Morocco, the UAR and the Provisional Government of Aigeria, and was dedicated to a militant brand of neutralism. Its Charter proclaimed their adherence to non-alignment and their support of Lumumba against Kasavubu and Morocco's claim over Mauritania, denounced any French-initiated consultation and referendum on Algeria, and avowed their determination to liberate the remaining colonial territories in Algeria. As far as African unity was concerned, the Casablanca group members tended to urge an immediate political integration of the African states.[107]

Four months later, the Monrovia group was born as a result of a meeting between the heads of states of the twelve French-speaking countries of the Brazzaville group.[108] Later, it was joined by Ethiopia, Liberia, Libya, Nigeria, Sierra Leone, Somalia, Togo and Tunisia. In contrast to the Casablanca group, the Morovia group stressed on the respect of national sovereignty of the African nations and the principle of non-interference in their domestic affairs, and opposed immediate political integration and the acceptance of anyone leader in tile promotion of continental cooperation. It advocated instead a functional approach to unity, beginning with economic cooperation between the African states on a regional basis. The group recognised Mauritania, favoured friendly cooperation with Western countries and the method of pacific settlement of international disputes, and supported the Kasavubu government and the United Nations action in the Congo.[109]

Tunisia's increasing participation in African affairs in 1960, was prompted by the birth of a host of new nations, by the new significance of Africa in international politics, by the desire to "keep pace with events" and, last but not least, by the desire to make new friends in compensation for its temporary rejection by the Arab world.

Tunisia's position *vis-a-vis* the United Nations, the Congo and African unity, and its recognition of Mauritania were chiefly responsible for its being left out of the Casablanca Conference. Its adherence to the Monrovia group was meant to get itself out of its political isolation among the African states, and to seek a closer alliance with those moderate African countries which shared most of Tunisia's ideas about African and world affairs. Yet, in order to preserve its freedom of action and to avoid antagonising its Maghribieu brothers, especially neighbouring Algeria, Tunisia carefully avoided to commit itself strictly to any rigid group's policy. Thus, Tunisia boycotted the Lagos meeting (Nigeria- January 25-30, 1962), convened by the Monrovia group because Algeria was not invited.[110]

Tunisia's decision to remain aloof from the Lagos meeting and its denouncement of rivalling political grouping in Africa was also prompted by the fact that the Bizerte episode had provided Tunisia with a golden occasion to return to the Arab League and to make peace with its Maghrebian neighbour and the African nations outside the Monrovia group.

From 1962, onward, the situation both in Algeria and the Congo began to ease, differences between the two African blocs began to diminish. Among the African countries there was fairly general agreement on a campaign to press the United Nations into further action over South Africa, Southern Rhodesia, and the Portuguese colonies.[111] The climax of this general consensus and of the desire to patch up differences among Africans occurred in May 1963, when leaders of both the Casablanca and Monrovia groups met at Addis Ababa (Ethiopia) to proclaim the dissolution of their rival groupings in favour of the new organisation, the Organisation of African Unity (OAU).[112]

The prevailing opinion at Addis Ababa was against colonialism and in favour of the principle of African unity. As to the method to achieve this unity, Tunisia found itself among the majority.

As early as 1961, Bourguiba had, during his trip to the United States, warned the latter against endorsing pan-African propaganda. He said that Africa was a "geographical notion", not a unitarian political entity; "there (was) not one Africa, but there (were) many Africas;" and that unity sentiment was growing but vast differences between North Africa and Africa South of the Sahara still stood in the Way of unity effort.[113]

At Addis Ababa, Bourguiba, again, voiced his familiar position. He warned the conference against hasty improvisation 'of all-African unity which, he said, could not be imposed by force or by "subversion by those ambitious for domination," and suggested a step-by-step approach to African unity. Appeal for immediate action on unity was voiced by President Nkrumah of Ghana and Prime Minister Obote of Uganda, but the militants had lost most of their valuable allies. President Sekou Toure of Guinea, in an effort to heal the rift between his country and the former French colonies had allied himself with the moderates.[114] President Nasser of the UAR also dissociated himself with Nkruaah' policy when he said that unity could not come overnight.[115]

Other principles regulating relations among African states, the preservation and consolidation of the independence and territorial integrity of the individual states, non-intervention in the internal affairs of the individual states, and pacific settlement of disputes were also adopted at the Addis Ababa conference.[116]

At the Second Summit Meeting of the OAU at Cairo in July 1964, these principles were, again upheld. Nkrumah remained almost the lone advocate of the immediate establishment of a federal union of all independent African states. But the principle of gradual approach to African unity had been firmly established and practiced. When President Nyerere of the United Republic of Tangauyika and Zanzibar (now Tanzania) attacked the illusory characteristic of Nkrumah's plan the audience gave him a standing ovation.[117]

Nasser, again, declared: "The UAR shares the hopes of President Nkrumah for the realisation of African unity. But unity becomes a very difficult process when one comes to its application. Because the factors necessary for the establishment of unity should be assured before this unity could be realised." He urged "Let us begin from the beginning," and advocated an intellectual rapprochement, planning co-operation, money exchange and trade among the African nations.[118] This was very similar to what Bourguiba had advocated and practiced all along. But Bourguiba had no illusions about planning co-operation on a continental basis; he wanted to start it on a regional basis. As far as Tunisia was concerned, Maghribian co-operation should get top priority. With regard to all others African states with which Tunisia had no special ties, it would like to cultivate friendly relations and to exploit the possibility of fruitful co-operation. Tunisia favoured an exchange of men and ideas among African nations to encourage mutual understanding and tolerance which would serve as the basis for African unity.

There had been elaborate efforts on the part of the Tunisian government to bring government and student leaders, congresses, youth groups and trade unionists to Tunisia. The idea was to present to the African countries a showcase of an efficient, purposeful society in Tunisia which had successfully adapted itself to the requirements of modem life by incorporating into its culture the relevant Western values while remaining true to its African heritage. Banking on the appeal of its model of development, Tunisia hoped to play the role or an intellectual middleman, a cultural carrier, transmitter and interpreter between Africa and Europe.[119] This role and Tunisian prestige have been increasingly shared since 1960, by other former French colonies headed by leaders of Bourguiba caliber such as Leopold Senghor of Senegal and Felix Houphouet-Boigny of the Ivory Coast. However, Tunisia's modest objective and cautious diplomacy has earned for itself the friendship of almost all African countries, allowed it to keep pace with events in Africa, while concentrating its energy in the effort of nation-building and laying the foundation of Maghrebian unity.

Tunisia's Relation with India

India's independence in 1947 gave a big boost to the process of national liberations in whole of middle-east and north Africa and after independence, adhering its policy of non-alignment, its opposition to imperialism and apartheid, and its support to the liberation movements, India extended all type of assistance except military aid, to almost all the freedom struggle movements.

India has traditionally maintained cordial and friendly relations with Tunisia since establishment of diplomatic relation in 1958. The first resident Indian mission at the level of Cd'A was established in Tunisia in 1963. The Tunisian embassy in New Delhi was set up in 1981.

When the Tunisian struggle for independence from France took an ugly shape, the Indian representative in the United Nations, A.K. Chadha, said in the United Nations General Assembly on 22nd October 1953 that if the Franco-Tunisian problem was not settled in accordance with the principle of the United Nation Charter, the Tunisian people would be driven to desperation. He further said that the French policy in Tunisia as contrary not only to the basic interests of the Tunisian people but also to the best interests of France itself. Moreover, if the problem was not solved, it could lead to increased tension between French and the Tunisian government and their people.[120]

Though Tunisia was at last granted independence in March-1956, freedom alone could not heal the sufferings and grievances of the Tunisian people because of the presence of mighty French troops in Tunisia even after her independence. The French government was not prepared to leave Tunisia as she served many national interests of the former. The presence of French troops in Tunisia caused great resentment among the nations of the world. Most of the countries condemned French obstinacy in refusing to withdraw its troops from Tunisia. India was also one of the staunch critics of the presence of the French troops in Tunisia. C.S. Jha, the Indian representative, in a letter to the president of the UN General Assembly, said on 27th July 1961:

> We, the undersigned representatives wished to convey to you our deep concern at the situation now prevailing in Tunisia. The situation has been considered by the Security Council which has adopted an interim resolution calling for an immediate cease-fire and the withdrawal of all armed forces... we consider that this resolution should immediately be put into effect without any reservations or qualifications.[121]

In the UN General Assembly, the Permanent Representative of India, C.S. Jha, said on 21st August 1961:

> To my delegation it is clear that the status of Tunisia as a sovereign independent state and her membership of international community give her a position no way inferior to any other member of the UN—a position which does not admit of any infractions of her sovereignty except in accordance with her own free will and judgement... There can be no justification for the continued presence of French forces in the face of the dear and unequivocal stand of Tunisian government and its people. The only question is of the orderly evacuation of such forces through peaceful negotiations. It is imperative that such negotiations be undertaken immediately, so that situation in Tunisia is already grave and dangerous and which not only involves relation between France and Tunisia but it is a source of deep concern throughout Asia and Africa, should not be further aggravated... The presence of foreign troops on the territory of a state without a latter's consent and agreement is not permissible and that such presence violates the sovereignty of that country...[122]

Tunisia and India both hold, more or less, the same position on many international problems. Both the countries have demanded the withdrawal of Israel from the occupied Arab land and recognition of the rights of the Palestinian people.

Despite immense possibilities of co-operation between the two countries, not much has been done by them to improve their relation in political as well as in other field. The leaders and policy-makers of the two countries have not shown much enthusiasm in improving their relations. There have been very few visits of high level political delegations to each other's country.

In March 1967, the Tunisian Minister for Justice, Mogni Salim, visited India. He met M.C. Chagla, Minister of External Affairs. Besides other issues, the two leaders discussed the Kashmir problem also. Mogni Salim said that the Kashmir dispute should be settled between two countries in 'a friendly spirit in accordance with the Tashkant Agreement which has been signed by India and Pakistan after the 1965 war.' He denied that Tunisia had ever taken the position that the Kashmir problem should be settled on the basis of principle of self-determination as demanded by Pakistan for the people of Kashmir.[123]

Tunisia had been exporting rock phosphate to India even before Tunisia attained her independence in 1956. This naturally formed the basis of trade agreement between the two countries signed in 1960. Under the agreement, the two countries agreed to a barter trade covering a wide range of commodities. Almost at the same time, the State Trading Corporation (STC) of India entered a rupee clearing agreement with Tunisian office, Commerce de Tunisionne (TOC), under which Tunisia agreed to buy Indian goods in exchange of a rock phosphate. This agreement worked well. There was a time when there used to be an exchange of only Indian tea and jute for the Tunisian rock phosphate. Now India's export to Tunisia covers tea, pepper, jute goods, cotton and textiles, diesel motors and agricultural pumps, cotton yarn, a number of steel items and steel machinery, raw tobacco, rice, finished leather, fine chemicals, polyethylene, machinery. Tunisia exports to India the rock phosphate, triple super phosphate, cork wood and cork products, lead, mercury and non-ferrous metals. In the present times, Tunisia exports olive oil, dates, leather, and wiring harnesses to India. Efforts are made for further diversifying the range of these exports.

An agreement of friendship and technical and scientific co-operation between Tunisia and India was signed on 24th June 1965 at Tunis. Ismail Khellil, Director of International Cooperation signed on behalf of Tunisia and S.Than, Director of Foreign Trade, Ministry of Commerce signed for the Government of India.[124]

TUNISIA

Cultural Agreement with Tunisia

The Following is a brief summary of the Cultural

Agreement signed between India and Tunisia on 24th June, 1969 in New Delhi.

A Cultural Agreement between India and Tunisia was signed in New Delhi on 24th June 1969. This followed the discussions that were held earlier on various aspects of the Agreement between Mr. Habib Bourguiba, Jr. the Foreign Minister of Tunisia and Professor V.K.R.V. Rao, Minister of Education and Youth Services, Government of India. The two ministers signed the agreement on behalf of their respective Governments.

The two Governments have agreed to promote and develop as far as possible the relations in the fields of education, science, culture and sports, in order to contribute to better knowledge of their respective cultures and activities in these fields.

The agreement also envisages exchange of teachers, research scholars, technicians as well as exchange of cultural and artistic programmes between the radio and television stations of the two countries. It also includes exchange of groups of youths and groups of journalists.[125]

Indo-Tunisian Joint Communique

The following is the text of Joint Communique issued in New Delhi on June 25, 1969 at the end of the visit to India of His Excellency Mr. Habib Bourguiba, Foreign Minister of Tunisia:

At the invitation of Mr. Dinesh Singh, Foreign Minister of India, His Excellency Mr. Habib Bourguiba, Foreign Minister of Tunisia, visited India from June 20 to 24, 1969. During his stay H.E. the Foreign Minister of Tunisia was accorded a warm and cordial reception. He called on the President and the Prime Minister of India and held talks with the Foreign Minister, the Minister of Foreign Trade and Supply, the Minister of Tourism and Civil Aviation, the Minister of Industrial Development, Internal Trade and Company Affairs, and the Minister of Education and Youth Services.

The talks covered a variety of subjects of common interest including the present international situation and the friendly bilateral relations between the two countries. The talks were held in an atmosphere of great friendliness. They revealed a general similarity of views between the two sides and contributed to the bringing about of closer mutual understanding. The Foreign Minister of India expressed his great appreciation of the rapid progress being made in Tunisia under the leadership of President Bourguiba. The Foreign Minister of Tunisia who visited Bhakra Dam, the Nangal Fertiliser Factory and the Indian Agricultural Research Institute, expressed great appreciation of India's achievements under leadership of her thus Prime Minister.

The two Foreign Ministers expressed their conviction in the continuing validity of the policy of non-alignment which has made a positive contribution to the cause of peace and international cooperation. They also stressed the importance of the acceptance of the principle of peaceful co-existence in accordance with the United Nations Charter.

The two sides reiterated their firm opinion that an early conclusion of a comprehensive treaty on general and complete disarmament, both nuclear and conventional under effective international supervision, would be a vital contribution to the maintenance of world peace and security. They voiced their concern that there had been little progress so far in this direction and expressed the hope that 18-Nation Disarmament Committee would give urgent' consideration to this important matter.

The Foreign Minister affirmed their faith in the principle of resolution of differences between States by peaceful negotiations and without resort to force. In this spirit they expressed the hope that India and Pakistan would settle their difference peacefully and that in the interest of the sub-continent the relations between India and Pakistan would soon register significant improvement.[126]

The two Foreign Ministers expressed deep concern at the continuing occupation of the Arab territories by Israel. They stressed that while a comprehensive solution should be found by implementation of the Security Council Resolution of November 22, 1967, any delay in withdrawal by Isreali forces from the occupied territories was fraught with further dangerous possibilities. The two Foreign Ministers reiterated the full support of their Governments to the legitimate rights of the Palestinian people.

The two sides expressed the view that a solution to the Vietnam problem can be found only through peaceful negotiations on the basis of the 1954 Geneva Agreements and hoped that the current talks in Paris would lead to an early settlement.

The Foreign Minister expressed the solidarity of their Governments with all countries and organisations struggling against the racialist and colonialist policies, pursued by South Africa, Rhodesia and Portugal. They declared their conviction that these policies which are in direct contravention of the U.N. Charter should be brought to a speedy end.

The two sides also noted the imperative need for the developing countries to raise the living standards of their people as rapidly as possible. The two Foreign Ministers urged the advanced nations to pursue more constructive trade policies and show a deeper understanding of the role of trade in development in order to reduce dependence on credits. The Foreign Minister of Tunisia and the Indian Minister successfully explored the possibilities of expanding trade between India and Tunisia. Both sides expressed their keen interest in an increasing exchange of their respective goods and products.

The two sides examined the possibilities of economic and technical co-operation in various fields. It was decided that measures should be taken in pursuance of the Agreement on Friendship and Technical, Economic and Scientific Co-operation concluded between India and Tunisia in 1955, to strengthen technical and economic co-operation between the two countries.

The two sides emphasised the necessity of developing closer cultural contacts in all fields. The Foreign Minister noted the great and diverse achievements of civilisation in their countries and resolved to develop co-operation in many sided cultural activities in this spirit the two Governments conclude a cultural agreement. The Foreign Minister of India stated that the Government of India would welcome the establishment of a resident Tunisian Mission in India to consolidate the increasing collaboration between the two countries in all fields. The Tunisian Foreign Minister accepted the idea in principle and stated that a Tunisian Mission would be established in India at a suitable opportunity.

The Foreign Minister of Tunisia referred to the invitation which the President of Tunisia had extended to the Prime Minister of India to visit Tunisia and conveyed the hope of His Excellency the President of Tunisia that the Prime Minister would find it possible to visit Tunisia soon. The Prime Minister expressed her thanks for the kind invitation and assured the Foreign Minister that she would in consultation with the Tunisian Government find a suitable opportunity to visit Tunisia. She requested the Foreign Minister to communicate her acceptance of the invitation to the President of Tunisia in the context of the desire of both Governments to strengthen the friendly relations already subsisting between them.

His Excellency the Foreign Minister of Tunisia extended an invitation to the Foreign Minister of India to visit Tunisia. The Foreign Minister of India was happy to accept the invitation.

The two Foreign Ministers expressed deep satisfaction at the visit of the foreign Minister of Tunisia and the opportunity it had afforded for a friendly exchange of views further strengthening the existing ties of friendship and understanding and cooperation between the two countries.[127]

Trade Agreement with Tunisia

The following is the text of a Press release issued in New Delhi on June 29,1969 on the Trade Agreement signed between India and Tunisia.

A trade agreement between India and Tunisia was signed here today. This follows the discussions held by a

Tunisian Trade Delegation, led by Mr. Naceur Ben Amor, Director of Foreign Trade, Government of Tunisia (who accompanied the Foreign Minister of Tunisia, this Excellency Mr. Habib Bourguiba Jr. to New Delhi) with an Indian Trade Delegation led by Mr. S.K. Singh, Director Foreign Trade. These talks were held in a spirit of friendliness and mutual understanding.

The two delegations have agreed that the continued closure of the Suez Canal should not be permitted to affect their bilateral trade, the two delegations considered various ways and means for recommencing their bilateral trade.

India has agrced to the resumption of shipments of rock phosphate from Tunisia. Tunisia has agreed to import from India will immediate effect non-traditional items, particularly iron and steel products and engineering goods (Foreign Affairs Round).

TUNISIA

Vice President M. Hidayatullah's Speech at Dinner for Mrs. Wassila Bourguiba:

Following is text of the speech by the Vice President Mr. M. Hidayatullah, at the dinner in honour of the first Lady of Tunisia Mrs. Wassila Bourguiba in New Delhi on November 3, 1982:

It gives me great pleasure to welcome Her Excellency Madame Wassila Bourguiba and other distinguished members of her party this evening. We have been looking forward to this visit and are happy that it was possible for Your Excellency to accept our invitation. We would have greatly welcomed the President, His Excellency Mr. Habib Bourguiba but appreciate and understand his inability to come. President Bourguifaa is highly admired and respected in India as a valiant fighter for Independence and a champion of the cause of the oppressed and the downtrodden. I hope Your Excellency will convey our warmest regards and good wishes to him.

Tunisia and India share many things in common. Our two people are no strangers. Both our countries have struggled to obtain independence and have faced the gigantic task of bestowing the benefits of Independence and modernisation to our peoples. India has watched with admiration the successful Tunisian efforts to build their country. You have progressed not only in industrial and economic but also in social and cultural spheres. The friendly and cordial relations that have existed between our two countries have been strengthened by the signing of Indo-Tunisian Trade Agreement and the establishment of a Joint Commission. The Indo-Tunisian Cultural Exchange Programme signed in November, 1978 has brought the people of the two countries culturally closer still.

Tunisia and India share a common political outlook and ideal and both are devoted to peace and the principles of Non-alignment. Our support for Arab cause comes from principles and values dear to us and has been firm and consistent. We are confident that Indo-Arab friendship, based on shared ideals will promote mutual interests and continue to thrive in the years to come.

Your Excellency, we hope that your visit will lead to a better understanding between our peoples and will be an important step in consolidating the already warm relations we share with each other.

Excellencies Ladies and Gentlemen, may I now request you to join me in raising your glasses in a toast for the health and happiness of His Excellency Mr. Habib Bourguiba. Her Excellency Madame Wassila Bourguiba to the progress and prosperity of the Tunisian people and to the continued strengthening of the ties of friendship that binds us together.

Text of Mrs. Bourguiba's Speech

The First Lady of Tunisia, Mrs. Wassila Bourguiba said:

Mr. Vice-President, your generous hospitality, your words of welcome, the tribute you have just paid President Bourguiba, and through him the Tunisian people honour us greatly and go straight to our hearts. It strengthens our conviction that distance means little when esteem and friendship are as strong and constant as they are between our two peoples and when the foundations of the bonds which unite our countries are as solid and unalterable as was the wish of the founders of our two Nations, Pandit Nehru and President Habib Bourguiba.

The thoughts and actions of these two men who were, not only leaders and liberators but also founders of modern States have left their imprint on the course of the Century and continue to guide us and illuminate the path way to the future.

Bourguiba, as Nehru built a modern State which was the culmination of a long and bitter struggle.

PEACE AND SECURITY

The vision of these two men and their choice of a socialism based on the advancement of man a model for development which does not restrict independence and a strategy which does not hinder the vital interests of peace and international security these three options are living proof of a profoundly fraternal and conciliatory vision of human destiny.

The historical bonds woven between them by a common struggle grew stronger with the passage of time, through the choice of Non-Alignment one of the cornerstones of Tunisian and Indian Policy.

This choice, which assumes its significance through the trials to which the people of the Third World are constantly subjected, has allowed us to conceive and maintain a wide open co-operation based on a common interest with all nations of the globe.

Excellency India and Tunisia have at all times defended just causes advocating dialogue and negotiation for the settlement of conflicts. This principle has served as a common denominator in their support for the Palestinian cause which is at the heart of the Middle East problem and which constitutes a major concern of the international community and more particularly of the Non-Aligned Movement.

PALESTINE PROBLEM

The Palestinian problem which President Bourguiba has dubbed the "greatest injustice of the 20th Century" had matured today indeed at the height of a most cruel and abominable ordeal President Yasser Arafat never ceased to proclaim his willingness to bring about peace through negotiation and in accordance with the United Nations Resolutions. Today more than ever he appeals for the recognition of the legitimate rights of the Palestinian People within the framework of international legality that is within the framework-of a solution which takes into account the dignity of all concerned parties.

This is what had been advocated all along by the Non-Aligned Movement.

Beyond substance, this approach is vivid proof of the greatness of Mahatma Gandhi's eternal teachings.

We in Africa have not forgotten this path, either. The drama which afflicts millions of Africans in the Southern part of our continent had always been a great preoccupation for us as well as for India. Indeed, it was Mahatma Gandhi himself who was the first to denounce the legality of the racial discrimination which was instituted as a State supported system in South Africa and Namibia. This case for the defense of a flouted right clearly demonstrates the common stand of our two countries and the community of struggles which unite India and Africa.

NON-ALIGNMENT

Excellency one of the founders of the Non-Aligned Movement, Tunisia like India had not ceased to strive for its development, integrity and which inspire our action, it is a common vision of our own destiny and that of humanity which we strive to express. We in Tunisia are, therefore, particularly pleased that the next Non-Aligned Summit will be held in New Delhi, this return to grassroots will no doubt contribute, under the clairvoyant guidance of Mrs. Indira Gandhi, in stilling our movement with renewed strength.

Excellency Ladies and Gentlemen, I invite you to raise your glasses to His Excellency Mr. Mohammad Hidayatullah and Mrs. Hidayatullah to the health of Mrs. Indira Gandhi to the well being of the great Indian nation and to the friendship between the Indian and Tunisian peoples.

The following is the text of press release issued in New Delhi on February 22,1990 on Indo-Tunisian Joint Commission meeting:

The third meeting of the Indo-Tunisian Joint commission on Trade, which opened here yesterday, is scheduled to conclude tomorrow with the signing of the agreed minutes of the deliberations in the presence of the Commerce and Tourism Minister, Mr. Arun Nehru and the Minister of National Economy of the Republic of Tunisia, Mr. Moncef Belaid. The three-day deliberations will cover all aspects of bilateral trade including joint ventures and co-operation in tourism. During his discussion with Mr. Arun Nehru last evening, Mr. Belaid urged India to explore the possibilities of availing the preferential arrangements which Tunisia enjoys with EEC for enlarging its exports to that region. EEC accounts for the bulk of Tunisia's external trade with most of its goods enjoying duty free access to West Europe.

The Joint Commission between the two countries was set up under the Indo-Tunisian Trade Agreement of 1976 to review the progress of bilateral trade and draw up plans for the future expansion of trade and commercial relations.

The first and the second meeting of the Joint Commission were held in 1980 and 1988 respectively.[128]

Notable among the exchange of visits in the past was that of the Prime Minister Smt. Indira Gandhi in April 1984, followed by that of PM Narasimha Rao in 1992 former Prime Minister paid a visit to Tunisia in 1999.

The government of Tunisia recognises that fundamentalism is a threat to democracy and has been a participant in joint international efforts to check the menace of fundamentalism and terrorism. In October 1995, the two countries issued a "joint declaration on Combating

International Terrorism, Drug Trafficking and Organised Crime," The two countries have taken a similar stand on this issue in international fora.

Tunisian leaders have always expressed admiration for India's democracy and its leaders and openly acknowledged the strong support India extended to Tunisia in its freedom struggle. Two countries share a respect for secularism and moderation is an avowed hallmark of Tunisian foreign policy.

The institutional framework between Tunisia and India is strong. In fact, the two countries, who celebrate fifty five years of diplomatic relations this year, have signed several agreements with covering various sectors of economic activities; There is a Joint Commission at Ministerial level. A mechanism for Foreign Office Bilateral Consultation also exists between the two countries. In addition, there are several joint working groups which have been meeting regularly (Bio-technology, Science and Technology, Information and Communication Technology, SMEs, Pharmaceuticals, Textiles).

In April 2012, the eleventh session of the Tunisian-Indian Joint Commission was held here in New Delhi and was co-chaired by Tunisia's secretary for state for Americas and Asia Hedi Ben Abbes and Vice Foreign Minister of India E. Ahmed. This session was an occasion to emphasise the Tunisian commitment to strengthen bilateral co-operation, particularly in the area of Information Technology, Communication, Science, Investment and Tourism.

His Excellency Mr. E. Ahmed paid an official visit to Tunisia at the invitation of the Government of the Republic of Tunisia from 5th to 7th November, 2012. During his visit, Mr. Ahmed conveyed the greetings of the Indian leadership and the good wishes and felicitations of the people of India to the government and the people of Tunisia on the successful non-violent revolution for dignity and freedom led by the Tunisian people followed by an orderly transition process.

Tunisia has been reliable supplier of phosphates for decades, it constitutes the main Tunisian product exported to the Indian market. Olive oil, dates, leather, and wiring harnesses are also exported from Tunisia to India. Efforts are made for further diversifying the range of these products.

India exports a wider range of products. Significant among them being, rice, tea, tobacco, finished leather, fine chemicals, polyethylene, machinery, articles of iron and steel, electronic goods and yarn.

A Tunisian-Indian joint venture in Tunisia launched in 2006 for manufacturing Phosphoric Acid will be commissioned soon. The total annual production of the plant will be 360,000 tons of phosphoric acid.

The new Tunisia is keen in further developing its relations with India in all fields. The new environment will have a positive impact on business and will offer new opportunities for investments and development on stronger basis of transparency and equality.

The promising areas of co-operation between the Indian and Tunisian business circle exist in many sectors such as auto-industries, information technology, business processing outsource, biotechnology, pharmaceutical and textile etc...[129]

References

1. Wilfred Knapp, *North West Africa: A Political and Economic Survey,* (Oxford, Oxford University Press, I977), p. 342.
2. Wilfrid Knapp, *Tunisia,* (London, Thomes and Hudson, I970), p. 10.
3. Mohammed Abed Jabri, Evolution of the Maghrib Concept: Facts and Perspectives in H. Barakat, *Contemporary West Africa* (London, Croomhelm, 1985), p. 64.
4. R.K. Ramazani, "Cultural Change and Intellectual Response in Algeria, Tunisia, and Iran", *Comparative Studies in Society and History,* No. 2, January 1964, pp. 225-226.
5. John P. Entelis and Mark A. Tessler, The Maghrib: An Overview, in David E. Long and Bernard Reich, *The Government and Politics of the Middle East and North Africa,* (Boulder, Westview Press, 1986), pp. 372-75.

6. Samir Amin, *The Maghrib in the Modern World,* (Harmondswoth, Penguin, 1970), p. 108.
7. *Ibid.*
8. Charles-Andre Julien, *L'Afrique du Mord in Marche,* (Paris, Julliard 1952), p. 23 as quited in H. Baraket *op.cit.,* No. 3, p. 66.
9. *Ibid.*
10. *Ibid.*, p. 67.
11. Alal al-Fasi, *The Independence Movements in Arab North Africa,* (New York, Octagon Books 1970), pp. 26-30.
12. *Ibid.*
13. Hassan Syed Suliman, *The Nationalist Movements in the Maghrib,* (Upsala, Scandinavian Institute of African Studies 1987), p. 41.
14. H. Barakat, *op.cit.,* No. 3, p. 68.
15. Alal at-Fasi, *op.cit.,* No. 10, p .395.
16. David E. Long and Bernard Reich, *op.cit.,* No. 5, pp. 375-76.
17. John Ruedy, *Historical Influences on Infra-Regional Relations in the Maghrib* in H. Barakat. *op.cit.,* No. 3, pp. 87-103.
18. *Ibid.*
19. H, Barakat *op.cit.,* No. 3, p. 68.
20. Wilfrid Knapp, *Tunisia op.cit.,* No. 2, p. 164.
21. H. Barkat, *op.cit.,* No. 3, p. 76.
22. Charles-Andre Julien *op.cit.* No. 8, p. 26.
23. H. Barkat, *op.cit.,* No. 3, p. 72.
24. *Le Monde* 12 Aout 1961.
25. *Keesing's Contemporary Archives,* January 19-26, 1957, p. 15329.
26. At the Tangier Conference, Bahi Ladgham represented the Neo-Destour, Ferhat Abbas represented the FIN, and al-Fassi represented the Istiqlal of Morocco. Libya only sent observers to the Conference.
27. Hameeda Akhund, The Maghrib in Search of a Union. *Pakistan Horijon,* Vol. 11, No. 2, June, 1958, p. 79.

28. *Ibid.*

29. Conference de I'Unite" a bulletin published by the Under-Ministry of Information and Orientation of the Tunisian Republic 1958, as quoted in Mohammed Abed Jabri, in *Evolution of the Maghrib Concept: Facts and Perspectives* in V.H. Barakat *op.cit.*, No. 3, pp. 73-74. *see also Keesing's Contemporary Archives* June 7-14, 1958, p. 16227; Tibor Kerekes, ed., *The Arab Middle East and Muslim Africa,* (New York: Frederick A. Paraeger, Publications, 1961), p. 89.

30. Jean and Simone Lacouture, Le Maroc a I'epreuve, Paris, Editions du Seuil, 1958, p. 358, as quoted in H. Barakat *Ibid.*, p. 75.

31. Nevill Barbour, "The Maghrib Liberated, II, *The World Today,* Vol. 19, No. 9, September 1963, p. 397.

32. *New York Times,* July 21, 1958.

33. Lois A Aroial and Richard P. Mitchell, *The Modern Middle East and North Africa.* (New York, MacMillan, 1984), p. 330.

34. *Keesing's Contemporary Archives,* September 16-23 1961, pp.18327-328.

35. Goronwy Rees, *"The Green, The Encounter",* September 1960, p. 39.

36. George W. Shepherd, "Tunisia and Arab Nationalism," *Current History,* Vol. 35, No. 212, July 1959, p. 33.

37. *Le Monde,* 18, 19 Juillet 1961.

38. Mohammed Abad Jabri, *op.cit.,* No. 3, p. 77.

39. *Tunisia's Constant Solidarity with Algeria,* (H. Bourguiba's speech on the eve of the GPRA departure for Algier. July 2, 1962), Tunis: Secretariat of State for Cultural Affairs and Information, 1962), p. 11.

40. Clement H. Moore, "Bourguibism in Tunisia," *Current History,* Vol. 44, No. 257, January 1963, p. 40.

41. O.P, Gallagher, "Ramadan in Tunisia: Aspects and Tunisian Republic," *American Universities Field Staff Reports,* Vol. VI, No. 1, April 15, 1960, pp. 13-14.

42. Mohammed Abad Jabri *op.cit.,* No. 3, p. 78.

43. *Ibid.*, p. 79.

44. *Ibid.*

45. Ideological Report Adopted by the Convention of the National Union of Popular Force, 1962.
46. "The first permanent consultative committee" was created in October 1964 for the purpose of co-ordinating the economic development plans of the four Maghrib countries and helping Tunisia, Algeria, and Morocco to establish a common policy toward the Common Market, As of 1967, the committee had achieved neither goal. However, its creation did lead to the creation of other permanent committees in the fields of education, telecommunications, commerce, transportation, and tourism. As of 1967, these committees had not succeded in carrying out thier most ambitious projects such as the creation of a customs union and of a North African airline; however, they were able to co-ordinate railroad, transportation, to establish uniform mail and telephone rates, and to create a North African office for the exportation of alfalfa. For detail *see* David and Marina Ottamay, *Algeria: The Politics of Socialist Revolution* (Los Anglis, University of California Press, 1970), p. 245.
47. *New York Times,* January, 19-21, 1963.
48. *New York Times,* May 25, 1964.
49. Brain Foster, "Tunisian Problems", *Contemporary Review.* Vol. 192, September 1957, p. 141.
50. H. Bourguiba, *Signs of an Improvement in International Relations,* (Tunis: Secretariat of States for Information and Tourism, 1961), p. 27.
51. *New York Times,* June 21, 1957.
52. *Ibid.*
53. H Bourguiba, *Bizerte Has Served the Cause of the Nation and Brought the Arab Peoples Together,* (Tunis: Secretariat of State for Cultural Affairs and Orientation, Dec. 1963), pp. 7-8. For detail see also Samuel Merlin. *The Search for Peace in the Middle East* (London, Thomas Yasaloff. 1968), pp. 289-92.
54. C. Gallagher. "A Note on Northern Africa," *American Universities Field Staff Reports,* Vol. X, No. 4, June 1964, p. 14.
55. *Jeune Afrique* 6 Juillet 1964.
56. Loma Hahn, "North Africa: A New Pragmatism", *Orbis,* Vol. 8, No. 1, Spring, 1964, p. 139.

57. *Jeune Afrique,* 6 Juillet, 1964.
58. *New York Times,* October, 4, 1964.
59. *The Washington, Post,* November 2, 1964.
60. L.M. Kenny, "The Goal of Arab Unification," *International Journal,* Vol.19, No. 1, Winter, 1963-64, p. 50.
61. N.A. Parks and M.T. Husayn, *The Crescent in Crisis,* (Lawrence/University of Kansas Press, 1955), p. 138. Bourguiba's reaction on the question of Arab Unity and Formation of Arab League see Samuel Merlin *op.cit.* n. 53, pp. 306-12.
62. L.M. Kenny, *op.cit.,* No. 60, pp. 55-57.
63. Henry Siegman, "Arab Unity and Disunity", *The Middle East Journal,* Vol. XVI, Winter, 1962, pp. 49-52.
64. H.A.R. Gibb, "The Future of Arab Unity", in Philip W. Ireland, ed. *The Near East* (Chicago: The University of Chicago Press, 1953), p. 73; also Henry Siegman, *op cit.,* No. 63, p. 52.
65. C.F. Gallegher, "Tunisia", in G.M. Carter, ed., *African One-party States* (Ithaca, New York: Cornell University Press, 1962), p. 79.
66. H. Bourguiba, "Building a New Tunisia", *American Universities Field Staff Reports.* Vol. II, No. 1, January 30, 1961, p. 9.
67. Kenneth Perkins, *A History of Modern Tunisia.* (Cambridge, Cambridge University Press, 2004), p. 142.
68. SCIAS/GEN/INF/8I, pp. 56, as quoted by Yassin-EI-Ayouty. *The Organisation of African Unity after ten years* (New York, Prager 1975), p. 53. (Speech of Bourguiba in OAU Summit). See also Samull Merlin *op.cit.,* No. 53, pp. 306-12.
69. Tamfig Y. Hasou, *The Struggle for the Arab World,* (London, KPI Ltd, 1985), p. 15, and Hussein, A Hassouna, *The League of Arab States, and Regional Disputes,* (New York, Oceana Publications, 1975), pp. 3-23.
70. Pierre Rossi, *Bourguiba's Tunisia,* (Tunis, Editios Kahira, 1967), No. 49, p. 184.
71. Memorandum addressed to the Third Arab Summit meeting held at Casablanca on 13th September 1965. For detail see Samuel Merlin *op.cit,* no. 53, pp. 162-181.

72. *New York Times,* November 24, 1955.
73. *Ibid.,* November 21, 1955.
74. *New York Times,* November 21, 1955.
75. *Ibid.,* November 21, 1956.
76. *Ibid.,* March 7, 1958.
77. H. Bourguiba, "We choose the west," *Orbis,* Vol. 12. No. 4. Fall, 1958, p. 315.
78. *Keesing's, Contemporary Archive,* November 8-15, 1958, p. 16485.
79. *Ibid,.*
80. *New York Times,* November 24, 1958.
81. *Ibid,.* November 28, 1958. For detail Study of Bourguiba relations with Nasser see Samuel Merlin, *op.cit.,* No. 53, pp. 297-324.
82. C.F. Gallagher, "North African Crossroads-part III: The Tunisian Hour, *American Universities Field Staff Reports,* Vol. VII, No. 4, May, 1961, p. 7.
83. C.F. Gallagher, "Tunisia," in G.M. Carter, ed., *op.cit.,* No. 65., p. 80; *New York Times* January 31 and February 1, 1961.
84. H. Bourguiba, *Signs of an Improvement in International Relations,* (Tunis: Secretariat of State for Information and Tourism, 1961), pp. 5-6.
85. *Keesing's Contemporary Archives,* September 30-November 7, 1961, p. 18346.
86. *LeMonde* 22 August, 1961.
87. In contrast to the support he had received from the Egyptian communists at the time of the Bandung Conference (1955), before leaving Cairo to attend the Belgrade Conference (1961), Nasser received a message from the militants of the (JAR extreme left denouncing: "You have left the peaceful road of positive neutralism to adopt non-alignment policy putting on the same level the socialist nations and the bloc of imperialistic and colonialist powers." *(Le Monde,* 2nd September 1961).
88. *New York Times,* January 17, 1964.
89. *Keesing's Contemporary Archives,* September 30, November 7, 1961, p. 18346.

90. *Ibid.*

91. H. Bourguiba, *Bizerte Has Served the Cause of the Nations and Brought the Arab Peoples Together,* (Secretariat of State for Cultural Affairs and Orientation, 1963), pp. 8-9. (underlines added).

92. *Ibid.,* pp. 7-11. See also. Samuel Merlin *op.cit.,* No. 53, pp. 306-12.

93. C.F. Gallagher, "The Tunisian Way: Moderation and Progress in the Maghrib," *American Universities Field Staff Reports,* Vol. IX, No. 11 November, 1963, p. 14.

94. Kenneth J. Perkins, *Tunisia crossroad of the Islamic and European Worlds,* (Boulder, Westview Press, 1986), p. 160-162. See also. Samuel Merlin *op.cit.,* No. 53, pp. 88-143 and 325-345.

95. *Ibid.*

96. Anthony Sylvester, *Tunisia,* (London, The Bodley Head, 1969), p. 192. See also, Samuel Merlin *op.cit.,* No. 53, pp. 88-143 and 325-345.

97. *Ibid.*

98. H. Bourguiba, Jr., "The Foreign Policy of Tunisia," in J.E. Black and K.W. Thompson, eds., *Foreign Policies in a world of change,* (New York: Harper and Row, Publishers, 1963), p. 370.

99. H. Bourguiba, "Nationalism: Antidote to Communism," *Foreign Affairs,* Vol. 35. No. 4, July 1957, p. 653.

100. H. Bourguiba, "The Independence of Ghana," *The Advancement of Africa.* (Tunis: Secretariat of State for Information, n.d.), pp. 41-42, and 47. (hereafter referred as The Advancement of Africa).

101. *Ibid.,* p. 42.

102. *Ibid.,* p. 51.

103. Catherine Hoskyns, "*The* African States and the United Nations, 1958-1964, *International Affairs,* Vol. 40, July 1964, pp. 466-467.

104. *The Advancement of Africa, op.cit.,* No. 100, p. 56.

105. *New York Times,* December 9, 1958.

106. *New York Times,* April 15, 1960.

107. John Crutcher, "Pan Africanism: African Odyasey, "*Current History,* Vol. 44, No. 257, January 1963, p. 5.
108. The group was created in December 1960, and consisted of the Ivory Coast, Dahomey, Niger, Upper Volta, Cameroon, Central African Republic, Chad, Congo-Brazzavile, Galbon, Malagasy, Mauritania and Senegal.
109. John Crutcher, *op.cit.,* No. 107, p. 6; Boutros -Ghali, "The Addis Ababa Charter, "*International Conciliation,* No. 546, January 1964, p. 7.
110. *Keesing's Contemporary Archives,* April 14-12, 1962, p. 18708.
111. Catherine Hoskyns, *op.cit.,* No. 103, pp. 47I-473.
112. *Ibid., p. 467; Keesing's Contemporary Archives,* June 15-22, 1963 p. 19465 Member of the (OAU: Algeria, Burundi, Cameroon, Central African Republic, Chad, Congo (Brazzaville), Congo (Leopoldville), Dahomey, Ethiopia, Gabon, Ghana, Guinea, Ivory Coast, Liberia, Libya, Madagascar, Mali, Mauritania, Morocco, Niger, Nigeria, Rvanda, Senegal, Sierra Leone, Somalia, Sudan, Tanganyika (Now Tanzania), Togo, Tunisia, Uganda, United Arab Republic, Upper Volts.
113. *New York Times,* May 12, 1961.
114. *New York Times.* May 1, 1963.
115. *Keesing's Contemporary Archives, op.cit.,* No. 112, p. 19465.
116. E.C. Schwarzenbach, "A Report on the Africans' Addis Ababa Conference", *Swiss Review of World Affairs, July* 1963, p. 10.
117. *New York Times,* July 21, 1964.
118. *Jeune Afrique,* 3 Aout 1964.
119. C.P. Gallagher "Tunisia", in G.M. Carter, ed., *op. cit.,* No. 65, p. 81.
120. Krishan Gopal and Kokifa Krishan Gopal, West *Asia and North Africa, A Documentary Study of Major Crisis,* 1947-48, (V.I. Pub., New Delhi, 1918), pp. 354-55.
121. *Ibid.*
122. A. Appodarai, *select document in India's Foreign Policy, 1947-72* (Oxford university press, New York-985), Vol. 11, pp. 387-93.

123. The Statesman (Delhi), 7 March 1967.
124. Foreign Affairs Record, Vol. 11, No. 6, June 1965, pp. 131-32.
125. Foreign Affairs Record.
126. *Ibid.*
127. *Ibid.*
128. *Ibid.*
129. Ambassador of Tunisia H.E. Tarek Azouz. Tunisian Embassy, New Delhi, May, 2013.

3 Tunisia and France

Tunisia's links with Europe go as far back as the 10th century when a French Counsel was resident in this country from 1577. But the early 18th century saw it emerge as a politically conscious State whose independence as recognised by many of the important Western Powers like England, France and Austria-Hungary and even accepted by the Turkey of that time, some of whom concluded political and commercial treaties with Tunisia. This chapter focussed on the policy pursued by France before and after independence.

Among the countries of that region, Tunisia showed far greater political awareness and a more vigorous political leadership than several others. In 1857, an enterprising ruler by the name of Ahmed Bey initiated a policy of reforms and formulated what came to be known as the Fundamental Pact or Constitution containing a proclamation defining human rights, such as equality before the law for all the inhabitants of Tunisia without any distinction of class, race or religion, liberty of conscience and worship and freedom to canyon such normal activities, as trade.[1] A complete system of legal codes, civil, penal and commercial, without distinction or discrimination, was established. Income 'and-expenditure' came to be regulated through a regular budget, and a court of accounts set up for its control.[2] These policies were pursued by two successive rulers, Mohamed Bey and Sadek Bey. But other factors were at work running counter to these progressive measures. One was the trouble with the tribesmen which interrupted the working of the reforms, the other, the French plans for getting complete control over the entire North African region. After France took over Algeria in 1830 and began expanding, according to French admission, their policy towards Tunisia underwent quick changes. On grounds of ensuring security to Algeria, France began to intervene to an increasing extent in Tunisian internal affairs.

Tunisia's fate was sealed at the Congress of Berlin in 1878. Italian and French rivalry had reached a high pitch. Italy considering it had a major claim on Tunisia because of its large national community settled in the Regency; France, on the other hand, held the view that possession of Algeria gave her prior rights. The French were all the more aggressive in view of the major defeat they had suffered at German hands in 1870. Britain was now less adamant in its opposition to France: not only would a further weakening of the latter endanger the balance of power policy to which Salisbury and Disraeli clung after recent Russian encroachments on Turkish sovereignty, but Britain needed "international acquiescence in its presence in Cyprus. At the Congress, Britain made a tentative suggestion that France be given a free hand in Tunisia. This was upheld by Bismark who thus hoped to assuage France's wounded pride and turn its' attention from its lost provinces of Alsace and Lorraine. Moreover, as Bismark foresaw, this would be driving the wedge into French and Italian solidarity, and indeed, as his astute statesmanship had foreseen, Italy joined the Triple Alliance (Germany, Austria, Italy) in 1882.[3] The change of attitude was signified locally and indirectly by the forced retirement in 1879 of Sir Richard Wood on the flimsy pretext of administrative reorganisation involving a necessary 'general massacre of aged official innocents' as a Foreign Office official put it. The French were not deceived, and extended wholehearted thanks for being rid of the staunchest supporter of British and Turkish interests in Tunisia. In spite of Italian objections and a strong anti-colonial feeling in France, the imperial power prepared to move in.[4]

The last and quite minor problem which remained was for France to devise some sort of *casus belli.* In a most opportune fashion, it was found that a border tribe, the Khrumir, was guilty of some misdemeanours and the French

Parliament voted credits for "border operations'. The Bey's offer to deal with the problem himself was refused, and two French columns crossed the Algero-Tunisian frontier on 24th April 1881, whilst a third landed at Bizerta. Roustan pointed 'out to the Bey that he had to choose between abdication or signing a treaty establishing a French Protectorate. Under duress the Bey signed the Treaty of Bardo on 12 May 1881.[5]

Which he did without consulting his High Council of Tunisia thus violating the 1861 Constitution by impugning the integrity of his country. His action was thus not only a political betrayal but also judicially illegal.[6] Under the Treaty terms France underwrote the Tunisian external debt by which, the International France Commission was replaced by a French controlled Financial Department. After that the, French simply started taking over the country.

Article 2 of the Treaty said: The occupation will cease when the French and Tunisian military authorities have by mutual agreement recognised that the local government is in a state to guarantee the maintenance of order',[7] The other articles further stipulated that the existing treaties between Tunisia and France as well as between Tunisia and other European countries would continue.

The illusions were thus maintained that the State continued as before, that the intervention was temporary and that only the rights of external sovereignty were conferred upon. France, that is, the French diplomatic and consular agents, henceforth, became responsible for the protection of Tunisian interests abroad and the French Resident-General, the intermediary between Tunisia and the other foreign governments, while the War and Navy Departments were entrusted to French Military leaders. Tunisia thus became a French Protectorate.

The 'progressive expansion of 'French control continued and culminated in the 1883 Treaty of Mersa under which the Bey undertook, in order to facilitate the fulfillment of the Protectorate, to carry out those administrative, judicial and financial reforms that the French Government may consider useful. This covered the subjects left untouched by the Bardo treaty. In addition the French Government had the right for its own benefit to lay down the amount of taxes; their scale and mode of collection and the right to regulate the use of the Tunisian revenues.[8] The wide interpretation of these terms as stated in the decree of the President of the Republic made clear that it assigned to the Resident-General practically full powers: "To take over with the approval of the French Government of all decrees issued by the Bey". "A Second Presidential decree which followed a year later and also as before a unilateral act, reinforced the powers of the French representative in Tunisia and made him 'the depository of the power of the Republic of Tunisia". In other words for all practical purposes, these successive prerogatives made the French Resident-General the real head of the Tunisian affairs. In fact, he alone had now the power to give executive force to the laws and preside over the Council of Ministers. Soon a Secretary-General was installed whose duties were stated as co-ordinating the technical services and actually had control over economic plans and the personal expenses of the Bey. Tunisian sovereignty was thus completely undermined by what the French defined as 'a protectorate of continuous creation'. It is interesting to note that the French authorities have always maintained that France had the right to act unilaterally according to the Mersa agreement, while actually these prerogatives were written into the Treaty by the French themselves for their own advantage. It is also significant that this Treaty was never sanctioned by the French Parliament.[9]

Penetrating light is thrown on these episodes by the debates that took place in the French Parliament when Jules Ferry, the head of the French Government, asserted before the Senate 'We want from him (Bey) neither his territory nor his throne. Clemenceau on the opposition side was equally eloquent. He was then a Radical Deputy and fully aware of the business and financial influences at work in precipitating these aggressive acts. 'In all this, I see only men who wished to do business and make money. It is not on such grounds as these we had to commence a struggle with the Bey and bring about the crisis that fed to this expedition', he declared in the Chamber of Deputies. "You have violated the Constitution and have come here to confront the Chamber with a *fait accompli.* You have spent large sums and declared war without consulting Parliament."[10]

An open avowal that this was a premeditated plan is to be found in *Politique Francaise en Tunisia* by Estournelles de Constant, one of the men involved in it. He writes: "The Bey thought to be doing well in asking our advice and we replied with alacrity to this courtcousing situation in which Tunisia found itself, and from which if seemed impossible to extricate without outside aid-foreign assistance. The Beys put themselves in the position of allowing us to guide them fearing our displeasure and thus achieved their ruin".[11]

From now on France seems to have contrived to assure to herself mastery in every field of life, which included wholesale importation of French personnel and the stimulation of an artificially inflated French colony that could only be sustained by concessions and lucrative jobs at a heavy cost to the State.

Although no large-scale colonialisation occurred, as it had in Algeria, the French administration placed the European settlers' interests first and subjected Tunisia to so-called reforms that were clearly not in the interest of the Muslim population.[12]

On the other hand, the French settler population remained much smaller than its counterpart in Algeria, never exceeding seven per cent of the total Tunisian population. It also penetrated the country's economic and commercial life with far less intensity. For example, the fertile and commercially prosperous area of the Sahel, along the central-eastern coast of the country, was left largely in Tunisian hands.[13]

Tunisian Nationalism

Tunisia was the first of the three North African countries to be influenced by modern nationalism and France.

Tunisian nationalism took shape in response to French rule. Tunisian thought about the nature, structure and purpose of government was influenced by contact with France; the ideals of self-government, which would surely have emerged anyway, took their particular form from contact with France; the ideology of Tunisia as part of France evoked, counter-feelings of the independent nature of a Tunisian community.[14]

From the first, the French occupation had to come to terms with a complicated system of Islamic land ownership. One of the first actions of the French protectorate was to establish a legal framework for the acquisition of land in a European manner. It did so by an Act of 1885, which was based on the Torrens Act, passed for similar purposes in different conditions in Australia. It was the first in a series of legislative acts 'which made possible the private acquisition of land. The problem of mainmort was got round and eventually pushed aside by replacing the yearly payment by a single lump payment.[15]

The application of this legislation was of major importance in Tunisian development. Its immediate practical effect was to make colonisation possible; it had a far deeper impact on society. The administration of the 1885 Act was put in the hands of mixed tribunals, so that French and Tunisians sat side by side deciding claims to ownership. They came from very different backgrounds and represented different systems of law. Their association provided fresh insight and fresh knowledge, which contributed on the one side to an understanding of European law and on the other to an awareness of Islamic civilisation. More important for the future, it set an example of the acquisition of right by legal means which could be extended to the political sphere and contribute to the building of a nationalist movement. Later it also provided a legal framework in which young Tunisians could defend the interests of the under privileged in their society, defending in a court of law the rights and status of share croppers and the like, developing thereby a social philosophy intertwined with the demand for political rights. Bourguiba's early career was spent in this way.[16]

Local administrators—the caids—who exercised administrative, judicial and tax gathering powers were protected from upheaval, disorder and expropriation in a way they had not been before the French came; but their position was not one to which rating young ambitious Tunisians would want to succeed. Nationalist aspirations would bring them into conflict with the old order of their own society as well as imperial rule. The apparatus of the State was essentially French and protected settler interests; but the more truly French, and therefore reforming and democratic it became, the more it would meet resistance from its own settlers—without being able to meet the full demands of the nationalists by the surrender of real power.[17]

These sources of tension were only increased by the development of education. Immediately after the occupation it was suggested by no less than Jules Ferry, the creator of lay education under the third republic that schooling for the Europeans could be left in the hands of Lavigerie and his missions, and that a greater effort should be made to teach the Tunisians French, and practical trades.

The standard traditional Muslim education, even when the reforms which a young (for the most part French educated) generation introduced in the twentieth century are taken into account, remained low.[18]

The education most worth aspiring to for young Tunisians was, therefore, Sadiki College followed by higher studies in France. The political effect of this was immense. It created an elite with a strongly developed national sense, aware of French values. It bought them into contact with the efficiency of French institutions—a degree of efficiency which they found attractive but was hardly likely to overawe them; it also introduced them to a France which was only weakly represented in the protectorate—the France of progressive ideas, a socialist party and intellectual freedom.[19]

It was a Sadiki graduate, who in 1888 founded the first Tunisian non-official Arabic language newspaper, *al Hadira.* A group centred on the newspaper also founded an institute in 1896, called the *Khalduniya* (after the medieval historian and philosopher) designed to provide modem studies for Zitouna students. Out of the *Khalduniya,* 'frew' the important movement of the turn of the century known as the Young Tunisians, with its own news paper, *Le Tunisien,* founded in 1907 (An Arabic version followed under the direction of Taalbi in 1909. Even so the movement was not nationalist. It accepted the French protectorate, and sought the extension of the benefits of the protectorate to Tunisians in every way. They wanted more French education, not to the exclusion of Arabic but as the means to modernisation and to give Tunisians greater access to government employment.[20]

After the World War I, the Tunisian nationalists were incited by external factors to intensify their action.[21]

In search of a French commitment to apply to Tunisia the principle of self-determination included in President Woodrow Wilson's Fourteen Points, a delegation of former Young Tunisians travelled to Versailles in 1919 to meet with the peace commissioners. The group's failure to win concessions prompted one of its members, Abd alAziz Thaalbi; to write *La Tunisie Martyre,* a short book outlining a philosophy at odds with the Western sympathies of the pre-war Young Tunisians. Thaalbi, who had studied at Zaituna, had earlier worked for Salafiyya—inspired reforms but had never agreed with the Western proclivities of the more secular of the Young Tunisians. The central thesis of his work was that Tunisia had enjoyed a golden age in the nineteenth century, which the imposition of foreign rule had cut short. As evidence of Tunisia's pre-colonial accomplishments, Thaalbi offered the 1861 Constitution, which he urged the Bey to restore. He rejected Franco-Tunisian cooperation, arguing that the French presence had brought only harm to the country. After a brief detention following the publication of *La Tunisie Martyre, Thaalbi* assumed the leadership of the newly created and still loosely-organised Dustur (constitution) party.[22]

France did introduce some reforms in 1922, centring around the creation of a Grand Council with separate

Tunisian and European sections. Reflecting the realities of power, if not of demography, the council's European members outnumbered their Tunisian counterparts. Colons elected most of the European representatives, but local advisory councils, organised at the same time and controlled by French officials or carefully selected Tunisians, appointed the Tunisian component of the Grand Council. Besides these obvious shortcomings, the council lacked meaningful legislative power. The Dustur roundly rejected this system, which fell far short of its minimum goals.[23]

At the end of 1924, a Tunisian memorandum was transmitted to the French government by Destourian delegation which once more put forward the Tunisian claims.[24]

This strident yet syncretic nationalism—for it unconsciously embodied the ideals of the society it attacked —was an indispensable ingredient of the national self-awareness which must precede independence. Yet, the nationalist movement as a whole was fall of confusion/and false starts. The Destour party itself had no clear plan of action. It lacked the nerve and the resources to be an out and out revolutionary party vowed to the overthrow of the protectorate, and it lacked the political acumen to make political capital out of otherwise trivial incidents. It drew up a long list of 'demands' and then rested its case. Although its branch organisation spread in the 1920's it was ineffective in building widespread popular feeling into a mass party. The leaders of the Destour came primarily from Tunis and were drawn from the traditional governing class of religious lawyers and well to do merchants. The new atmosphere of the twenties with the protests of the elite being taken up by ordinary people, but such people only partially organised by the Destour.[25]

As L. Brown has suggested, the formalistic legalism characteristic of the Destourian leaders' political manoeuvers was inspired by their contacts with the west, but was "supported by the attitudes of the traditional society". This legalism enabled them to undertake political action on behalf of the Tunisian society without totally committing themselves either to the action itself. They were not and could not be revolutionary either socially or politically and they tended to ignore the political importance of the new intelligentsia and social groups that appeared through the educational and economic impact of the protectorate. Without mass organisation, and as its leaders remained isolated in their exclusive social milieu, the Destour party lacked the resilience necessary for withstanding political repression. Thus since the imposition in January 1926 of restrictions on the press and political activity, the Destour party languished in passivity.[26] The weakness of the Destour was amply demonstrated by its aloofness from the flowering of national working class organisation.[27]

Neo-Destour and Nationalism and France

It was at this time, in the middle of these confused and conflicting initiatives in modernisation and nationalism, that a new party emerged under the leadership of Habib Bourguiba. Its novelty did not lie in a reconciliation of the ideological differences between different strands of Tunisian thought; it was rather in organisation and tactics. It was assisted in this by the economic situation, which continued to deteriorate and was made very much worse when the world slump struck France and its colonies in 1932—at a time too of bad harvests, which have always been powerful catalysts in political history.

The traditional leadership of the Destour ran into the sand during the 1920's. Having done so much to create nationalist feeling and to express a nationalist case they were unable or unwilling to proceed further. Younger men—Mahmoud Materi, Tahar Sfar and Habib Bourguiba—pressed impatiently for a more vigorous and demanding attitude and for action against the protectorate. They ran a new newspaper, *La Voix du Tunisien,* in which they angrily attacked the French president, Doumergue, during his visit of 1931; two years later they founded a new paper, significantly called *L Action Tunisienne.* In March 1934, the final break came, and at a historic conference held at Ksar Heltal the Neo-Destour party was formed.[28]

Unlike the leaders of the Destour, Bourguiba and his well-educated peers did not reject the West. Neither did they accept the steady frenchification of their country, seeking it as part of a process leading to French assimilation of Tunisia. They chafed at their exclusion from the upper levels of the bureaucracy and resented efforts to increase the number of French citizens in Tunisia, both by promoting French colonisation and by enacting legislation artificially enlarging the French population. Shortly after the war, the government bestowed automatic French citizenship on all Europeans born in Tunisia. This policy not only swelled the so-called French population, it also united Europeans of various ethnic backgrounds by erasing, at least in theory, distinctions between Europeans of French and non-French ancestry. Since 1923, Tunisians meeting certain educational and financial criteria had also been encouraged to adopt French citizenship. To do so, however they had to renounce their right to trials in accordance with the-precepts of Islamic law, which few Tunisian Muslims, even westernised ones, were prepared to do.

The Neo-Destour Party announced conference of 1933, that is, the achievement of an independent and sovereign Tunisia, remained the basic policy of the party. At the same time, the party decided to proceed to its realisation in stages. As an initial step it pressed for a return to, the spirit and the letter of the occupation statutes, which either had not been respected or had been mutilated in a manner contrary to its original purport and this with the understanding that French trusteeship was not intended to be permanent. In pursuance of its aim the party urged the speedy implementation of the following reforms:

1. Abolition of the "colonial allowance". (This is an allowance amounting to one-third of the basic salary paid to French employees in Algeria, Tunisia, and Morocco).
2. Cessation of official colonisation of the land.
3. Compulsory education for all.

4. The setting up of elected municipal councils.
5. Appointment of Tunisians to various government jobs, including a greater share in pivotal posts.
6. A more effective relief programme.
7. Anti-usury legislation.
8. Abolition of the Grand Council and its replacement by a duly-elected Tunisian parliament and a government responsible to it.[29]

In this Congress, Bourguiba put forward a programme in which he expressed once more the demands of the party for an elected parliament with universal suffrage and added: "The independence of Tunisia, completed by treaty of friendship and of union with the great French Republic, securing for France the interests of the whole foreign colony, will be the ideal of the Tunisian nationalist movement".[30]

Neo-Destour party was the political expression of the new elite. It embodied the spirit of a new generation which was both progressive and Tunisian Muslim ambitious and mobile "but retaining its roots in the home village or town, of humble social background but determined to succeed in the face of a system that still favoured the established aristocracy. It was predominantly a Sahilian movement. Most of its leaders came from the Sahil, including Bourguiba, and when in 1934 these leaders rebelled against the leaders of the Destour, they symbolically did so at the party congress held in the Sahil at Qsar Hilal (Ksar Hellal).[31]

The main thrust of Bourguiba's speech at the Ksar Hellal Congress was that the new team had greater credibility among the French authorities. He also made the point that it was precisely the ability of the new team to have the ear of the government in France that led the Executive Commission of the Destour Party to fear them.

Ainsi done, le Resident General ne trouve comme interlocuteur que M. Ahmed Essafi et ses amis, pendant que les chefs du mouvement qui etaient parvenus a faire entendre lew voix aux Conseils du Gouvemement Francais etaient ecartes et empeches de prendre une part quclque minime qu'elle fut, aux pourparlers.[32]

Finally, he asked for the mandate to pursue their principal objective: *"la liberation de notre patrie".*

The "new" Destour thought to have solved the problem of political survival by the new organisational plan which was adopted. This new plan called for a double-tiered leadership; the Bureau Politique, which was the effective Executive Commission, and the National Council, which stood ready to replace the Political Bureau with a new team if the Bureau Politique became incapacitated for one reason or another. The support that Bourguiba had lent to M'Hamed Chenik and which had cost him the friendship of Ali Bouhajeb paid off at this time, as Chenik'was able to provide financial backing, both directly' and through the Agricultural Cooperative, which rallied many small land-owners to the Neo-Destour.[33]

As this historical overview of the split shows, the differences between the "Archeo-" and the "Neo-" Destours was not on the ideological level nor was it between "traditionalists", on the one hand, and "modernists", on the other, since the leaders of the two Destours were basically of the same background. Both were within the modernist stream, heir to the pre-Protectorate reformist tendency of Shdykh Qabadu and Khayr al-Din, of Bechir Sfar, Ali Bash Hanba and Ab delaziz Thaalbi. At this critical juncture in the history of the Tunisian Nationalist Movement, a simple gesture brought out the crucial importances of Islam. The'new team was requested to be sworn-in on the Quran and it was only after this symbolic gesture that they were accepted as legitimate leaders.[34]

In the absence of a national trade unionist movement, the Neo-Destour party could attract into its ranks those Tunisians who might have expressed their labour grievances through the confederation generals Tunisianne du Traviel (C.G.T.T). And when in 1946, the *Union Generate des Travilleurs Tunisiens* (U.G.T.T.) was founded, it became until independence the political ally of the Neo-Destour.

The Neo-Destour came into being as a result of the dissatisfaction of the new Tunisian elite with the Destour political leadership. Its leaders introduced into Tunisian politics not so much a new political aim (for the aim of independence was implied if not always explicit in the Destourian position), but a new style of action, a greater sense of mission and commitment, and the will not only to achieve independence but also[35] the New-Destour developed its organs and spread its influence under the continuous threat of suppression. The-party was formally banned six months after its foundation and remained illegal for the following twenty years.[36]

The very nature of the new party, its desire to appeal to the Tunisian masses and to use them to defy the French-guaranteed that it would not be tolerated. By late 1934, Bourguiba and most of the other top Neo-Destour leaders had been arrested and sentenced to internal exile, usually in the Sahara. In the months immediately after the Ksar Hellal Congress, however, Bourguiba and his colleagues had devoted their attention to structuring the Neo-Destour into tightly knit cells, a technique they borrowed from the Communists and one that allowed the party to continue functioning without its leaders. Consequently, the French decapitation of the Neo-Destour failed to destroy it. Indeed, it proved a tactical blunder enhancing the public image of the party and that of its imprisoned organisers. Neo-Destour militants, backed by former supporters of the CGTT, mounted demonstrations during 1935 an 1936, eventually forcing the recall of the hated Peyrouton.[37]

The First Franco-Tunisian Experiences and 1938 Crisis

With the appointment of Ajmand Guillon as a new French resident in Tunisia in March 1936, an era of relaxation and what Destourians called "the first Franco-Tunisian experience began.[38] Bourguiba several times put forward his party's programme and explained it, notably in a memorandum sent to Pierre Vienot[39] in August 1936, in a public speech at Tunis and in many articles in L'Action. In fact, the Neo-Destour hoped that France would react in

Tunisia as it had done in Syria and as Britain had already done in Egypt. But Bourguiba admitted that the independence of Tunisia could not be immediately recognised as this would presume that public opinion was already prepared in France as well as in Tunisia, while this was not yet the case.

Consequently, Bourguiba proposed a series of measures for future development towards independence beginning with the abolition of the privileges given to the French in Tunisia. Moreover, he demanded "the substitution of the actual despotic regime based on pleasure by a constitutional and democratic regime that permits people to participate in power, to take an active part in the making of laws and in the voting of the budget and added: "The institution of universal suffrage and the extension of powers to the Grand Council in this sense could be the beginning of a deeper reform in the direction of the democratisation of the regime"[40]

This marked generally the first stage of the "Franco-Tunisian" experience. However, the situation deteriorated with the fall of the Ministry of "Leon-Blum in France in June 1937.

As for the nationalist action, strikes and serious incidents took place since March 1937 between the Tunisian workers and the forces of the police.[41] Then the Destourians decided, in November, on a strike in solidarity with the victims of French repression in Algeria and Morocco. Bourguiba made a call for the struggle in an article published in L'Action under the title of "Unconsciousness or Cynicism" in which he wrote: "...general counter-offensive in all the fronts ... The country is decided for the struggle. It is also ready for all the sacrifices that this struggle entails... [42] At the same time and on the occasion of the announcement of the budget for 1938, the Neo-Destour withdrew its confidence from the resident-general".

In fact political agitation extended in April 1938 to all parts of Tunisia and a general strike was held as well as a huge demonstration led by Mongi Slim and Ali Balhaouan. Many people were killed due to the intervention of the police:

twenty-two according to the residence and 200 according to Neo-Destourian. Then two thousand militants were arrested and martial law was proclaimed.[43] Bourguiba and his companions were accused of conspiracy against the State security and were referred to a military justice.

Henceforth, Bourguiba and his companions, until their return to Tunis in 1943, would only know the different prisons in Tunisia and France, and finally Rome. The Tunisian nationalist movement once more entered an era of underground activities. It was then that Bourguiba was given the title *"Le Combattant Supreme"*, and during his absence, the main leader of the clandestine organisation of the party was al-Habib Thamer. The most important activity of the party during this period consisted in the continuous demand for the liberation of prisoners and recall of the main points of the Destourian programme.[44]

Tunisia and the Second World War

The extreme repression of 1938 quietened nationalist agitation. As at the same time Fascist agents became very active amongst the Italians in Tunisia, thus reviving the Tunisians' fears of Italian colonial ambitions in the country, the French presence started to appear, at least momentarily, an advantage. The relative lull in political activity continued even after the fall of France and the arrival of a Fearing immediate complications in the North African zone, had the Neo-Destour leaders, Bourguiba and his chief colleagues, removed forthwith to Marseilles from where they were later transferred to Lyons. These unhappy events however had serious repercussions on the war situation for the mobilised. Tunisian troops in the French army revolted and refused to leave for the front unless the political activists were released and conditions restored to normal. The civil population backed up the demand that unless negotiations were opened to settle the terms under which Tunisians could honourably participate in the war, that is, steps taken to set Tunisia on the road to freedom, the Tunisians would have no truck with this war.[45] Until the beginning of November 1942, when Allied troops landed in Morocco and Algeria, and soon afterwards Tunisia became the theatre of major military operations, mass usual activities remained curtailed because of the tight restrictions imposed.

Within six months Munsif Bey's standing overshadowed that of any political leader in the country. Even Bourguiba's political future might have been different had the Bey remained in power. But he was deposed on 14 May 1943 by the Free French authorities a week after the Allied forces entered Tunis. He was accused to collaboration with the Axis, but the more likely reason for his removal from the throne was his attempt to shake off French control.

Bourguiba from his prison in Marseilles took a definite stand against collaboration with the Axis. In a message, he smuggled from his prison in August 1942. He urged the Neo-Destour Political Bureau to enter into relations, and coordinate their political action, with the Free French, leaving until after the war about the question of Tunisia's independence. Bourguiba was sent to Rome by the Germans at the beginning of 1943, where the Italian government tried to obtain a statement in favour of the Axis from him. In his speech on the Rome radio not say a word in favour of the Axis powers.[46] After the liberation of Tunis, Bourguiba immediately made a call entitled "For a Franco-Tunisian block" directed against the Axis powers.[47]

The end of the war did not herald any change that was likely to bring Tunisia nearer to independence. In order to solicit international support for Tunisia, Bourguiba left the country secretly in March 1945, went to Egypt, where he hoped to obtain help from the newly founded Arab League, then spent two years touring Asia, Europe, and the United State. In Tunisia, where the (U.G.T.T.) was founded in 1946, there was a tendency towards coordinating the action of the various anti-colonial groups in a National Tunisian Front. A Congress was held on 23rd August 1946 in which the Destour, Neo-Destour, and U.G.T.T. took part and adopted a manifesto.[48] The broke in to disrupt the meeting as Salah b. Yusuf (Youssef), then the secretary-general of the Neo-Destour, was delivering his address. Before the gathering dispersed, the leaders present had time to pledge themselves to work for Tunisia's independence. In the face of the demonstrations, strikes, and other forms of agitation which followed, the French made minor concessions accompanied by the police repression. In July 1947, a new Tunisian government was formed, with Mustafa Ka'aḳ as prime minister, in which the number of Tunisian ministers was made equal to the French. This did not seem to make any significant difference since real authority remained in the hands of the Resident-General.

In theory the protectorate treaty did not abrogate the Bey's sovereignty, and for this reason protectorate officials acted in the Bey's name. In practice, however, the French settlers in the country were made to share in the Bey's sovereignty by being given the opportunity to form the Consultative Conference.[49]

When France responded to the nationalists' demands in 1945 with only minimal compromises, Bourguiba concluded that Paris would not of its own accord to beyond insignificant concessions. Faced with a choice between promoting violence inside the country or attempting to generate enough external support to pressure France into reconsidering its Tunisian policies, Bourguiba opted for the latter course.[50] He left the country in April 1945 going first to Cairo to lobby at the newly created Arab League. For the next four years, Bourguiba travelled throughout the Middle East, as well as in the United States, where influential labour organisation sympathised with the Neo-Destour because of the nationalists' links with trade unionism. In November 1946, he gave the French ambassador in Cairo a note entitled "France in face of the Tunisian problem? In which he stated: "What Tunisia claims is the status of a sovereign state, attached to France by a treaty of alliance freely negotiated in order to guarantee to the latter its strategic, economic and cultural interests. An elected constiuent assembly will give the country a modern democratic constitution.."[51] Hence, Bourguiba opted for the method of states to realise the goal of the independence of Tunisia from France.[52] In 1948, Bourguiba helped found the Committee for the

Liberation of the Arab Maghrib, an agency headquartered in Cairo that coordinated contacts among nationalist leaders from all of France's North African Possessions. The concentration of the Arab world on Palestine in the postwar years, however, made it difficult for the North Africans to command very much attention from their fellow Arabs.[53]

Quest for National Self-determination in Tunisia

The achievement of at least nominal independence in eastern Arab countries after World War I, and the example of the nationalist movement in Egypt inspires Tunisians with a greater national consciousness.

India's independence in 1947 gave a big boost to the process of national liberation in whole of Middle East and North Africa.

From 1950, the question of co-sovereignty became the major bone of contention between the French and Tunisian nationalists. In August 1950, Muhammad Shanniq was made to form a new government of nine Tunisians and three French. The formation of the government was understood to herald political changes of significance, and so the Neo-Destour agreed to take part in it. Salah b, Yusuf, the party's secretary-general, became the minister of justice. The French reforms which were announced soon afterwards involved upgrading the prime minister by having his orders countersigned not by the French secretary-general of the government but by the resident. The Grand Council was, henceforth, to have equal French and Tunisian membership. The settler organisation *Rassamblement Francaise de Tunisie* had for some time insisted that only a joint Franco-Tunisian sovereignty would be compatible with the dominant interests, the French had in the country, and the French government up-this viewpoint.[54] Prime Minister Shanniq and three other Tunisian Ministers went to Paris in October 1951 to demand Tunisian independence and the recognition of total Tunisian sovereignty, while remaining close cultural, economic, and military relations with France.[55] The French government's reply given on 15 December was that a fruitful

Franco-Tunisian association required French participation in Tunisia's governmental institutions.

Although the Neo-Destour gained official recognition in August 1951, the party showed no signs of subservience. Bourguiba took the view that the concept of co-sovereignty fell short of Tunisian aspirations. He insisted upon a completely Tunisian government; an assembly reflecting demographic realities and not unfairly weighted to protect European interests, CIS all previous experiments at a legislative body had been; and the more rapid incorporation of Tunisians into the bureaucracy. He forcefully rejected a French proposal for municipal elections in which colons would vote but at the same time tried to assure the French that a nationalist government would not ignore their legitimate concerns.

Bourguiba's protestations did not sway the colons. More unified than ever before, they had formed their own party, the *Rassamblement francaise de Tunisie*, to guard against any additional changes in the status quo. The vehemence of their protests undermined the continuation of the 1951 reform efforts, which might otherwise have found some middle ground between the French and the nationalists, particularly since France was moving in such a direction. In addition to the mounting domestic popularity of the Neo-Destour, France could not indefinitely ignore international pressures for decolonisation in the post-war era. Bourguiba tried to capitalise on this situation by again travelling abroad as a spokesman for Tunisian nationalism. Neo-Destour attempts to internationalise the Franco-Tunisian dispute culminated when Ben Yusuf went to the January 1952 meeting of the UN Security Council in Paris to place Tunisian grievances before the world body.

The atmosphere in Tunisia after January 1952 was not conducive to compromise or to the acceptance of the partial solutions the French were proposing. Police repression was countered by demonstrations and strikes. The U.G.T.T. and the Neo-Destour formed a united front for the following three years, and Farhat' Hashshad (Hached); 'the founder of the

U.G.T.T., served on the clandestine Political Bureau of the Neo-Destour from 1952.[56] Whereas most of Neo-Destourian leaders were in prison. Hashshad was-kept free because of his international connections through the U.G.T.T. membership in the International Confederation of Free Trade Unions. From 1952 Tunisian guerrillas *(fellaga)* also operated from mountain bases against French settlers. The settlers countered by forming their own terrorist organisation, the Red Hand, which attacked Tunisian political leaders still at liberty. Its most important victim was Farhat Hashshad who was assassinated on 5th December 1952.[57]

Violence eventually led the French government to give in. On 30th July, 1954 the Mendes-France government adopted a project of granting autonomy to Tunisia. On the 31st Mendes-France went to Tunis to explain the new policy and to ask the Bey to choose a new government to negotiate the form of Tunisian independence.[58] The negotiations made slow progress and were interrupted when the government of Mendes-France fell on 5th February 1955. When they were resumed on 15th March Bourguiba was allowed to take part in them, and soon acted as the leader of the Tunisian side. The *fellaga* had intensified their action in the second half of 1954, and it appears that the continuation of terrorism was a decisive factor in leading the French government to allow Bourguiba join in the negotiations. An agreement on granting autonomy to Tunisia was concluded with Bourguiba on 22nd April 1955, and on June 3rd, 1955, he signed a convention with France proclaiming Tunisia's internal autonomy. The secretary-general of the party, Salah Ben Youssef, denounced the autonomy convention with France as a "step backward" and openly attacked Bourguiba. Instead, Ben Youssef called for immediate Tunisian independence within the framework of pan-Arabism.[59] Ben Youssef had the support of strongly religious and conservative groups, as well as of urban elements that sympathised with his espousal of a radical Arab nationalism drawing inspiration from Nasserism in Egypt. On the other hand, Bourguiba, who represented moderation and an attachment to specifically Tunisian (as opposed to broader

Arab-Islamic) virtues and possibilities, had the support of educated, Western-trained elites from the Sahel and Tunis.

In the bitter and personal confrontation that took place between these two charismatic leaders, Bourguiba prevailed because of the overwhelming support of the party and the crucial backing of the trade-union movement, headed by Bourguiba's ally, Ahmed Ben Salah. Ben Youssef organised a guerrilla insurrection in the south, but this was quashed with the help of French troops.

Thus, in the first years of autonomy and independence, Bourguiba was able to establish his supremacy not only in the party but also in the formal machinery of the state. In April 1956, he became prime minister, leading a government in which sixteen of the seventeen ministers belonged to the Neo-Destour. In July of the following year, Bourguiba became head of state as well, when his government abolished the powerless and unpopular monarchy of the Bey and proclaimed Tunisia a republic.

Beyond the priority given to the task of building over nation-building, international problems had continued to plague Tunisia throughout the 1950s and until the end of the Algerian War. In the first place, regional considerations complicated relations with France. In the second place, the United States alternated between willingness to intervene in the previous dominions of its Allies and a hands-off policy.

Relations with France passed through several crises. The first occurred at the end of October 1956, following the kidnapping of Ahmed Ben Bella and his companions, who were on their way to meet Bourguiba and Mohamed V in Tunis. Almost at the same time, the French participation in the combined British-Israeli-French attack against Egypt also exacerbated relations. The two crises allowed Bourguiba to pressure France in order to limit the Algerian war was to become among the foremost concerns of the new Tunisian government and may have delayed the process of economic development which was to become the overriding issue during the 1960s.

In February 1958, the French forces attacked the frontier village of Sakiet Sidi Youssef and killed some eighty Tunisians, including children. It took the intervention of the United States and Great Britain to smooth things over between France and Tunisia. Nonetheless, the United States made it clear at this time that it considered North Africa within the French sphere of influence. When Bourguiba returned from an exploratory trip to the United States, having received only minimal economic aid, he had to concede that France remained the "international scene".[60]

On the French scene in May 1958, De Gaulle came to power and on 30th January 1961, he received Bourguiba at Rambouillet. The idea was to test the lay-out for Algerian autonomy on terms similar to those that had been worked out for Tunisia. Bourguiba was encouraged to believe that he was being considered as future leader of a United Maghrib.[61] But Bourguiba was placed in a dilemma. He could not allow the stationing of French troops on Tunisian soil and, at the same time, aspire to being acknowledged as a leader of the Maghrib as a whole. The French authorities either did not understand his dilemma or had other priorities. Consequently, when the Bizerte crisis reached its apogee in June 1961, they did not evacuate their troops but only gave assurance of a future withdrawal.

In July 1961 fighting broke out between Tunisian and French troops over the Tunisina demand for France's evacuation of the large naval base at Bizerta, on Tunisia's northern coast. After nearly two years, the French departed in March 1963. The confrontation enhanced the prestige and popularity of Bourguiba in the eyes of his own people and the world community.

The Bizerta Crisis

The border issues between Morocco and Algeria as well as the dispute between Tunisia and Algeria had led to armed clashes. Bourguiba had first attempted to rectify the Tunisian border before Algerian independence at a time when the question did not openly involve the two countries. The persistence of the issue, and Bourguiba's attempts to resolve it, however, has placed a heavy burden on Algerian-Tunisian relations since Algerian independence: The resolution of the issue and the appearance of new leadership of Tunisia, including Mohammad Masmoudi as Foreign Minister, may be signs of a new "post-Bourguiba" era and the abandonment of the "Bourguibist" technique of policy-making. The Bizerta crisis not only demonstrates Bourguiba's dissimilation of his real objectives in the summer of 1961, but it also illustrates the inefficiency of Bourguibist politics in the multilateral relationship of the post-colonial Maghrib.[62]

Following Tunisia's accession to independence, the Tunisian Government engaged in negotiations with France with a view to achieving the withdrawal of all French forces from Tunisian territory.[63] February 1958, the Tunisian Government pressed its demand for evacuation of the base after the bombing of Sakhiet Sidi Youssef, which it considered a retaliation for Tunisian support to Algerian fighters.[64] Eventually, by an exchange of letters between the French and Tunisian Governments on June 17, 1958, it was agreed that France would maintain on Tunisian territory only forces *"qui s'y trouveront en vertu d'accords negocies entre les deux Etats,"* and that negotiations would take place for the establishment of a "regime provisoire" over Bizerta, pending the conclusion of an "accord definitif."[65]

The proposed negotiations over Bizerta did not, however, take place. As a result, when President Bourguiba met President de Gaulle at Rambouillet on February 17, 1961, the former raised the question of evacuation of the base.[66] President de Gaulle subsequently stated that it had then been agreed to postpone any decision until after the termination of the Algerian war.[67]

Toward the end of June 1961, a crisis broke out between the two countries in connection with the extension of the runway of the military airfield on the base. President Bourguiba set out the position of his government in a Note delivered on July 6, 1961, by his Chief of Cabinet to President de Gaulle. In his Note, the President of Tunisia requested the French Government to reconsider in a realistic way the

French position *vis-a-vis* the problem of the base. President Bourguiba pointed out that the French policy should take into account of France's withdrawal from most African ex-colonies, as well as the decreased importance of the base under the changing strategic consideration of the era.[68] He further stressed that the action to increase the length of the runway of the military airfield, revealed the French Government's intention to maintain and even to aggravate the status quo. Finally, he urged the French Government to accept the principle of evacuation, and reaffirmed Tunisia's determination to achieve that end by all means at her disposal.[69]

During the following days, mass demonstrations took place throughout Tunisia in support of the national demands. On the other hand, on July 17, the French Charge d'Affaires in Tunis delivered a memorandum to the Tunisian Foreign Ministry, whereby the French Government categorically rejected all Tunisian demands for evacuation and declared that it considered the demonstrations as an unacceptable premeditated pressure against it.[70] On the same day, President Bourguiba announced to the Tunisian National Assembly that a blockade would be established against the Bizerta base as from July 19.[71] This was followed by a meeting of the French cabinet at the end of which the Minister of Information stated that the French Government had decided to strengthen the French forces in Bizerta with new parachute regiments.[72]

On July 18, Tunisian volunteers began the blockade of the base and set up road blocks between the various installations.

On July 21, the French troops opened an offensive against the town of Bizerta, occupied the barracks and bombarded the Casbah area where many civilian casualties were reported. Eventually, on July 22, after the Security Council issued an appeal for a ceasefire, the French Government announced that its Commander had received instructions to enter to contact with Tunisian authorities for that purpose.[73]

On July 20, 1961, the Tunisian Government requested an urgent meeting of the Security Council to consider France's acts of aggression which infringed the sovereignty and security of Tunisia and threatened international peace and security.[74] The Security Council met on July 21 to consider Tunisia's complaint. The Tunisian representative, though not a member of the Council, was invited to participate in the Council's debate. He declared that, according to the Franco-Tunisian agreement as enclosed in the exchange of letters of June 17, 1958, France was to keep no armed forces on Tunisian territory beyond those agreed upon between both countries. Not only had France violated that agreement, but she had also been committing premeditated armed aggression against Tunisia which was justified, under its right of self-defence, in taking measures to banish from its territory the threat of aggression supported by foreign forces.[75]

The French delegate stated that it was rather his government which might have complained of acts of aggression against French forces. He pointed out that the exchange of letters of June 1958, while arranging for the evacuation of French troops from the rest of Tunisia, provided for the negotiation of a provisional agreement to ensure the maintenance of the base until a permanent agreement could be concluded. The French Government had proposed that talks should be opened on the subject, but negotiations were never entered into.[76] When the Council resumed its discussions on July 22, the Secretary-General of the United Nations drew the attention of the Council to the threatening development of the situation. He emphasised that in accordance with the Secretary-General's obligations under Article 99 of the Charter, he considered it his duty to appeal to the Council to consider taking an intermediate decision pending further consideration of the question. Such decision should call for an immediate ceasefire and a return to the *status quo ante*, without prejudice to the final outcome of the Council's deliberations.[77] In accordance with the Secretary-General's suggestion an interim resolution was submitted by Liberia, which called for an immediate ceasefire and a return of all armed forces to their original positions.[78] The resolution was adopted by ten votes to nil, with France not participating in the voting.

On the same day, two other resolutions were submitted to the Council: one by Liberia and the United Arab Republic, calling for the immediate withdrawal of those French forces which had been introduced into the base since July 19, the return to their original positions of troops which had left those positions, and immediate negotiations for the speedy evacuation of all French forces from Tunisia.[79] The second resolution, sponsored by the United Kingdom and the United States, urged France and Tunisia to refrain from any action which might lead to a further deterioration of the situation and to negotiate promptly a peaceful settlement of their differences.[80] However, neither resolution received the required majority of seven affirmative votes for adoption.

On July 20, i.e., during the French counter/attack, Tunisia presented its case to the Security Council. The resolution on which the Council finally agreed called for an immediate ceasefire and a return of all troops to their initial bases. The resolution was a defeat for Tunisian policy since it did not sustain the Tunisian demand for the complete withdrawal of all French troops from all parts of Tunisian territory. Instead, Tunis was required to withdraw her troops to Fort Saint. France, as in the case of the Algerian war, demonstrated her disregard for the United Nations.

On July 23, President Bourguiba invited the United Nations Secretary-General Dag Hammarskjold to visit Tunisia for a direct and personal exchange of views on the situation.[81] In accepting the invitation, the Secretary-General pointed out, however, that since the problem was still before the Security Council, the substance of the problem was outside his personal competence.[82] Thereupon, he flew to Tunis on July 24, where he held talks with Tunisian officials. On July 26, the Secretary-General visited Bizerta, where he discussed the situation with the Tunisian acting Governor of Bizerta, but was refused meeting by the French Commander of the base.[83]

Meanwhile, in a change of letters, dated 25th and 26th July, 1961 between the Secretary-General and the French Foreign Minister, the Secretary-Genera! pointed out that he had received no reply from France concerning the interim resolution adopted by the Council and that no contact had yet been established between the French and Tunisian authorities in Bizerta.[84] On the other hand, the French Foreign Minister asserted in his reply, that the Secretary-General's views seemed to reflect the Tunisian Government's views and that the French Government had agreed on a ceasefire when the French forces had attained their objectives.[85] To this accusation, the Secretary-General replied in another letter on July 27, that his attitude was based exclusively on the interpretation of the duties of the Secretary-General, the principles of the Charter, and the intentions which he assumed were held by all members of the Council who voted for the interim resolution.[86]

On July 27, 1961, Tunisia requested another meeting of the Security Council on the ground that the interim resolution of the Council had met with a refusal by the French military forces to comply with it.[87] On the following day, France informed the Security Council that the cease-fire at Bizerta was being observed and that the restoration of normal conditions in Bizerta would be agreed upon through direct talks with Tunisia rather than by action undertaken by the Council.[88]

The Security Council was reconvened on July 28, and following the debate that took place, three draft resolutions were submitted to the Council. The first resolution, sponsored by Ceylon, Liberia and the United Arab Republic, expressed serious concern that France had not complied fully with the interim resolution and invited France to do so immediately.[89] The second resolution, submitted by the same three countries, invited France to enter immediately into negotiations with Tunisia with a view to the rapid evacuation of French forces from Tunisia.[90] A third resolution, introduced by Turkey, expressed concern that the interim resolution had not been fully carried out, called for its immediate and full implementation, and urged early negotiations between France and Tunisia for a peaceful settlement of their differences including a definitive settlement of the Bizerta question, with due regard for Tunisian sovereignty.[91] However, none of the three resolutions submitted to the Council obtained the required majority for adoption.

On August 7, 1961, a request for the convening of a special session of the General Assembly to consider the Bizerta situation was submitted to the Secretary by 47 member states.[92] The special session opened on August 21, and was boycotted by the French delegation. The representative of Liberia introduced a draft resolution co-sponsored by 32 countries. In its operative part, the resolution:[93]

1. Reaffirmed the Security Council's interim resolution and urged France to implement fully its first operative paragraph;
2. Recognised the sovereign right of Tunisia to call for the withdrawal of all French armed forces present on its territory without its consent;
3. Called upon the governments of France and Tunisia to enter into immediate negotiations to devise peaceful and agreed measures in accordance with the principles of the charter for the withdrawal of all French armed forces from Tunisian territory.

During the debate that took place in the Assembly, the Tunisian representative referred to the exchange of letters between France and Tunisia on June 17, 1958 and held that the mere promise of an agreement was not a basis on which to assert a French right to presence in Bizerta.[94] Some delegates attacked the Franco-Tunisian Agreements as being, "unequal" and therefore, invalid in international law,[95] while others ignored the existence of agreements between the parties, and argued that Tunisia's right to demand the evacuation of French troops from her territory was inherent in her sovereignty.[96]

Eventually, the resolution submitted to the Assembly was adopted on August 25 by 66 votes to nil, with 30 abstentions.[97]

Arab League Support

When the League Council met on July 20, 1961 to consider Kuwait's application for membership of the League, the United Arab Republic representative raised the question of "the French armed attack that had taken, place on the people of Tunisia."[98] After a lengthy expose by the Tunisian representative on the background of the Bizerta situation,[99] the League Council, upon a motion put forward by the United Arab Republic delegation, adopted the resolution, which stated that it vigorously denounces this French imperialist aggression against its sister people of Tunisia, proclaims that it whole-heartedly upholds its sister state Tunisia in the battle against French imperialism and supports it in its struggle to free itself from the French imperialist forces."[100] "The resolution was communicated by the League to the United Nations.[101]

Upon his arrival in Tunisia on July 28, 1961 the Secretary-General held a series of meetings with President Bourguiba and senior government officials, during which the crisis was discussed as well as the effectiveness of Arab solidarity. The Secretary-General reported to the Council about his consultations with President Bourguiba and Tunisian officials, and his visit to the Tunisian armed forces and civilian casualties.[102] Moreover, he pointed to the Council resolution of July 24, which provided for the pursuance of the Bizerta question in the United Nations and other international circles, until the final withdrawal of French forces. Since the current Council meeting was taking place on August 15, shortly preceding the General Assembly meeting due to be held on August 21, the Secretary-General proposed the adoption by the Council of a resolution expressing full support for Tunisia which once reported to the United Nations, would carry weight during the consideration of the case by the Assembly.[103]

The proposal of the Secretary General was unanimously agreed upon by the member states' representative and the

Council adopted the following draft resolution submitted by the United Arab Republic representative:

> "The League Council learned about the latest developments concerning the French aggression on Tunisian territory, and the convening of the United Nations General Assembly to a meeting on August 21 for the consideration of the question.
>
> The Council reaffirms the determination of the Arab member states to continue supporting their sister Tunisia and helping her with all means towards the liberation of her territory. Further it expresses its thanks to the friendly nations for their support to Tunisia in her just struggle".[104]

The crisis arose out of the armed clash that occurred in connection with the presence of French troops in the Bizerta base. Thus, viewed in a broader context, the conflict was but one phase in the process of withdrawal of all. French forces from Tunisian territory, upon Tunisia's achievement of independence. This aspect of the crisis provided a basis for the intervention of the League of which the basic policy under its pact's provisions had been to promote complete independence of all Arab people.

A settlement of the Bizerta crisis came about when on September 5, 1961, President de Gaulle held a press conference at which he reaffirmed France's recognition of Tunisian sovereignty over the base. Moreover, he called for the negotiation of a *modus vivendi* for Bizerta, and the reaching of an agreement on the conditions for using the base during the continuing dangerous world situation.[105] The border problem he continued, was of no concern to Tunisia. "The Tunisian press reacted sharply, declaring that the resumption of the battle was inevitable in order to achieve national goals.[106] On the other hand, in a press conference on September 8, 1961, President Bourguiba expressed his satisfaction that President de Gaulle had recognised Tunisia's sovereignty over the base and the principle of the evacuation of Bizerta. He declared that Tunisia would accept the negotiation of a *modus vivendi* that might provide for the temporary remaining of French troops while subsequent negotiations would determine the date for complete evacuation.[107]

On September 17, a mixed commission comprising senior officials of the French and Tunisian governments met in Bizerta to negotiate a *modus vivendi* on the spot. An agreement was eventually signed on September 29, by virtue of which French troops would withdraw to their positions prior to the outbreak of fighting.[108] Accordingly, French troops withdrew from the town of Bizerta to the naval base.

Talks on the evacuation of the base and a final settlement of the Bizerta question opened in Rome in December 1961 between representatives of both governments. The discussions were resumed at ministerial level in Paris from January 16-20, 1962.[109] As a result of such talks, the French Government decided to evacuate the base installations at Menzel-Bourguiba which were formally handed over to Tunisia on June 30, 1962. This step, undertaken by the French Government, together with the subsequent ceasefire in Algeria and the achievement of its independence, led to the resumption of diplomatic relations between France and Tunisia on July 20, 1962.[110] Finally, the last French forces completed withdrawal from the Bizerta base on October 15, 1963.[111]

These events confirmed French reluctance to endanger her future presence, at the Algerian base of Mers El Kebir by concessions on Bizerta. They also confirmed the notion that Bizerta was a secondary problem for Tunisia; the solution followed a settlement of the Saharan problem that favoured Algeria.

The Bizerta incident, which followed so closely on Bourguiba's visit to the United States, did not seriously disturb relations between the two countries. The break with France was neither total nor final. In May 1966, fresh commercial agreements were signed which gave free entry to a certain number of Tunisian goods, including a small quantity of wine. Above all the Tunisian educational system continued to depend on France assistance. In March 1968, there were three thousand Frenco teachers in Tunisia. One half of the university teachers were French. Tunisian students continued to go to France for higher degrees and young professional men for shorter periods of vocational training. Under French law a certain number of conscripts can undertake overseas service in developing countries instead of military service, and of such young men then were some 900 in Tunisia, many of them as teachers. Civilian employees, teachers and technical experts—are paid more than they would be in France, but one-third of their salary comes from the French government.[112]

In 1969, France helped Tunisia attain associate membership in the European Economic Community,[113] and Tunisia actively sought better relations with France as it began to experiment with a more open economy in the 1970s. Since then contacts have centred on economic matters, most notably development aid, investments, and military assistance. Arabization has decreased the need for French-speaking teachers, but French technical help in agricultural, public-works, and public-health projects has been substantial. French firms' connections with Tunisia, some of which predate the protectorate, have kept France the primary supplier of Tunisian imports, even during times of political tensions. France also provides the bulk of Tunisia's military material and much of the advanced training for its armed forces.[114]

Although Paris and Tunis have not always agreed on specific policy decisions, France has consistently characterised the political situation in Tunisia as preferable to any probable alternatives. France made the strength of its commitment to the Bourguiba regime clear in the aftermath of the Gafsa raid by rushing additional military equipment to Tunisia along with a promise of military intervention if necessary to guarantee the integrity of the country's frontiers. Business has also dominated Tunisia's post-independence dealings with other Western European states, although none of those nations has approached France in terms of the magnitude or intensity of its contacts with Tunisia.

The connection with France and the assistance Tunisia received, therefore, remains close, is solidly based on widespread French culture in Tunisia and is generally the subject of amicable speeches on both sides of the Mediterranean.

For Bourguiba the French legacy was almost as much a part of the Tunisian identity as was Arabness. As a student in France, he had absorbed a romantic imagery of nationalism, justice, equality, and humanism that he believed to be at the root of French civilisation. As Derek Hopwood put it, "He had acquired from his stay in Paris an undying affection for France, bourgeois, reformist, lay France, and he wanted to instill those values into Arab Muslim Tunisia".[115]

Bourguiba had a genuine regard for French culture made this stance more attractive to him, it is true. Nevertheless, the way in which he always sought to appeal to liberal circles within France and to distinguish them from those Frenchmen supporting the colonial system was an effective weapon of the weak against the strong.[116] French civilisation could offer the values and strategies needed for modernisation; the synthesis of Tunisian and French culture could provide the means for social regeneration and evolution. He acknowledged that, while he had happily assimilated aspects of French identity, the transformation would not be as easy for a whole society. He knew that he could not hurry Tunisians through the process or force upon them too many cultural adoptions from the former colonial power. Nonetheless, he strove where possible to retain and develop strong cordial relations with France and to ameliorate lingering resentments from the colonial era.[117]

In Sum, Tunisia has consistently demonstrated a close affinity to France, with whom it maintains extensive cultural, educational, and commercial ties. Although the United States is perhaps regarded as the world's pre-eminent military power, Bourguiba and his generation of Gallicised elites consider France the most influential cultural, intellectual, and "spiritual" force. Economic and military ties between the two countries have increased because neither de Gaulle nor Bourguiba lost his sense of history or proportion, permanent and irreparable break did not result from a momentary aberration. Though Bourguiba in private has expressed bitterness and disappointment at the strong French measures against his country, publicly he has voiced his trust in and loyalty to France.

Short History of Pierre Mendes

Pierre Mendes-France was born on January 11, 1907 at Paris. He was born into a Jewish family and was educated at the University of Paris, graduating with a doctorate in law and becoming the youngest member of the Paris Bar Association in 1928. In 1924, he joined the Radical Socialist Party, the traditional party of the French middle-class centre-left.

In 1932, Mendes-France was elected to the National Assembly as a deputy for the Eure department. He was the Assembly's youngest member. His ability was recognised at once, and in the 1936. Popular Front government of Leon Blum, he was appointed Secretary of State for Finance. When World War II broke out, he joined the French Air Force. After the French surrender to Nazi Germany, he was arrested by the Vichy government authorities and sentenced to six years' imprisonment on a fallacious charge of desertion, but on 21 June 1941, he escaped and succeeded in reaching Britain, where he joined the Free French forces of Charles de Gaulle.

After serving with the Free French Air Force, Mendes-France was sent by Gaulle as his Finance Commissioner in Algeria, and then headed the French delegation to the 1944 monetary conference at Bretton Woods. When de Gaulle returned to liberated Paris in September 1944, he appointed Mendes-France as Minister for National Economy in the provisional government.

But Mendes-France soon fell out with the Finance Minister, Rene Pleven, when Mendes-France favoured state regulation of wages and prices to control inflation (while

Pleven favoured free market policies). When de Gaulle sided with Pleven, Mendes-France resigned. Nonetheless, de Gaulle valued Mendes-France's abilities, and appointed him as a director of the International Bank for Reconstruction and Development, and as French representative in the United Nations Economic and Social Council.

In 1947, when normal French politics resumed under the Fourth Republic, Mendes-France was re-elected to the National Assembly. He first tried to form a government in June 1953. But he was unable to gain the numbers in the Assembly. From 1950, he had been a consistent opponent of French colonialism, and by 1954, France was becoming hopelessly embroiled in major colonial conflicts: the First Indo-China War and the Algerian War of Independence. When French forces were defeated by the Vietnamese Communists at Dien Bien Phu in June 1954, the government of Joseph Laniel resigned, and Mendes France formed a government. Among his ministers was the young Francois Mitterrand.

Mendes-France immediately negotiated an armistice with Ho Chi Minh, the Vietnamese Communist Leader. There was he said, no choice but total withdrawal from Indo-China, and the Assembly supported him by 471 votes to 14. Nevertheless, nationalist opinion was shocked. and Roman Catholic opinion opposed abandoning the Vietnamese believers to Communism. A tirade of abuse, much of it anti-Semitic, was directed at Mendes-France. (Mendes-France is a Sephardic Portuguese name).

Jean-Marie Le Pen, then a Poujadist member of the Assembly, described his "patriotic, almost physical repulsion" for Mendes-France.

Undeterred, Mendes-France next came to an agreement with Habib Bourguiba, the nationalist leader in Tunisia, for the independence of that colony by 1956, and began discussions with the nationalist leaders in Morocco for a French withdrawal. He also favoured concessions to the nationalists in Algeria, but the fact that there were a million Pied-noirs there meant that there could be no easy way out of that situation. The future mercenary Bob Denard was convicted in 1954 and sentenced to fourteen months of jail for an assassination attempt against Mendes-France.

Mendes France hoped that the Radical party would become the party of modernisation and renewal in French politics, by passing the SFIO. An advocate of greater European integration, he helped bring about the formation of the Western European Union, and proposed far-reaching economic reform. He also favoured defence co-operation with other European countries, but the National Assembly rejected the proposal for a European Defence Community, mainly because of misgivings about Germany's participation.

His cabinet fell in February 1955. In 1956, he served as Minister of State in the cabinet headed by the SFIO leader Guy Motlet, but resigned over the issue of Algeria, which was coming to dominate French politics. His split over Algeria with Edgar Faure, Leader of the conservative wing of the Radical party, led to Mendes-France resigning as party leader in 1957.

Fifth Republic

Like most of the French left, Mendes-France opposed de Gaulle's seizure of power in May 1958, when the mounting crisis in Algeria brought about a breakdown in the Fourth Republic system and the creation of a Fifth Republic. He led the union of Democratic Forces, an anti- Gaullist group, but, in the November 1958 elections he lost his seat in the Assembly. In 1959, he was expelled from the Radical party, whose majority faction supported de Gaulle.

Mendes-France then joined the Unified Socialist Party (*Parti Socialiste Unifie* or PSU), a small party of the intellectual left. He made an unsuccessful bid to regain his seat in the National Assembly representing Eure in the 1962 election.

In 1967, he returned to the Assembly as a PSU member for the Isere, but again lost his seat in de Gaulle's 1968 landslide election victory. In accordance with the PSU, Mendes France expressed sympathy for the sentiments and actions of the student rioters during the "events" (les evenements) or May 1968, a position unusual for a politician of his age and status. In an unorthodox move, De Gaulle's socialist opponent, Gaston Defferre, had designated him Prime Minister-elect prior to the election, but no avail for either. When Mitterrand formed a new Socialist Party in 1971, Mendes France supported 'him, but did not attempt another political comeback.

Shortly, before Mendes France died in 1982, he witnessed the coming to office of Socialist President Francois Mitterrand.

References

1. Kamladevi Chattopadhya, Nationalism in *Tunisia. Foreign Affairs Report,* Vol. 1, Nos. 1 and 2, July-August, 1952, p. 2.
2. *Problem of Tunisia, Political Status.* Tunisian Destour Party Cairo, as quoted in Kamladevi Chattopadhya. *Ibid.*
3. Magali Motsy, North *Africa 1800-1900,* London, Longman, 1984. p. 199.
4. *Ibid.*
5. For Text of the Treaty of Bardo *See* A.M. Breadley, *The Last Punic War. Tunis. Past and Present* (London, William Backward 1992) Vol. 1, pp. 313-315.
6. *Problem of Tunisia op.cit.,* n. 2.
7. *Ibid.*
8. *News from France,* French Embassy, New York, 15th October 1951.
9. *Problem of Tunisia, op.cit.,* n. 2.
10. Kamladevi Chattopadhya, *op.cit.,* n. 1, p. 3.
11. *Ibid.*
12. John P. Entelis and Mark A. Tessler, Republic of Tunisia, in David E. Long and Benrnard Reich (Ed.) *The Government and Politics of the Middle East and North Africa* (Boulder, Westview Press I986), p. 435.
13. *Ibid.*
14. *Ibid.,* p. 113.
15. *Ibid.*

16. Charles C. Harber, Tunisian Land Tenure in the Early French Protectorate. *Muslim World,* Vol. 63, No. 4, October 1973, pp. 307-15.
17. *Jami* Y.M. Abun-Nasr, *History of Maghrib,* 2nd ed. (Cambridge: Cambridge University Press 1975).
18. Wilfrid Knapp—*Tunisia* London, Thames and Hudson, p. 119.
19. *Ibid.*, p. 120.
20. Stuart E, Brown, *The Young Tunisians* (unpublished Ph.D. Dissertation, Institute of Islamic Studies, McGill University, Montreal, Quebec, 1976), cited in Norma Salem, *Habib Bourguiba, Islam and the creation of 'Tunisia* (London, Croom Helm, 1984), p. 25.
21. These factors were the anti-colonialism of the United States (i.e., Wilson's 14 points) and Soviet Russia (after 1917 revolution), the nationalist Egypt of Sa'ad Zagloul (1919 revolution), and the establishment of a local parliament and a government council in both Tripolinia Cyrenaica in Libya (June and November 1919 respectively).
22. Wilfred Knapp, *Tunisia, op.cit.*, n. 2, p. 1, 27; Norma Salem, *Habib Bourguiba, op.cit., Ibid.*, p. 50.
23. Kenneth, J. Per Kins, *Tunisia: Crossroads of the Islamic and European Worlds,* (Boulder, Westview Press, 1986), p. 98.
24. The text of the memorandum is *reproduced* in H. Bourguiba's book in Arabic: *Introduction to the history of the nationalist movement,* Tunis, 1962, p. 55. as quoted in Hassan Sayet-Saliman. *The Nationalist Movements in the Maghri* (Uppsala, The Scandinavien institute of African Studies, 1987, p. 19.
25. Clement Henry Moore, *Tunisia Since Independence: The Dynamics of one-party Government,* (Los Angeles, University of California Press, 1965), pp. 28-29.
26. L.C. Brown and Micaud, Charles, *Tunisia: The Politics of Modernisation,* (New York, Praeger, I964), pp. 38-45.
27. Clement Henry Moor. *Tunisia Since Independence op.cit.*, n. 25, p. 29.
28. Anthony Syluester, *Tunisia,* (London, Badley Head, 1969), pp. 47-48.

29. Alal-al-Fasi, *The Independence Movements in Arab North Africa* (New York, Octogoa Books, 1970), p. 69.
30. H. Bourguiba, *La Tvnisie et la France,* Paris, 1954, p. 58. as quoted Hassan Sayet Suliman *op.cit.,* n. 24, p. 20.
31. Norma Salem, *Habib Bourguiba, Islam and the Creation of Tunisia,* London, Croom Helm, pp. 95-96.
32. Habib Bourguiba, *Hayati Aral Jihadi* (My life, My opinion, my struggle), (Tunis, Ministers de l'information, 1978), p. 299. The French Translation of the Arabic Test of Bourguiba's Speech as published in *Al-nahdah* (10-15 March 1934) is to be found Histories 11. pp. 26-32 as quoted by Norma Salem *op.cit.,* n. 31, p. 96.
33. *Ibid.*
34. *Ibid.,* 97.
35. Jarair M. Aban-nasr, *op.cit.,* n. 17, pp. 345-46.
36. *Ibid.*
37. Kanneth, J. Per Kins, *op.cit.,* n. 23, p. 104.
38. H. Bourguiba, *La Tunisie et la France.* pp. 77-173, as quoted in Hassan Sayet Salim an, *op.cit.,* n. 24, p. 21.
39. Pierre Vuenot was State Secretary for foreign affairs in France and was also in charge of affairs of the protectorates and mandates of the Levant
40. H. Bourguiba, *La Tunisie et la France,* Hassan Sayet Saliman, *op.cit.,* n. 24, p. 21.
41. Felix Garas, *Bovrguiba et al Naissance d'une nation,* Paris, 1956, 109-110 as quoted in Hassan Sayet Suliman, *Ibid.,* p. 22.
42. H. Bourguiba, La *Tunisie et la France, op.cit.,* pp. 162-163, as quoted in Hassan Sayet Suliman, *Ibid.,* p. 22.
43. Felix Garas *op.cit.,* n. 41, pp. 118-119.
44. R. Le. Toumeau, *Evolution Politique de l'Afrique du Word Musulmane* 1920-1961 Paris, A Colin 2nd ed. 1962. p. 90, as quoted in Hassan Sayet Saliman, *op.cit.,* n. 24, p. 22.
45. Kamladevi Chattopadhyay, *op.cit.,* 1, p. 9.
46. For the Text of the Speech sec. H. Bourguiba, *La Tunisie et la France,* pp. 182-84 as quoted in Hassan Sayet Suliman *op.cit.,* n. 24, p. 23.

47. *Ibid.*
48. For Text of the Menifesto *see* Alal Al-Fasi, *The Independence Movement in Arab North Africa, op.cit.*, n. 29, pp. 75-77.
49. Clement Henry Moor, *Tunisia Sines Independence, op.cit.*, n. 27, p. 283.
50. Hassan Sayet Suliman, *op.cit.*, n. 24, p. 46.
51. R. Le. Toumeav *Evolution Politique op.cit.*, n. 44, pp. 115-116.
52. *Ibid.*
53. Kenneth J. Perkins, *op.cit.*, n. 23, p. 111.
54. R. Le Toumeau, *op.cit.*, n. 44, p. 119.
55. A. *Balhaonan, Revolutionary Tunisia* (in Arabic), Tunis, pp. 142-143, as quoted in Hassan Sayet Suliman, *op.cit.*, n. 24, p. 48.
56. A Balhaonane, *op.cit.*, n. 55, pp. 216-17, 229.
57. R. Le Toumeau, *op.cit.*, n. 44, p. 130.
58. *Ibid.*, p. 134.
59. *Ibid.*, pp. 135-136.
60. *The New York Times,* 17 December 1956.
61. Logic, Dwight L. Ling, *Tunisia: From Protectorate to Republic,* Bloomengton, (Bloomington Indians University Press, 1967), p. 201.
62. Werner Klaus Ruf, The Bizerta Crisis: A Bourguibist attempt to resolve Tunisia's border problems, *The Middle East Journal,* Vol. 25, no. 2, 1971, pp. 201-11.
63. Statement by the Tunisian representative before the Council of the League of the Arab States, Minutes League Council (l.C.) Extraordinary Session held in Cairo on July 24, 1961, p. 308.
64. *Ibid.*
65. Letter from the Tunisian representative to the President of the Security Council, dated July 21, 1961: United Nation's Documents, S/4869.
66. Letter of President Bourguiba to General de Gaulle, dated July 6, 1961: United Nations *Documents,* S/4871.

67. Samuel Merlin, *The Search for Peace in Middle East* (London, Thomas Yosaloff, 1968) pp. 422-424.
68. Statement by the Tunisian representative: Minutes of L.C. Extraordinary Session, July 24, 1961, p. 310.
69. *Ibid.*
70. *Ibid.*, p. 311.
71. *Ibid.*
72. *Ibid.*
73. Keesing Contemporary Archives 1961-62, pp. 183-44.
74. Letter of July 20, 1961 from the 'Permanent Representative of Tunisia to the President of the Security Council—*United Nations Documents,* S/4862.
75. *United Nations Security Council Official Records S.C.O.R.* 16th year, 961st meeting, July 21, 1961, p. 2.
76. *Ibid.*, p. 10.
77. *Ibid.*, 962nd meeting, July 22, 1961, pp. 1-2.
78. *United Nations* Documents S/4880.
79. *United Nations* Documents S/4878.
80. *United Nations* Documents S/4879.
81. *United Nations Documents,* S/4885.
82. *Ibid.*
83. See the letter of Hammarskjold to Foreign Minister *Conve de Murvillle* of July 25, 1961 , and the letter of de Murville to Hammarskjoold of July 26, 1961. Both have been published by the press services of the French embassies. Cf. *Le Monde,* July 28, 1961, as quoted and in *Keesing Contemporary Archives,* 1961-62, p. 18344.
84. *United Nations Documents,* S/4894/ Add. 1.
85. *Ibid.*
86. *Ibid.*
87. *United Nations Documents,* S/4893.
88. *United Nations Documents,* S/4897.
89. *United Nations Documents,* S/4903.
90. *United Nations Documents,* S/4904.
91. *United Nations Documents,* S/495.

92. *United Nations Documents,* A/4831.
93. *United Nations Documents,* AS/L.351.
94. *United Nations Documents,* A./PV. 996, August 21, 1961, p. 32.
95. See, for instance, speech of the Czech representative: *ibid.* 1000, August 23, 1961, p. 28.
96. See, for instance, statement by the representative of Ceylon: *Ibid.* August 21, 1961, p. 31.
97. United Nations *Documents,* Resol. 1622 (S-111).
98. League of Arab States : Minutes of L.C. 35th Ordinary Session, July 20, 1961, p. 46.
99. *Ibid.,* p. 47.
100. League of Arab States Resoi. no. 1778, 35th Ordinary Session, 8th meeting, July 20, 1961.
101. Letter of July 21, 1961, from the U.N. Secretary-General to the President of the Security Council, enclosing the text of the telegram addressed to the former by the Secretary-General of the Arab League: United Nations *Documents,* S/4872.
102. League of Arab States: Minutes of L.C., 35th Ordinary Session 9th Meeting, August 15, 1961, p. 59.
103. *Ibid.*
104. *Ibid.,* p. 60.
105. See also. Samuel Merlin *op.cit.,* n. 67, pp. 424-425.
106. *La Presse and Le Petit Matin* (Both Tunis, September 6, 1961. As quoted in *Kissing Contemporary Archives* 1961-62, p. 1934.
107. See also. Samuel Merlin *op.cit.,* n. 67, pp. 424-425.
108. *Keesing Contemporary Archives,* 1961-62, p. 18349.
109. *Ibid.,* p. 18609.
110. *Ibid.,* p. 18948.
111. *Ibid.,* 1963-64, p. 19696.
112. Wilfrid Knapp. *op.cit.,* n. 18, pp. 180-181.
113. R.K., Ramazani, The European Community and the Middle East—in Collin Leagum, *Middle East Contemporary Surveys, 1976,* p. 49.

114. Kenneth J. Perkins, *op. cit.*, n. 23, pp. 165-66.

115. Derek Hopwood, *Habib Bourguiba of Tunisia: The Tragedy of Longevity,* Hampshire, England: Macmillan, 1992, p. 142.

116. C. Carl Brown, Bourguiba and Bourguibism Revisited: Reflections and Interpretation, *Middle East Journal,* Vol. 55, no. l, winter 2001, p. 54.

117. Emma C. Murphy, The Foreign Policy of Tunisia, in Raymond Hinnebusch and Anoushiravan Ehteshami ed. *The Foreign Policies of Middle East States*, Boulder, Lynne Rienner, 2002, p. 239.

4 Tunisia and the Cold War

Tunisia, like other states which became independent in the late forties and fifties, entered an international environment characterised by intense Cold War competition. Since then, new power centers have emerged, and the competition for the allegiance of the new states of Africa and Asia has moderated.

For most of the states of Africa and Asia, self-reliance would require acceptance of poverty as the price of independence. On the other hand, complete acceptance of a continuing dependence on a single foreign power for development and security was incompatible with the forces of nationalism which brought the new states into being in the first place.

Therefore, the problem of foreign policy for the new states was to devise means of maximising external assistance while protecting their newly-acquired sovereignty. The typical foreign policy strategies of the new states in the post-war period reflect these requirements. Regionalism was one such strategy, particularly popular in Africa and the Arab world. Through regional economic and political integration, groups of states could pool scarce resources and thus minimise their individual dependence on extra-regional powers. Most of the regional integration efforts in these areas have failed because of national rivalries within the region, competitive economies, lack of essential resources, and insufficient political commitment for unification. Hence, this chapter focussed on the policy pursued by Tunisia during Cold War period.

Non-alignment was the most popular foreign policy stance for the newly-sovereign states of Africa and Asia. The term "non-alignment" covered a multiplicity of individual policies. The non-aligned states insisted on total decolonisation and "rejected membership in great power alliances. They took advantage of the nuclear stalemate and the competition between the two Cold War blocs to seek aid from both sides without commitment to either. 'Abd al-Nasir's Egypt in the late fifties and early sixties was the prototype of the no-naligned or "positive neutralist" state.

Independence through non-alignment works only to the extent that great powers are willing to compete for the allegiance of the non-aligned state. Egypt was in a strong position to practice non-alignment because both the United States and the Soviet Union considered it politically strategic. States less strategically located from the point of view of the great powers and less politically influential—for example, the smaller states of sub-Saharan Africa, benefitted less from non-alignment.

Non-alignment is also limited by the degree of dependence on external assistance. Egypt's dependence on Soviet military assistance for its conflict with Israel in the late sixties undermined any Egyptian claim to non-alignment and finally resulted in alliance.

Similar circumstances have led most of the new states of Asia and Africa to practice a modified form of non-alignment. While rejecting formal alliances with any great power and diversifying their sources of aid, they developed stable relationships with one or several states: the United States, the Soviet Union, China, or various European states including the former colonial powers. Because of the existence of several sources of aid, these new states have enjoyed a greater independence from external influence than an exclusive aid relationship would have permitted.

Time and again, the Tunisian "policy-makers have-emphasised" the "non-commitment" or "non-alignment aspect of Tunisian foreign policy. In a short essay written in 1963, Habib Bourguiba, Jr., then Ambassador to the United

States," briefly explained this principle of Tunisian foreign policy as follows:

> We believe that any international policy should not in any way jeopardise freedom, justice, and dignity of individuals on one side or the other. We believe that the "law of the jungle" must be eliminated from international relations. As long as certain powers will continue to act in this way, international peace will be threatened; and if peace is constantly threatened, nothing valuable can be achieved by men in this, our world, let alone the risk of blowing it up once and for all.
>
> This is why Tunisia considers that her first duty is to co-operate in maintaining peace everywhere in the world and support all forms of peaceful co-operation between all nations. Since she believes that the United Nations Organisation is one of the best means to promote such co-operation, she favours a powerful United Nations Organisation and backs its action everywhere.
>
> As a former colonised nation Tunisia stands for the principle of complete and total decolonisation for all people. We back all nations still colonised be they from Africa or any other continent. Opposition to colonialism is a question of human dignity which goes far beyond geography or race. Co-operation is certainly a better relationship than domination. No nation is entitled to rule another nation.
>
> Another principle of our foreign policy, linked to the first two, is self-determination. We believe that liberty should be given to the peoples to freely choose their destiny. However, this liberty must be limited in order to prevent any fractioning, hence weakening of former colonised nations.
>
> Another aspect of our foreign policy is non-alignment. We believe that the best way for the developing countries to work for peace and eliminate the Cold War is to abstain from being integrated militarily or politically

> into either of the two blocs which are challenging each other in pursuing our support. We do not say we are neutral, because complete neutrality is impossible. But we try to approve of this or that bloc in so far as it acts in accordance with highly acclaimed moral principles on one particular issue. Similarly, we might side with the other bloc on another issue, If it happens that one of the two blocs is, during a certain period, more often on the side of justice, we shall be more often on its side, without systematically supporting it on any issue. That is what we understand by non-alignment.
>
> Last but not least, while standing for the rights of the individual, for peace and international co-operation, for decolonisation and self-determination, for non-alignment, we try to keep the respect of all nations by the only weapons we have at hand: moderation, seriousness, good-will, good sense and loyalty to high principles, whatever the immediate consequence might be. These pragmatic efforts to avoid any excess, any extremism are essential to every young nation.[1]

Non-alignment in Tunisian Foreign Policy

The policy of non-alignment as described above is, in fact, a relatively new feature of Tunisian foreign policy. It is the last stage of a development process. In 1956, it would have been inconceivable to think of non-alignment as a guiding principle of Tunisian foreign policy. Bourguiba had made it clear that: "I am against neutralism and I think it is in our interest to join the NATO. We are an integral part of the Occident and the free world."[2]

This open alignment with NATO was reaffirmed a year later when Bourguiba wrote:

> Tunisia's natural sympathies are with the democratic and liberal nations, and its economic interests demand that it trade with its neighbours. In as much as the free world and the communist world are two opposite camps, Tunisia belongs to the former. Thus, so far it has seen no need to join any defensive alliance against

communist aggression, but if it felt threatened it would not hesitate to do so.[3]

But enthusiasm with NATO seemed to wane by the end of that year when some of the countries (the United States, the United Kingdom, Belgium, and Italy) hesitated to sell needed arms to Tunisia in deference to France, but negative attitude towards the Soviet Union and other communist nations still, persisted. At the 'moment, the Tunisian leader found "absolutely no advantage in approaching the Soviet camp or in doing anything that might augment its prestige or justify its pretensions of defending (Tunisian) sovereignty.[4] Thus, a Russian arms offer was rejected,[5] because Bourguiba did not have faith in communism and Soviet Russia which always strove for "the conquest of the globe".[6] This position could hardly be labelled non-alignment.

As far as one can recall, a distant connection between Tunisian foreign policy and today's non-alignment was discerned at the time of the Accra Conference of eight independent African nations when Tunisia joined with the other participating countries in the agreement, to adopt a common foreign policy of "non-entanglement with big powers".[7]

But it was the Sakiet incident and the second crisis over the problem of arms shipment to Tunisia in 1958, that prompted Bourguiba to announce publicly and unilaterally the adoption of the principle of "non-commitment" of Tunisian foreign policy. In retrospect, Bourguiba saw past co-operation between his country and the free world as a "lesser evil", no more no less. In 1958, the assistance of the once suspected communist nations was no longer rejected, but sought after, for Tunisia had decided to "procure arms anywhere they might be obtained," and that these arms would "not necessarily be of Western origin."[8]

Actually, Tunisia only approached Czechoslovakia and Yugoslavia, not the principal opponent of the United States, Soviet Russia—for a possible arms deal. This was immediately dropped after the United States had guaranteed that it would ship weapons to Tunisia regardless of France's reaction. Despite the Tunisian declaration of 1958, in favour of non-commitment, in the eyes of the majority of other non-committed nations, Tunisia's behaviour during the ensuing period 1958-1960, was still too pro-Western to qualify itself as a genuine non-committed nation. Consequently, Tunisia's name was not included in the initial list of the non-aligned nations to participate in the Belgrade Conference in September 1961.

As Tunisia grew and became sure of herself, her relations with the outside world increased. By 1961, Tunisia had established diplomatic relations with many newly independent nations in Asia and Africa and became more receptive to Afro-Asian politics. As a small and developing nation, Tunisia wanted to find herself in the company of the emerging countries whose influence was increasingly felt in international politics, but she could not share their emotional and, at time, erratic, anti-colonialism. On the other hand, she was trapped in an ideological alliance with the West, particularly with the United States, which had proved utterly ineffectual in solving the outstanding problems caused by obsolete Western imperialism. Powerless among the Western powers, feeling rejected by the Afro-Asian countries. Tunisia was in no position to work effectively for the realisation of her major national objective; decolonisation in Tunisia (French troops still stationed at Bizerte), let alone decolonisation in the world and the preservation of democratic values.

In the aftermath of the Bizerta crisis, Bourguiba received the invitation to the Belgrade Conference of non-engaged countries which had previously been denied him. Bourguiba, no doubt, badly wanted that invitation to boost his position among Tunisian Leftists, but the invitation was not based on any substantial change in Tunisian policy. According to the definition of non-alignment, proposed by the preparatory conference in Cairo in June, 1961. Tunisia was a non-aligned nation before Bizerte. Its foreign policy was based on peaceful co-existence and non-alignment; it consistently supported national independence movements; it belonged to no multilateral, bilateral or regional military alliance; the Bizerta base was not ceded in the context of a great power conflict and Tunisia had challenged the continued existence of the base. In fact, invitations were issued to a large extent on the basis of the preferences of the organisers of the conference, Tito and 'Abd al-Nasir, and on those of the original invitees. It is likely that Tunisia was originally black-balled by Abd al-Nasir and that the Tunisian-Egyptian reconciliation after Bizerta made Tunisian attendance at Belgrade possible.

At Belgrade, Bourguiba emphasised the familiar themes of his foreign policy: non-alignment, an independent policy based on Tunisian national interests, peaceful co-existence, non-intervention in the internal affairs of other states, support for a strong United Nations, support for Chinese admission to the UN, nuclear disarmament, de-colonisation international aid for development. Rejoined a minority of the speakers at Belgrade in criticising the resumption of let nuclear tests by the Soviet Union on the eve of the conference.[9]

There was a change of form, but not of substance. There was a shift in the method of foreign policy, not in objectives which remained the consolidation of national sovereignty and the preservation of human dignity. Therefore, the adoption of non-alignment in itself was not contradictory to Tunisia's attachment to Western democratic principles. Bourguiba pointed out that:

> In practicing non-alignment, Tunisia does not renounce friendship. But she places her attachment and her fidelity to principles beyond her preference and her affinities. Everywhere and always she tries to moderate her reaction and let reason prevail over passion.[10]

Tunisia's attachment and fidelity to principles beyond her preference and affinities earned for herself a place among the non-aligned countries. But her impartial application of these principles which stressed upon moderation and reason imbued Tunisian foreign policy with a distinct characteristic which, to many other non-aligned nations, seemed to be more lenient to the West and, at times, verged on a pro-Western stand.

Undoubtedly, there was subtle change, as a result of Tunisia's switch from pro-Western position to non-alignment. Friendship with the West remained intact, but Tunisia did not now have any computation to act contrary to Western desire. She had refrained from communism and had tried to better her relations with the communist nations.

Tunisia has kept herself out of all formal alliances to ensure her freedom of action. She participates in the Arab League, but acts independently of it. She is a member of the Afro-Asian caucusing group at the United Nations, out is not bound by the position of the majority.[11] She belonged to the 'Monrovia group, but boycotted its Lagos meeting to protest the failure of the group to invite Algeria.

On the other hand, Tunisia tries to cultivate friendship with all states. She is among a very few Arab countries which had been able to maintain sound relations with both the aggressively republican states and the suspiciously defensive monarchies of the Arab world. She was widely respected among the Afro-Asian countries. Although she had special relations with the United States which has in Tunisia its greatest per capita commitment for Africa (roughly US $15.00 per capita per year) and one of its deepest ethical engagements anywhere in the world, and with France whose technical and educational contributions are impressive. Tunisia has sought and received considerable contributions from other Western countries like Italy, West Germany, Denmark and the Netherlands. Sweden, looking, for a pet country for its experimental aid project, has unofficially adopted Tunisia as the underdeveloped country in which it proposes to make its major assistance effort. With the communist nations, relations run the gamut from formally correct (as in the case of Communist China) to cordially warm (as in the case of Yugoslavia). Trade has been exchanged with Czechoslovakia and Bulgaria, while the Soviet Union has provided Tunisia with credits and technical assistance.[12]

It is on the third point-commitment to important issues of the time that Tunisia stands out as a special case of non-aligned nations. Tunisia shares with other non-aligned countries their position with respect to many broad principles concerning economic development of new nations, nuclear disarmament, peaceful co-existence, the emancipation of oppressed people, etc. But she often disagrees with many of them when these common principles are put into practice. Tunisia was a member of the Monrovia group which the majority of the Belgrade nations did not seem to consider as their comrade: while all members of the militant Casablanca group were invited, only three members of the Monrovia group (Ethiopia, Somalia, and Tunisia) attended the Conference. The choice of association clearly indicated the moderate brand of Tunisia non-alignment.

This is also shown by Tunisian voting record at the United Nations. It was calculated that on eighty important roll call votes in plenary and committee sessions of the fifteenth and sixteenth General Assemblies (1960-1961), Tunisia voted 20 times in agreement with the United States, 23 times in agreement with the Soviet Union, 26 times in agreement with neither, and 11 times with both, with 24 abstentions. Whereas other non-aligned nations such as Morocco voted only five times in agreement with the United States, 37 times 25 times with neither, 11 times with both, with 21 with the Soviet Union, 25 times with neither, abstentions; the UAR had a record of, respectively, 4, 37, 28, 11, 24; and Ghana, 11, 33, 25, 11, 23.[13]

In other words, compared with the majority of other non-aligned nations, Tunisia was relatively more pro-Western.

Tunisia's Relations with United States

When Tunisia obtained its independence in 1956, the United States was the first great power to recognise the young nation, and was among the first countries with which Tunisia sought to establish diplomatic relations. In the main, Tunisian-American relations have been characterised by friendship and mutual respect. Temporary deviations from this pattern tended to stem from outside influence rather than from the initiative of either of the partners.

Historical Foundation: Pre-independence Relations

History records various contacts between the United States and the Regency of Tunis which began as early as in the eighteenth century.

The control of the Mediterranean Sea by the Barbary States (Morocco, the Regencies of Tripoli-Algiers, and Tunis) and the American need to navigate in peace in Tunisian waters brought them together and on March 26, 1799, the first treaty of friendship and guarantee of freedom of navigation of American vessels in the Mediterranean was signed, between the United States and Tunisia.[14] Consuls were exchanged, followed by several years of uneventful relationship between the two countries.

Meanwhile, a change in the balance of power in the Mediterranean began to take shape. The Barbary States grew weaker while the United States was becoming a growing power and started to form its own fleet. After a naval demonstration before Algiers in 1815, American strength was recognised, and annual tributes in return for the freedom of navigation were ceased to be paid to the Barbary States. From then on, piracy became virtually inactive as the power of the West far outstripped that of the Barbary States. Tunis renounced piracy formally in 1819, and in 1824 signed with the United States an agreement putting the two signatories on a basis of equality and according most-favoured nation status. The period of American pre-occupation with North Africa because it was an obstacle to her trade with Europe and the Levant was over.[15] After France had established its protectorate over Tunisia, the consul mission of the United States became "nothing but an honorary post, one with no particular political objectives."[16] Direct diplomatic activities between the two countries virtually came to a stop.

The first World War took the United States out of its isolationist position and involved it in European politics. For a while, the Wilsonian principle, of the "right of self-determination of people" aroused great hope among subject people, including the Tunisians whose nationalism started to manifest itself, after, the war, in the form of the Destour party. But at the peace conference; Wilson's ideas did not prevail; the United States, again, resigned itself to fortress America; Tunisia was left unaided in its struggle for independence.

Only during the second World War did the United States pay serious attention to North Africa because of its strategic importance as a bridge to invade Europe.[17] In November 1942, the Americans led allied landings in North Africa. Tunis was chosen as the Headquarters of General Eisenhower, and generally Allied troops were received by Tunisians as friends and liberators.[18] Although freed by the Axis, Bourguiba, the Head of the Neo-Destour Party which was struggling against French colonialism for the independence of Tunisia, refused to throw his support to them, but instead urged the Neo-Destourians and the Tunisian people to cooperate with the Allies. By this move, he had predicted that the war would be won by the Allies, and hoped that when this was done, the Allied powers would remember Tunisian co-operation, and the Americans who were known for their aversion to colonialism would use their influence to effect decolonisation in North Africa.

Thus, in a letter dated June 1, 1943, and sent through the American General Consul, the Chief of the Neo-Destour party expressed to President Franklin D. Roosevelt of the United States, his "greatest hopes on the victory of the Democracies," reminded him of Tunisia's expectation that "fighting for a new and more human world from which racial prejudice would be forever banished, the great Democracies could not exclude from that world the colonised people, and in particular the Tunisian people who have no less right to live than their European and American brothers," and urged him to "see to it that Free France, who is fighting against Nazi slavery, does not treat the Tunisians as slaves and that she practices a policy more in conformity with her genius and traditions".[19]

The American response was that the war had to be won before any secondary issues could be settled, and the United

States was unwilling to jeopardise its relationship with France while the fight against the Axis powers continued.

When the war ended the same stand was taken in respect to the struggle between France and Tunisian nationalists for other reasons. The United States demobilised and, for a time, tended to let slide most external problems save those that concerned the Cold War. At that time, it was obsessed with strategic considerations, with building military pacts and bases; it was anxious to avoid offending France and, therefore, could give little, if any, support to the nationalist movement in Tunisia.[20]

This European orientation of American foreign policy naturally disappointed the Tunisians. However, on the whole, past experience with the United States had left a good impression on the Tunisians. Not only was the United States was suspected of pursuing any colonial ambition in the area, she was also greatly admired for her noble ideas embodied in the pronouncements of Wilson and Roosevelt which were readily embraced by the Tunisian elite who were culturally attached to Western thought. Furthermore, the Tunisians were grateful to America through sympathetic gestures of such men as the American General Consul, H.A. Doolittle, whose intervention on behalf of Bourguiba perhaps had saved the latter from being captured and tried by the French who falsely accused him of collusion with the Axis. Last but not least, they believed in the American "tradition" of supporting the underdog, and thought that the United States might be persuaded to support the Tunisian case.

In an effort to enlist American support, Bourguiba, in December 1946, made his first trip to the United States where he was received by Lois Handerson, the then Chief of the Africa-Middle East Office, and was introduced to Dean Acheson, but obtained no promise of support.

His second trip to the United States, accompanied by the Tunisian labour leader Ferhat Hached, was relatively more successful. The withdrawal of the UGTT (Union Generale des Travailleurs Tunisiens) from the communist-dominated Confederation of Free Unions earlier in the year had earned for Tunisia the respect of American labour unions. In September 1951, when Bourguiba and Farhat Hached attended the AFL congress in San Francisco they were warmly received and were pledged friendship and support by the American labour leaders.[21]

In this period an appeal was made to the American tradition of helping the political underdog, and emphasis was put on the strategic implication of the Tunisian struggle. Bourguiba admitted that "We are not unaware that we are militarily weak and strategically too important to do without the assistance of a great power" but, he warned, "I feel weighing my words carefully, that Tunisia would go through a dangerous and chaotic period which neither France nor Tunisia would be thankful for, and which would certainly not be a matter of indifference to those powers interested in the real peace and stability in the vital part of the Mediterranean world".[22]

Official support from the United States finally came, although slowly and reluctantly. In 1952, when the French Government adopted a new policy of repression in Tunisia and jailed Bourguiba, the United States decided to abstain "from voting for the inclusion of the Tunisian question on the Security Council agenda, but supported a mild Assembly resolution recognising Tunisia's ability to govern itself, and asked that both parties, refrain from doing anything that might aggravate the tense situation.[23]

In 1953, the Tunisian nationalists intensified their effort to win international support. Bahi Ladgham, a close collaborator of Bourguiba, was sent to New York to found the Tunisian Office for National Liberation to make contact with, and seek support of, the American labour and political leaders as well as of foreign-diplomatic circles. His effort was rewarded and in the full session of the United Nations, the, General Assembly adopted an Icelandic resolution recommending negotiations between France and Tunisia.[24]

Negotiations between the two parties soon began. Internal autonomy was granted to Tunisia in 1955. Shortly afterward, on March 20, 1956, Tunisia's independence was proclaimed. The United States was the first great power to recognise the new nation.

Tunisia's Relation with USA since Independence

In Tunisian foreign policy, the United States occupies a special position. It is commonly understood in Tunisia, that although the United States did not actively interfere on behalf of Tunisia's independence as the Tunisians had wished for fear of hurting France, it nonetheless had clearly expressed sympathy and support to the Tunisian cause. Other forces were at work to enhance American-Tunisian friendship. On the personal level, Ladgham's experience in the United States and the encouragement and assistance he got from his American friends had made this powerful man a strong advocate of a pro-American policy which, on the whole, had met with no considerable opposition from the other leaders of the Neo-Destour who were also admirers of American democratic principles. Politically speaking, association with the United States satisfied Tunisia's seemingly contradictory dual objective of diminishing French influence while remaining on the Western side "(an objective mostly motivated by cultural orientation)". Furthermore, with the American practice of foreign aid, Tunisia looked to the United States as an important source of finance for Tunisian economic development. In an earlier period, Tunisia also wanted to mobilise.

American support in its future bargaining with France on the remaining problems between the two countries and on the Algerian question in view of arriving at a peaceful solution, conducive to a possible Franco-Maghribian co-operation. In the wake of Tunisia's independence, Bourguiba, in an effort to capture American confidence, asserted his loyalty to the West and said:

> "I am against neutralism and I think it is in our interest to join the NATO. We are a part of the Occident and the free world".[25]
>
> We choose to collaborate with the great Western Powers so that we might be able to face a possible French attack.

> I am Western and I will remain so... Tunisia is a country weakened by French colonialism. She needs to lean on the friendship of a powerful country in order to consolidate her independence and continue her struggle.[26]

> The choice of Western friendship instead of Russia's was also based on the calculation that "once the Iron Curtain is lowered, there is no escape from the Communist grip. On the other hand, it is possible to leave the western camp at any time".[27]

Next, his first ambassador to the United States, Mongi Slim, explained to his American audience that (1) Tunisia "cannot have complete independence until the French troops are withdrawn;" (2) the Security of Tunisia "is not complete without peace in Algeria"; and (3) she wanted to be a "buffer state between the Arabic and European worlds".[28]

The implied message was clear in return for her loyalty to the West, Tunisia expected the United States to assist her to obtain the withdrawal of the French troops in Tunisia, to find a peaceful solution for the Algerian problem, and to build a bridge between the West and the Arab world.

But the immediate concern of the Tunisian Government was economic problems. In the midst of rising expectation, and as a result of newly-acquired independence, the Tunisian-Government was faced with serious problems of unemployment and population growth. It was calculated by an American survey team in 1956, that 100,000,000 dollars per year would be needed to replace the assistance formerly made available by France to the Tunisian economy. Now that France had resigned from Tunisia, she was only willing to contribute the equivalent of 57 million dollars.[29] Tunisia had to look elsewhere for aid. In July, 1956, during his stay in Paris, Bourguiba called upon Douglas Dillon, the American Ambassador to Paris, to explain to him Tunisia's economic needs, but made no specific request for aid.[30]

Two months later, almost simultaneously with the establishment of the Tunisian Embassy in Washington, the

Tunisian Government requested emergency wheat assistance from the United States.[31] In October, the unfortunate arrest of the Algerian leaders took place, resentment against France mounted in North Africa, the timing of the American grant of 45,000 tons of wheat in November seemed to be designed to show American sympathy and to allay Tunisian hostility towards the West. In the same month, Bourguiba decided to head the Tunisian delegation to the United Nations to mark the formal entry of Tunisia into the world organisation, to support the cause of Algerian independence, and to seek economic assistance from the United States.

At the United Nations, Bourguiba criticised both the Suez invasion countries were blinded by the Suez crisis, and even praised the United States for its attitude on Algeria.[32] This impartial position and his conduct of Tunisian struggle for independence which was characterised by moderation and reasonableness brought him deep sympathy from the United States. The Washington Post hailed his "calming influence" on North Africa.[33] Bourguiba was introduced by Ambassador Henry Cabot Lodge as "one of the men of whom the world can be proud, because of his love of peace among men and his work to promote the happiness of humanity."[34] But it seemed, in 1956, that the United-States was not prepared to go much further than verbal encouragement, lest France might interprete its move as an effort to displace French position in North Africa.

In December, Bourguiba returned empty-handed to Tunis. Instead of announcing a vast programme of American aid, he praised France especially her agreement to withdraw troops from Egypt. In order to allay French fear of his 'pro-American policy, Bourguiba declared before the Tunisian Constituent Assembly that,

> The moral support of the United States should not lead us to adopt an unfriendly attitude toward France... If we had thought of US aid, it was only to the extent that this might be used to complement French aid. We never had any thought of the United States taking over from France.[35]

The move was designed to dispel French suspicion, to ease the tension between Tunisia and France resulting from the arrest of the Algerian leaders, and to open the door for Tunisia's acceptance or French subsidies.

In January 1957, diplomatic relations were resumed between the two countries; the United States now found itself in a position to respond to Tunisia's request for help without having to take sides. In March, Vice-President Richard Nixon arrived in Tunis to represent President Eisenhower in the Tunisia/independence anniversary fete. Discussions on the quest for peace in North Africa and economic aid were held between the leaders of the two countries. On March 26, 1957, an American-Tunisian economic agreement was signed providing for $5,500,000 to finance development projects, technical co-operation, and the training of experts in Tunisia.[36]

To France, the American move was ominous. In a speech before the French Council of the Republic, Foreign Minister Maurice Faure, referring to Nixon's visit, declared that France's influence in Tunisia would not be replaced by US dollars and technicians, warned that American aid could be accepted only in agreement with France, and added: 'We ardently hope that America understands this in the very interest of North Africa.[37] Moreover, United States viewed France as the main source of economic aid to these countries and that any American aid could only be supplementary to that given by France. Even as late as the controversy over the arms shipment to Tunisia, Secretary of State John Foster Dulles indicated that the United States would have been happy, and would be happy in the future, if Tunisia would get arms from France. As he puts it, "the relations between France and Tunisia are historic, are many, and we would prefer to have the relationship carried out on that basis rather than upon an arrangement with other countries."[38]

It seems clear that Vice-President Nixon had the situation in Tunisia and Morocco in mind when he reported to President Eisenhower on his trip to Africa that "Africa is a priority target for the international Communist movement" and that "the Communist threat underlies, the wisdom and necessity of our assisting the countries of Africa to maintain their independence and to alleviate the conditions of want and instability on which communism breeds." Also, in obvious reference to France and its relations with Tunisia, he recommended that the United States should encourage the continuation of special ties between the independent states of Africa and European states "where they are considered mutually advantageous by the states concerned," but that "we should take them in account in formulating our own policies to the extent compatible with the fundamental requirement of conducting our own relations with those states on a fully equal... basis".[39]

In a sense the Nixon trip, despite the previously mentioned temporising statement concerning the priority of French interests in Tunisia represents a recognition on the part of American policy-makers that the United States must begin a new role in the area. The mere fact that he visited and Tunisia was an indication of heightened American interest in the problems of these two newly-independent countries. It reflected an awareness that the time had come for the United States to pursue a more independent policy in Northwest Africa, if the area were not to be softened up for a repetition of Soviet inroads into Egypt and Syria. Following the Nixon visit, the change in United States policy was felt with the stepping up of American economic aid and technical assistance to Tunisia by the agreement. But it was not until left September 1957.

Tunisia, the new agreement was expected to herald a new era in Tunisian-American relations. When it was announced that James P. Richards, the special envoy of President Eisenhower would tour the West Asia to determine the needs of the region and to see how the United States could help to implement the Eisenhower Doctrine (the Eisenhower Doctrine proclaimed American intention to help the West Asia countries to resist communist aggression by giving them necessary economic and military assistance), Tunisia awaited the visit with great expectation.

It was thought in Tunis that since President Bourguiba was highly respected in the United States, since Tunisia was a progressive nation and a staunch ally of the West, and since Tunisia had announced its support of the Eisenhower Doctrine, so it deserved American special treatment.

But deterred by French warning, the Richards mission's commitment to Tunisia fell short of Tunisia's expectation: it refused to grant any military aid to the latter,[40] and its three million dollars of pledged economic aid was described by Bourguiba as much smaller than that accorded by the mission to less populous and less friendly nations and particularly inadequate in view of Tunisia's economic problems.[41] In view of this, Bourguiba criticised the United States for being preoccupied by opportunistic considerations, for seeking to cure the Communist evil after it had reached critical proportions rather than preventive expenditures in countries whose government had chosen unequivocal alliance with the free world, and reprimanded it for supporting imperialism in Africa by solicitude for French sensibilities and by continuing disregard independent Tunisia as a "French sphere of influence".[42] Despite all the shortcomings of the Richards mission, Bourguiba asserted that Tunisia would not change its policy and that it continued to regard herself as "part of the free world closely tied to the United Slates".[43]

The rationale of Tunisia's pro-Western policy was explained at length in an article by Bourguiba in Orbis. He said that Tunisia chose the West because there was moral force, especially in the United States working against vestiges of imperialism. Bourguiba also stated that he did not have faith in Communism and Soviet Russia which "strove for the conquest of the globe." He could not, therefore, bring himself to "ask help from Russia against France or Great Britain for the mere sake of revenge and without thinking of the consequences".

In regard to the United States, Bourguiba declared candidly: "The Free World owes its existence to the protection of the powerful United States ...While we may not hesitate to criticise the United States whenever necessary, we cannot deny the fundamental facts or our survival.[44] Bourguiba's comment was not lost on the American policy-makers, who, were deeply impressed by his realism and statesmanship,[45] and who responded favourably to his call later in 1957. As a result of the arrest of the-Algerian leaders and the Suez crisis which slowed down Egyptian assistance to the Algerian nationalists. Tunisia dropped its policy of neutrality in the Algerian conflict to move closer to the FLN. This caused serious strain in Franco-Tunisian relations.[46] When French financial aid to Tunisia was suspended in May, 1957, Tunisia approached the United States and other countries for aid to balance the loss created by the suspension of French assistance.[47]

On May 28, it was reported that Egypt and the Soviet Union would offer aid to Tunisia; but the United States, warned by France that NATO would suffer if it tried to supplant France in North Africa, and reluctant for anger France refused to do anything substantial to ameliorate the Tunisian economic situations.[48]

Meanwhile, relations between France and Tunisia rapidly deteriorated. After the establishment of the FLN External Delegation Headquarters in Tunisia, FLN activities in Tunisia 'markedly increased and the possibility of the war spilling over into Tunisian territory as a result of the French practice of hot pursuit multiplied. Bourguiba proposed to strengthen his armed forces to ensure Tunisia's security. He first requested France to grant Tunisia 1,000 rifles. Naturally, this demand was rejected and, in August, France decided to suspend altogether arms delivery to Tunisia.[49]

Tunisia, then, called upon the United States, Italy, Belgium, and the Arab States for assistance. Upon French objection, Belgium and Italy refused to comply with Tunisian request. Egypt promptly tendered its assistance on September 16, 1957. The Tunisian Ambassador to Egypt stated on September 23, 1957 that this offer had been accepted, and that a Tunisian military mission would shortly visit Cairo to discuss details. On the following day, the United States gave President Bourguiba a written assurance that Western arms would reach Tunisia during October.[50] This decision was undoubtedly prompted by the fear that necessity might force Tunisia to accept arms from the Soviet Union through the intermediary of Egypt and from other Communist nations such as Yugoslavia with which Tunisia had signed a trade agreement in June, and Czechoslovakia whose trade delegation had recently visited Tunisia.[51]

After unsuccessful efforts to persuade the French Government to deliver arms to Tunisia, the United States and Britain officially announced their decision on November 14, "to ship arms and ammunitions to Tunisia, over the bitter protest of the French Government".[52] The United States issued a statement regretting that France found it impossible to associate itself with the project "despite the frequent consultations which have taken place on this subject," and maintaining that its decision "constitutes a recognition that Tunisia, as a free and independent member of the United Nations has the inherent right and obligation to provide for its internal security and self-defense," and that "the Western countries should provide to Tunisia', which has freely chosen to identify itself with the West, the opportunity to purchase its means of defence from Western sources."[53]

Although the arms shipment to Tunisia was a minor one,[54] United States had concerted its action with Britain to allay French fear that it planned to undermine French policy in Tunisia and increase American influence. The American decision to grant arms to Tunisia could be considered as a diplomatic victory for Bourguiba. For the first time, the United States had overridden the protest of its traditional ally to respond to Tunisia's call.

A pattern seems to have been established: each time relations between France and Tunisia deteriorated, Tunisia turned to the United States for support. The result was that as French influence in Tunisia declined, American commitment to the country increased. This was exactly what

Bourguiba wanted. He went about it in the early period of Tunisian independence by declaring against the vestiges of French colonialism in Tunisia and North Africa while showing himself a loyal supporter of Western democratic principles. This left the United States with little choice but to help Tunisia achieve her objective.

In the Spring of 1958, the Sakiet raid brought Franco-Tunisian relations to the breaking point. Roadblocks were set up and demonstrations were held throughout Tunisia to protest against French brutalities and to demand the evacuation of all French forces from the Tunisian bases. At the same time, the Tunisian Government lodged an official complaint with the Security Council of the United Nations. The United States was also notified of the situation; its diplomatic support was requested. Profoundly disturbed by the raid in view of its possible effects on relations between France and Tunisia, both friends of America, the United States with Great Britain offered their "good offices" to help find a means of reconciling the differences between the two parties.[55]

Bourguiba seized the opportunity to impress the Anglo-American mediators of the seriousness of the Algerian war and its repercussions in Tunisia. He told Britain and the United States of the threat to his position and to his pro-Western policy by anti-French and anti-Western sentiment in Tunisia resulting from French brutality and Western passivity, and warned that unless the, West, principally the United States, took a clear position "in favour of the victim of aggression and against the aggressor" it might have to face a possible change of leader and hence, of foreign policy in Tunisia. Such a change, it was intimated, would be detrimental to United States interest.[56]

Bourguiba also wanted to involve the United States and Great Britain in the Algerian conflict in the hope of bringing it to a sat is factory conclusion and of allaying the FLN fear that Tunisia might contract a deal with the West, a deal inimical to their interest which would, in turn, push them into the arms of Egypt.[57]

The United States and Britain privately assured Bourguiba that they would attempt to end the Algerian war.[58] Meanwhile, the Anglo-American good offices commission worked out a mutual agreement on the basis for direct negotiations between France and Tunisia whereby France recognised Tunisian sovereignty over Bizerta and accepted the principle of evacuation of all French forces from Tunisia, except Bizerta.[59] On June 17, 1958 in an agreement with the Tunisian Government, France pledged to withdraw her forces from all her installations outside. Bizerta, and to enter negotiations with the Tunisian Government not later than October 1, for a provisional agreement on the status of the Bizerta base over which Tunisian sovereignty would be recognised.[60]

If Bourguiba had succeeded in using Sakiet and Anglo-American support to get considerable concessions for Tunisia, he had failed to use it to internationalise the Algerian war. This displeased the FLN leaders, who concluded that Bourguiba was a pro-Western, and increasingly began to lean toward Nasser. Especially after the seemingly pro-Nasser coup in Iraq (also a strong FLN supporter) in July 1958, Nasser's influence clearly increased among the FLN leadership at the expense of Bourguiba's. Friction began to develop between the FLN and the Tunisian Government to the point that there was even rumour of an Algerian instigated coup in Tunisia.[61]

To protect Tunisia against "external pressure" the Tunisian Government decided to treble its armed forces to 18,000 men and to seek military equipment abroad. For fear of French "control" resulting from Tunisia's dependence for ammunition and spare parts, the Government rejected the French offer of arms shipment, but requested assistance from the United States and Great Britain.[62]

Disappointed by Western reluctance to sell arms to Tunisia without the approval of the French Government, Bourguiba declared, on November 13, 1958, that his government had decided to "procure arms anywhere they may be obtained" and that "these arms will not necessarily be of Western origin." His resentment against Western sensibility for France was clear when he emphasised:

> ...We are willing to take into consideration the offer of any country willing to deal with us on the understanding that we are not a member of the influential sphere of any great power... In order to prove that we belong to no particular zone, we are prospecting in all directions, irrespective of the political tendencies or orientation of the country willing to supply us with arms. It is not a question of future dispositions or blackmail but of dispositions already taken.[63]

If the Tunisian President did not design his speech as a blackmail, it did have a blackmailing effect on American policy-makers because almost simultaneously with this speech and his disclosure of Tunisian request of arms from Czechoslavakia and Yugoslavia, the United States, State Department announced that the United States was ready to sell arms to Tunisia without French clearance.[64] On November 25, the conclusion of the American arms shipment to Tunisia agreement was announced.[65] Again, Bourguiba had used American assistance to balance French influence in Tunisia and to remain on the Western side without having to identify, with French colonialism in Algeria.

On the economic and financial side, American aid to Tunisia steadily increased as French assistance decreased. In 1957, as a result of border incidents, and serious friction between the two countries, France stopped its aid to Tunisia, only to resume it in 1962 on a smaller scale, and seemed to settle on cultivating cultural ties with Tunisia. The American assistance programme in Tunisia was a combination of financial aid, technical cooperation, and American surplus of agricultural commodities. Financial aid consisted of dollar and hard currency grants and development loans from various sources. Dollar grants were made for commodities imports, purchase of equipment, and for financing-specific projects. Hard currency grants involved the use of the proceeds of sales of American agricultural commodities to other countries (Italy, Germany and France) to buy in those countries goods needed by Tunisia in its development programme. Loans were made for financing specific projects and for purchases of equipment and materials.

Technical cooperation (labelled since 1961 "development grants") was provided in a variety of fields, such as agricultural development, skills training, water resources development, education, management training, communications, tourism, civil aviation, housing, industrial development and employment services. The United States also used the Tunisian currency engendered from the sale of American surplus agricultural commodities in Tunisia to make grants and long-term loans, and for its own needs in Tunisia.[66]

In 1959, American aid programme to Tunisia was further expanded with the extension of the ICA Investment Guaranty Programme to Tunisia to attract private investment in the country, and with the additional loans accorded the Tunisian National Railways by the American Development Loan Fund."[67] The year ended with the visit of President Eisenhower in December, 1959.

During Eisenhower's stay in Tunisia, the Tunisian President talked to him about the necessity to end the Algerian war, confided with him his projects to make Tunisia a progressive and developed nation, urged him to increase American economic aid to Tunisia, and frankly told him of his intention to take help from all countries, including Communist lands, because "no matter where it comes from, such help will reinforce us against Communism." He also assured Eisenhower: "Do not worry. No matter what happens we will be together, Tunisia and the rest of the free world".[68]

The American President was so impressed by Bourguiba's frankness and loyalty to the West that he seemed to have decided to make Tunisia a "pilot project", a show case for American aid. In March 1960, his Assistant Secretary for African Affairs, Joseph C. Satterthwaite, pleaded with Congress for increased development aid to that "vigorous and progressive Arab Government which aligns, itself courageously with the Western world," because "the

Bourguiba Government's success in this endeavour will have vitally important consequences for the neighbouring Arab areas as well as for many African countries".[69]

In October 1960, President Eisenhower, in response to a letter from President Bourguiba, expressed the willingness of the American Government to consider a request for increased assistance; he also suggested a high-level visit to Tunisia later in 1961.

American aid had been tremendously beneficial to Tunisia, especially during the first few years of its independence when there was a mass exodus of European technicians and entrepreneurs as well as a flight of capital from Tunisia. During this period, the Tunisian Government placed emphasis on the consolidation of its economic independence from France, and American aid was primarily used to achieve economic stability. When this first objective was achieved, the Government turned its attention to economic growth and found its efforts complicated and slowed down by the cumbersome procedure of American aid on an annual basis and the severe control of its use. Therefore, the Tunisian Government started to ask the United States for massive aid and reform in its aid procedure to allow long-range economic, planning in Tunisia aiming at achieving economic "take-off".[70]

In 1961, the change of administration took place in Washington. With the accession of John F. Kennedy to the American Presidency, Tunisia hopefully expected more positive support from the United States in its quarrel with France over Bizerte and over the Algerian conflict, because the Tunisians noticed, Kennedy, while still out against American neutral position in the North a senator had spoken African conflict,[71] and as President showed a keen interest and understanding of the new revolution in Africa and a marked departure from American heavy European orientation in dealing with problems of the area.

The years of 1960 and 1961 also witnessed the new birth of several African nations, their increasing influence in the United Nations, and their militant agitation against the remnants of colonialism. To keep in tune with the fervent nationalism of Africa and to retain leadership in African politics, Tunisia had to play down its pro-Western aspect of foreign policy and adhere more vehemently to the prevailing trend of non-alignment. Bourguiba explained that his country had adopted "non-alignment" because of "tacic or overt support of colonialism by the United States." Now that the United States was sympathetic to African aspirations, he was "optimistic and very satisfied" and hoped that enough away from the "President Kennedy's new policy will move far colonialists to let me come closer to the west".[72]

Basically, Bourguiba was a man of the West, but in fact, the geographic location of Tunisia was such that he could not ignore the feelings of his African friends. One of the main principles of Tunisian foreign policy was friendliness towards the United States; but how warm this friendship could be would have to depend on American foreign policy toward Africa.

There was no doubt that mutual respect between the leaders of the two countries and the new administration policy sympathetic to African nationalism—and favourable to long-term aid and economic planning were conducive to a warmer relationship between Tunisia and the United States.

In May 1961, at the invitation of President Kennedy, President Bourguiba arrived in Washington as the first Head of State to visit the United States under the Kennedy administration. His objectives were (1) to explain to the American policy-makers the necessity of his non-alignment policy, and the attachment of his country to democratic principles; (2) to seek American support for the fight against colonialism in Tunisia and Algeria; and (3) to impress the United States of the serious effort of the Tunisian people to develop their country and of the need for long-term aid to help finance Tunisia's "carefully conceived, multi-layer development programme placing maximum emphasis on the utilisation of Tunisia's own human and natural resources."[73]

In a speech to a joint session of Congress highlighting his visit, Bourguiba mentioned the common attachment to the principles of self-determination of all people and co-operation among free men as the "surest foundations" for co-operation between the United States and Tunisia, and rhetorically and aptly set down the basis of Tunisia's policy toward the United States. He said:

> "What your country needs are not satellites who vote with you automatically on all issues because they want your money, but friends who support you from conviction I can assure you that Tunisia will always tell you when we disagree with you, just as we will always applaud you when we believe you to be right. And we expect from you a reciprocal frankness.[74]

The United States understood and Bourguiba's visit was richly rewarded. The joint communique on May 5, 1961, between the two Presidents announced the United States support for Bourguiba's policy of non-alignment, their shared conviction on the "orderly process of decolonisation", their hope for negotiation and peaceful application of the principle of self-determination in Algeria, and pledged American sympathy for economic and social development aid in Tunisia.[75] The visit was followed by a series of agreements whereby the United States accorded Tunisia two 15-year loans totalling ten million dollars and twenty-five million dollars more in loans and grants outside regular aid program.[76] Washington also toyed with the idea of choosing Tunisia as a "model" for massive economic aid.[77]

This warming up process was suddenly interrupted by the Bizerte crisis when the United States, for fear of undermining Western unity in the face of the Berlin crisis, failed to side openly with Tunisia against France. Bourguiba talked of his "painful and extremely irritating" experience and his "severe shock" at Western neutrality.[78] But he also wanted to press the United States to interfere on behalf of Tunisia by directly sending his son, Ambassador Habib Bourguiba, Jr. and his deputy, Bahi Ladgham, to the United States to explain the Tunisian situation, and indirectly by threatening to embarass the United States by its action at the United Nations.[79] But many factors (American evaluation of the seriousness of the Berlin crisis, President de Gaulle's, personality and the internal politics of France...) worked to limit the effectiveness of Bourguiba's strategy. The United States refused to vote for a condemnation of France and urged negotiation between the two parties outside the United Nations. At Tunis, disillusion with American action was unmasked by an editorial in the weekly Afrique-Action which read:

> "The myth of an America, soldier of liberty charged with the divine mission of defending democracy everywhere with dollars, and if need be with atomic bombs has disappeared. The truth about America, the policeman of an imperialism at bay from Turkey to Korea, from Taiwan to Cuba, 'from' Algeria to Bizerte, is manifested itself in disarray and failure."[80]

This bitterness gradually dissipated with the conclusion of the Bizerte crises, because the Tunisians understood that it was the "pressure of the United States and other powers", "not of Tunisian armed forces, that had immobilised the French army in their barracks, that American conduct during the crisis had been governed by its preoccupations with international politics and by its role in NATO, and that all along the United States had assisted them generously" in their struggle against economic under-development.[81]

No sooner had a *modus vivendi* at Bizerte been signed between France and Tunisia than it was followed by the visit of Assistant Secretary of State G. Mennen Williams (October 16) and the arrival of an American mission in Tunisia to study economic development plans and American aid, to discuss ways in which the United States might participate in Tunisia's three-year plan.[82]

In 1962, the Algerian war came to an end, the Bizerte issue had been settled, the serious obstacles in the otherwise smooth and warm relationship between the United States and Tunisia were removed. Tunisia could devote most of her national energy to economic and social development.

She would not have to ask for any American political support which might put the United States into an awkward position and bring disappointment to Tunisia, yet, she still depended on economic assistance from the United States to insure rapid economic and social progress in Tunisia. Since 1962, the United States had pledged to contribute 180 million dollars for Tunisia's three-year development programme and had increased substantially its assistance to Tunisia.[83] Between fiscal year 1957, and fiscal year 1963, American economic assistance to Tunisia averaged about 50 million dollars a year, and so far as the United States was concerned Tunisia had proved deserving of all the aid she got.

Before 1980, the United States mainly provided Tunisia with economic assistance since Bourguiba kept his country's military down to a very modest size. Total United States economic aid to Tunisia since 1956 was over $1 billion; American officials have often cited Tunisia as a model of successful aid-assisted economic development was overtaken by national security concerns in 1980 when Libya organised an armed attack against the Tunisian mining town of Gafsa to spark an uprising against the government. Tunisian leaders had been trying for several years to improve the defensive capabilities of their country's 28,000-man military force, and in 1980-1981 they turned to the United States for help. The Reagan administration responded with about 100 million in military aid annually from 1982 to 1984; these funds went toward the purchase of American-made M-60 tanks, a squadron of F-5 jet fighters, ground-to air missiles, a radar system, coastal patrol boats, helicopters and armoured personnel carriers.[84] The American response was intended to boost the Tunisian military in the face of the Libyan threat. There were grounds for criticising the nature of the arms acquired, which were poorly suited to deal with internal subversion, but the choice of weapon systems came from Tunis, not Washington.[85]

Washington responded once again to Tunisia's appeal for help after nine days of violent bread riots swept the country at the end of 1983, and during the first week of

1984. The Reagan administration dispatched General Walters to Tunis; Walters took with him a pledge of an additional $5 million in Public Law 480 food assistance. Congress increased Economic Support Funds for the country from $1.5 million in fiscal year 1984 to $20 million in fiscal year 1985. At the same time, the United States Agency for International Development (AID) made a decision in mid-1984 to continue economic assistance to Tunisia. This reversed a decision in 1981 to phase out the AID programme in Tunisia over five years on the grounds that the country had reached a level of economic development—$1,400 annual per capita income—that no longer justified American aid.[86]

Military aid, meanwhile, was reduced to about $67 million for fiscal year 1985, and probably will be reduced further in the coming years. Although the current military aid figure was reduced considerably from the $111 million level of the previous year, more of this year's assistance is either grant aid or aid at concessional rates. The total economic and military aid for Tunisia declined from $125 million in fiscal year 1984 to $91.7 million in fiscal year 1985.[87]

Several key members of Congress believe that Tunisia, a moderate Arab nation threatened by Libya, deserves firm American support. President Bourguiba's health problems in the fall of 1984, underlined the possibility of some would say probability of a succession crisis in the 1930's. A prolonged crisis would tempt Libya to intervene. United States policy-makers would like to contribute to an orderly succession that will preserve Tunisia's independence and its moderate orientation.

In fact, the United States remains one of Tunisia's closest friends and greatest benefactors, and Tunisia, America's most respected ally in Africa. The two countries have been linked together by mutual respect, common ideology, coincidence of interests and fruitful co-operation which is to be expected to continue in the foreseeable future.

Tunisia's Relations with the other Western and Eastern Countries

Italy was second only to France as Tunisia's trading partner as far as bilateral commerce was concerned. Again, reasons of geography and history were bound to favour close relations between the two countries. Only some 10,000 Italian nationals still remained in Tunisia by 1968 as against home 70,000 in 1956, but Italian was spoken widely up and down the country and many Tunisians had some Italian blood or otherwise close relations with Italy. In architecture, industrial design and the arts Italian influence was felt increasingly, and many Tunisians were able to pick up Italian programmes on their television sets. Compensation for the nationalisation of Italian-owned firms in 1964 had been arranged by means of a package deal which involved large Italian participation in the development of Tunisia's oil resources. The ENI (Italian National Corporation) had agreed to share profits arising from such exploitation on a fifty-fifty basis, and offered other advantages in Tunisia's favour. Opening the oil installations at El Borma in November 1966, Habib Bourguiba could describe the arrangement made with ENI as a 'model' deal 'an original form of association, more equitable and more fruitful than the old system of royalties paid by one part to the other'. Subsequently, an agreement in principle was made with ENI to develop chemical industry in the south.

Relations with the German Federal Republic were exceptionally cordial, especially after Bourguiba had refused to toe the line laid down by Cairo in 1965 and break diplomatic relations with Bonn. The Germans were short of true friends in the world, and Bourguiba's gesture was appreciated. Moreover, both Libya and Morocco were encouraged by Tunisia's stand and Bourguiba's gesture was appreciated. Moreover, both Libya and Morocco were encouraged by Tunisia's stand and followed her example. But mutual sympathies went back further than that. The brief spell of German occupation in 1942-43 had left behind no bitter memories in Tunisia.

German efficiency had always had its admirers in Tunisia and German business methods and industrial products had a high reputation. Moreover, the West German export drive in Tunisia was being suitably oiled by economic and technical assistance. Development loans totalling' over £20 million had been granted between 1962 and 1967. Many imaginative projects could be carried out, including water barrage, irrigation 'schemes, pilot farms and ports and communications facilities. In 1968 some 500 Tunisians were studying in West Germany, many of them helped by the Bonn Government. In 1966, West Germany was third in the list of suppliers of goods to Tunisia, with an export value of just over £6 million. Increasingly, large numbers of German tourists in Tunisia were giving a new dimension to relations between the two countries.

"This was also true of Anglo-Tunisian contacts. As more British people visited Tunisia there was also a growing, interest in trade and other relations between the two countries. For many years in the past Tunisia had been regarded by British businessmen as a French province," offering little opportunity to outsiders. This view was clearly erroneous, but was nonetheless still widely held in British business circles. In the mid-sixties, Britain's shipments amounted to about five per cent of Tunisian imports, an about the same proportion applied to trade in the other direction. Britain sold mainly tractors and other vehicles, and machinery; Tunisia chiefly exported her iron ore, esparto grass, pulp and phosphates. But there were clearly opportunities for a substantial increase of these trade exchanges. Tunisia was keen on shipping more vegetables, such as onions, artichokes, potatoes and tomatoes, as well as citrus fruit and juice, to Britain at times of year when such produce might be less easily available from established suppliers. Wine, too, offered excellent prospects, for many British tourists were acquiring the of very good Tunisian white, red and rose products. Considering the fast rate of Tunisia's industrial development there were good chances for the expansion of British exports, of equipment and plant in particular. The tourist industry, especially in Djerba, was already attracting substantial British capital, and joint ventures in industrial development projects were feasible.

Very little British aid was given to Tunisia, but it was possible this would change if some particularly promising field could be found for an Anglo-Tunisian industrial partnership, preferably in an industry where Britain had some clear "advantage, perhaps in petro-chemical and artificial fibre industries. British plant and other products, had a high" reputation in Tunisia. The Davy-Ashmore blast furnace at El Fouladh had an excellent record after two years of operation. One of the most profitable and successful small enterprises in Tunisia, a jute factory, was equipped by a British company. The Tunis Hilton, another landmark, was built by a British firm.

Britain generally has a good press in Tunisia, and is considered by many Tunisians well worth studying. The President himself contributed to this by his references to Britain. The BBC, in both French and Arabic, has a very high number of listeners and reputation for accuracy of news and balanced comment. The British Embassy and its reading room are busy places, although nothing like their American counterparts. In 1968, thirty-two British people were working as teachers of English in Tunisia. In London, a small, but very active British-Tunisian society docs much to encourage interest in Tunisia by organising lectures and other activities.

When Tunisia became independent Russian leaders had already changed their attitude to the emergent nationalist regimes. These were now to be keenly wooed by promises of aid and otherwise. But in the case of the Maghrib, the Soviet Union was rather cagey, no doubt out of consideration for France, especially for the French Communist party, Yugoslavia alone among the communist countries supported Algerians and other nationalists in the Maghrib without any inhibitions, and this earned President Tito a moral prestige there that was unequalled by any other communist power. By 1957, Yugoslavia had already pledged aid to Tunisia to the tune of about £2 million.

It was not until August 1961 that the Soviet Union agreed to assist Tunisia in building a number of projects, and granted for this purpose a low-interest loan worth just over £19 million. The date of the agreement followed closely on that of the Bizerte incident. Hopes were running high in some Tunisian quarters that a new, important source of foreign aid was now found. In that year President Bourguiba was an honoured guest in Washington, patched up his quarrel with President Nasser, concluded his agreement with the Soviet Union and also attended the conference of unaligned nations in Belgrade. It was in that year, too, that a Tunisian was elected President of the General Assembly of the United Nations.

The plain truth was, however, that the type of product and equipment that Tunisia needed most could best be provided by western nations, and it was in any case very difficult to get something for nothing, from the Russians or anybody else.

All this is not to minimise the importance of good relations with the Soviet Union and the East, from the Tunisian point of view. Politically, friendly relations with the communist world widened Tunisia's room of diplomatic manoeuvre while they also helped to take some steam of the clamour of the left-wing element, notably students, for closer links with the East. The importance of trade with the communist world was on the increase in 1968. It then accounted for about ten per cent of Tunisia's total commercial exchanges and it was expected that it might rise to fifteen per cent although it seemed unlikely to go much beyond that. The advantage to Tunisia was that hard currency was not needed for products purchased in the East and also that these countries were often willing to buy such Tunisian products as might be difficult to place elsewhere. Several communist countries, including Yugoslavia and Czechoslovakia, had been granting Tunisia substantial credits for the purchase of their goods, interest charges being usually less than three per cent. Bulgaria seemed exceptionally active in Tunisia, considering the small size of this Balkan communist country. The Bulgarians had constructed the large Sports City in Tunis.

Tunisia opted to politically align itself with the West rather than the East during the Cold War. The still vigorous pursuit of co-operation with Eastern-bloc countries was never on the basis of ideological affinity but rather on the coat-tails of mutual advantage. Agreements with Yugoslavia, Poland, Bulgaria, Rumania, Czechoslovakia, and the Soviet Union were intended to improve trading possibilities and enlarge Tunisian options, not to indicate a political preference. Likewise Bouguiba's son was to tell the UN General Assembly in 1965 that, with regard to China.

Whatever the reservations which a number of us may feel about certain actions of the People's Republic of China, whatever some of us may feel about her international behaviour, it is nevertheless high time to allow this country, which is playing a big role in the world and which has acceded to the status of a nuclear power to take the place due to her among the member states. It is obvious that the absence of the People's Republic of China deprives us of the valuable contribution this country might make to the consolation of peace and security in the world.[88]

> On the question of the representation of China at the United Nations, Tunisia had remained silent and abstained from voting for its inclusion in the United Naions' agenda from 1956 to 1960, in deference to the West, particularly the United States. But she began to vote in favour of the participation of the People's Republic of China in the United Nations in 1961, the year when non-alignment became *de rigueur* in Tunisian foreign policy.[89]

Similarly, even though the Tunisian government had sounded off its intention to recognise Communist China since 1958,[90] it nevertheless refrained from doing so until 1964, when Tunisia became the tenth nation in Africa, after her Maghribian brother, Morocco and Algeria, to recognise it.[91] And this was done because of pragmatic considerations, not because of Tunisia's approval of Communist China's behaviour.[92] President Bourguiba bluntly told Chou en Lai, when he pledged to support China's admission to the United Nations, that some of Peking's attitudes "in all frankness and friendship have not failed to arouse doubts among us—whether it is a question of the United Nations, the resort to force to settle frontier problems or the Moscow (test ban) pact, which is regarded by almost all humanity as a promise of hope.[93]

Thus Bourguiba sought not to balance East and West but rather to extract the maximum possible from both, thereby reducing Tunisia's dependency on either. Even the pro-Western political alignment was as much about the latter's ability to contribute to Tunisia's modernisation as it was about any congruence of values or aspirations.

Tunisia and the United Nations

As regards the United Nations, Tunisia has been its staunch and loyal supporter since the day the small nation made its debut at the World Organisation in 1956, whereupon Bourguiba declared:

> ...although small, my country is firmly resolved to contribute, to the best of its ability, to the strengthening of the United Nations and the consolidation of peace so that the principles embodied in the Charter will cease to be meaningless platitudes but a living reality".[94]

Tunisia stood by its words. When the Congo crisis occurred in 1960, Tunisia promptly contributed a sizeable force (second only to India's) to the United Nations peace keeping force in the Congo.[95] As the situation enfolded resulting in bitter quarrel among United Nations members and slashing attack on it Secretary General by the communist and many African nations, Tunisia remained courageously firm in her support of the United Nations and its Secretary General. Speaking for Tunisia during the Fifteenth Session of the General Assembly, Ambassador reinstated that small states like Tunisia were interested in having a "coherent, strong and, in particular, an effective international organisation," and that Tunisia opposed "the division of the United Nations into three blocs, reduced to the status of offices or institutions. It was even more strongly opposed to the splitting of the United Nations executive into a sort of triumvirate.[96] This position was reaffirmed by

Tunisian Foreign Minister Mokaddem at the Sixteenth Session of the General Assembly,[97] and at the Belgrade Conference by President Bourguiba who declared:

> Despite its imperfections, the United Nations is the great hope of humanity, the supreme resort of small powers, the instrument without which there would be, among nations, only the law of the jungle.[98]

The importance of the United Nations in the foreign policy-making of Tunisia was described by Habib Bourguiba Jr. in the following words:

> The future of the United Nation—is most promising when it deals with the problems of the will of weak nations of the world because what it will undertake will not be questioned by the Great Powers. Everybody agrees that history is irreversible and that all nations should be political emancipated. The shrinkage of our world is also making, more and more urgent an active solidarity among nations, comparable to the solidarity among the citizens of a particular state. In promoting these two goals, no power and no regional organisation can replace the United Nations in the long run. Besides, while the U.N, is useful to all nations, it is most needed by the small and the weak, those who cannot take care of their own problems. It is better for them to accept an imperfect decision, than no decision at all.
>
> That is why we have dedicated all our efforts on the international scene to strengthening the UN. Our aim is to keep it working, whatever might happen. Because the more people are accustomed to it, the more they will need it, and the more powerful it will grow, for the benefit of all. This is the reason why we have always adopted moderate positions, with a better chance of acceptance, rather than extreme positions which would meet no wide approval but which would have given us the satisfaction to completely express our views".[99]

In sum, Tunisia having formally disengaged herself from any bloc commitment to be able to decide for herself "without any preoccupation other than that of preserving peace and international security, or of contributing to peaceful and fruitful co-operation between people."[100] Tunisia did not mean to have this freedom of action curtailed by her association with other non-aligned nations. Thus, at Belgrade, Bourguiba pleaded that the Conference should not be "regulated by a rigid system and permanent organisms which would make the non-aligned, sooner or later, a third bloc, supplementary factor of complications and antagonism.[101] But the preservation of the freedom of action was not the sole objective of Tunisian foreign policy. Tunisia regarded the adoption of non-alignment as a reaction to the rigid division of the world into two antagonistic camps, a sincere expression of "universal conscience, racked and tormented by the tragic prospects of human destiny,[102] and as the first step toward the creation of a *"force de frappe morale"* to reduce the danger of an ultimate collision between the two giants and to work for the accommodation between nations and for peace under law and justice.

References

1. Habib Bourguiba, Jr. *The Foreign Policy of Tunisia,* in Joseph E. Black and K.W. Thompson, eds. Foreign Policies in a world of Change (New York: Harper and Row, 1963) pp. 352-53.
2. Interview given to Thomas F. Brady of *The New York Times,* March 24, 1956.
3. H. Bourguiba, "Nationalism: Antidote to Communism", *Foreign Affairs,* Vol. 36, No. 4, July 1957, p. 651.
4. *The New York Times,* September 27, 1957.
5. *The New York Times,* September 19, 1957.
6. H. Bouruiba, "We Choose the West," *Orbis,* Vol. 2, No. 4, Fall, 1958, p. 316.
7. F. W. Blyden, III, "The Idea of African 'Neutralism' and 'Non-alignment'; An exploratory Survey", in Kurt London, ed., *New Nations in a Divided World,* (New York; Praeger, 1964), p. 156.
8. Speech at Sayda, November 13, *Embassay of Tunisia, Bulletin,* No. 23, November 21, 1958, pp. 4-12.

9. Address by President Habib Bourguiba, "Conference of Uncommitted Countries" (Belgrade, The Publishing House Jugoslavija, 1961), p. 12. *see also* G.H. Jansen *Afro Asia and Non-alignment* (London, Faber and Fabor, 1966) pp. 282-83, 385-86, 297.

10. *Conference of Head of State or Government of Non-aligned Countries, Belgrade September, 1-6, 1961,* (Belgrade, The Publishing House" Jugoslavija, 1961), pp. 73-81.

11. T. Hovet, *Jr., Africa in the United Nations.* (Evanston, Northwestern University Press, 1963), pp. 17-18.

12. C.F. Gallagher, "The Tunisian Way: Moderation and Progress in the Maghrib", *American University Fteld Staff Report (AUFS)* Vol. IX, No. II, Nov. 1963, p. 15.

13. Francis O. Wilcox, *UN and the Non-aligned Nations.* (Headlines Series, No. 155), (New York: Foreign Policy Association, 1962), pp. 28-29.

14. Secretariat of State for Information, *Tunisian-American Relations,* (Tunis: Tunisian Documentation Service, 1959), pp. 16-22.

15. C.F. Gallagher, *The United States and Africa,* (Cambridge, Mass: Harvard Unviersity Press 1963), pp. 234-235.

16. Secretariat of State for Information, *op.cit.,* n. 14, p. 39.

17. On the strategic importance of North Africa, Stephen B. Jones wrote: most intense colour should be applied to northern and north-eastern Africa, because of their location *vis-a-vis* Europe and south-west Asia, because they are part of the Moslem world, which extends into south-west Asia and includes the Persian Gulf oil fields, and because they flank the so-called British lifeline through the Mediterranean and Red seas". *(Africa and American Security,* New Haven; Yale Institute of International Studies, 1945, Mimeographed, p. 18).

18. Secretariat of State for Information, *op.cit.,* n. 14. p. 53.

19. *Ibid.,* pp. 58-60.

20. Gallagher, *op.cit.,* n. 15, pp. 238-239.

21. Secretariat for Information, *op. cit.,* n. 14, p. 16.

22. *Recent Development in Tunisia,* pamphlet published by the Neo-Destour of Tunisia, Paris, 1951, p. 18. Quoted by Lorna Hahn, "Tunisia: A Challenge to American Foreign Policy", *The Middle Eastern Affairs,* May 1954, p. 165.

23. Secretariat of State for Information, *op.cit.,* n. 14, p. 66.
24. Gallagher, *op.cit.,* n. 15, p. 239.
25. *The New York Times,* March 24, 1956.
26. *Keesing's Contemporary Archives,* November 8-15, 1956, p. 16485.
27. *Ibid.*
28. *The New York Times,* August 29, 1956.
29. *The New York Times,* March 21, 1956; US Congress, House of Representatives, *Report of the Special Study Mission to the Near East and North Africa,* Sub-committee on the Near East and Africa, 85th Congress, 2nd Session, Washington: Government Printing Office, 1958, p. 10.
30. *The New York Times,* July 10, 1956.
31. US Congress, *op.cit.,* n. 29, p. 10.
32. *The New York Times,* November 30, 1956; Gallagher, *op.cit.,* n. 15, p. 240.
33. Secretariat of State for Information, *op.cit.,* n. 14, p. 77.
34. *Ibid.*
35. *The New York Times,* December 17, 1956.
36. US Congress, Senate, Committee on Foreign Relations, North Africa and the Mediterranean, Report of Senator Mike Mansfield, 85th Congress, 2nd Session, Washington: Government Printing Office, 1958, p. 14.
37. The New York Times, April 3, 1957.
38. US Department of State Bulletin, Vol. XXXVII, No. 963, December 9, 1957, p. 920.
39. *Ibid.,* Vol. XXXVI, No. 930, April 22, 1957, p. 638. (Italics added).
40. US Congress, House of Representative, *op.cit.,* n. 29, p. 9.
41. *The New York Times,* May 11, 1956.
42. *Ibid.*
43. *Ibid.*
44. Habib Bourguiba, "We Choose the West", *Orbis,* Vol. 2, No. 4, Fall 1958, pp. 316-319.
45. James P. Richards (US Special Ambassador to the Middle East) said: "In car foreign policy, no Secretary of State or

Presidnet can ever forget that Bourguiba is a great statesman, that in his thinking and desires he is oriented to the West, that now and in the years to come he will be a potent figure in the final decision as to whether or not Africa will continue as a friend of ours and the West, *The New York Times*, November 17, 1957.

46. For details, see previous chapter on Tunisian's relations with France.

47. *The New York Times,* May 24, 1957.

48. Lorna Hahn, *North Africa: Nationalism to Nationhood,* (Washington: Public Affairs Press, (1960), p. 228.

49. *Keesing's Contemporary Archives,* (November 30-December 1957, p. 15883.

50. *Ibid.,* p. 15884.

51. *The New York Times,* September 25, 1957.

52. *The New York Times,* November 15, 1957.

53. *US Department of State Bulletin,* Vol. XXXVII, No. 962 December 2, 1957, p. 882.

54. The United States pledged to ship 500-M-l rifles and 50,000 rounds of ammunition, while Britain agreed to contribute 350 sterling sub-machine guns, 70 Bren guns and ammunition for both types of weapons.

55. Keesing's May 31-June 7, 1958, p. 16205.

56. Frank White, "Dilemma of a Leader Who Wanted to be our Friend," Life, February 24, 1958; p. 24.

57. *The New York Times,* March 19, 1958. Writing on Bourguiba's concern about Nasser's increasing influence among the Algerian leaders in 1958, Roger Stephane reported Bourguiba as saying:" ...What is going to be important is that the Americans understand this is the time to act on behalf of Algeria, otherwise the Algerians would swing to Nasser's side. Then what would become of Tunisia? What would become of Morocco? Do the Americans, does the Free World want to see the Republic of Nasser extend to Casablanca?"

58. *The New York Times,* March 21, 1958.

59. *Keesing's Contemporary Archives, op.cit.,* n. 55, pp. 16206-16207.

60. *The New York Times,* June 18-19, 1958.
61. *The New York Times,* August 13-16, 1958.
62. *The New York Times,* August 15, 1958; "Bourguiba's Speech at Sayda, November 13, 1958", Embassy of Tunisia, *Bulletin No. 23,* November 21, 1958, p. 2.
63. Bourguiba's speech at Nabeul, *op.cit.,* n. 62, pp. 9-10.
64. *The New York Times,* November 14, 1958.
65. *Keesing's Contemporary Archives,* February 7-14, 1959, p. 16637.
66. US State Department Bulletin, May 4, 1959, p. 637 and June 22, 1959, p. 920. Also: US Congress, Rouse Committee on Foreign Affairs, Activities of Private US Organisations in Africa. Hearings before the Subcommittee on Africa, 87th Congress, 1st Session, Washington: Government Printing Office, 1961, p. 229.
67. US State Department Bulletin, May 4, 1959, p. 637 and June 22, 1959, p. 920. Also: US Congress, Rouse Committee on Foreign Affairs, Activities of Private US Organisations in Africa. Hearings before the Subcommittee on Africa, 87th Congress, 1st Session, Washington: Government Printing Office,' 1961, p. 229.
68. *The New York Times,* December 20, 1959.
69. *US Department of State Bulletin,* April 18, 1960, p. 608.
70. Special Mission for Economic and Technical Co-operation, *op.cit.,* pp. 2-4. See also Habib Bourguiba, Signs of an Improvement in International Relations, Tunis: Secretariat of State for Information and Tourism, 1961, pp. 36-37.
71. Kennedy had said: "We have ignored the explosive situation in Algeria and neglected our anxious friends in Tunisia for too long, both in the United Nations and in our economic aid programme, while handling the Communists and the anti-American extremists every opportunity to pose as the champions of freedom." *The New York Times* (February 12, 1958).
72. *The New York Times,* February 6, 1961.
73. Bourguiba's speech to Joint Meeting of US Congress, May 4, 1961, Vital Speeches, June 1, 1961, pp. 487-489.
74. *Ibid.,* p. 488.

75. *US Department of State Bulletin,* June 5, 1961, p. 853.
76. *The New York Times,* June 28 and July 1, 1961.
77. *The New York Times,* July 1, 1961.
78. *The New York Times,* July 23, 1961.
79. *The New York Times,* July 21, 25, August 3, 4, 1961.
80. *The New York Times,* August 27, 1961.
81. Habib Bourguiba, *Explanations and Clarifications,* (Tunis: Secretariat of State for Cultural Affairs and Information, 1961), p. 39.
82. *The New York Times,* November 14, 1961.
83. *The New York Times,* July 29, 1962.
84. Howard Schissel, Tunisia Facing a Future without Bourguiba, *Africa Report,* Vol. 29, No. 6, November-December, 1984, pp. 68-71. *See also,* Richard B. Parker, Worth Africa: Regional Tensions and Strategic Concerns (New York, Praeger 1984), p. 60.
85. John Damis, United States Relations with North Africa, *Current History,* Vol. 84, No. 502, pp. 193-1961.
86. *Ibid.*
87. *Ibid.*
88. Pierre Rossi *Bourguiba's Tunisia,* (Tunis Editions Katha, 1967), p. 191.
89. The official position of the Tunisian government regarding the admission of Communist China to the United Nations was presented by Mongi Slim at a plenary meeting of the General Assembly of the United Nations. He said: "It is inconceivable that a country whose population represents one-fourth of the world population should continue to be barred from the deliberations and work of our Organisation.

    My Government, which has, hitherto, remained on the sidelines on this issue in the hope that an agreement would be reached between the parties directly concerned, feels that it must 'now reconsider its position and declare itself in favour of the participation of the People's Republic of China in the deliberations and work of our Organisations. *United Nations General Assembly Official Record (UNGAOR) Session, Plenary Meetings,* Vol. 1, New York, 1961, p. 301).

90. *The New York Times,* July 28, 1958.
91. *The New York Times,* January 11, 1964.
92. *Afrique-Action,* 9 Janvier, 1961, p. 6.
93. *Keesing's Contemporary Archives,* May 16-23, 1964, p. 20054.
94. Statement by M. Habib Bourguiba, Prime Minister of Tunisia, delivered at the Plenary meeting of the UN General Assembly, November 22, 1956. Publication No. 2, New York: Tunisian Permanent Mission to the United Nations, 1956, p. 4.
95. *The New York Times,* July 22, 1961.
96. United Nations General Assembly Official Record (UNGAOR), *Fifteenth Session,* (Part I), *Plenary Meetings,* Vol. 11, New York I960, p. 582.
97. Mokaddem's speech, *United Nations General Assembly Official Record (UNGAOR) 16th Session, Plenary Meetings,* Vol. 1., New York 1961, p. 297.
98. *Conference of Head of State or Government of Non-aligned Countries, op.cit.,* n. 10, pp. 73-81.
99. Habib Bourguiba Jr. *op.cit.,* n. 1, p. 372.
100. *Conference of Head of State or Government of Non-aligned Countries,* op.*cit.,* n. 10.
101. Mokaddem, *op.cit.,* n. 97, p. 298.
102. *Ibid.*

5 Economic Factors as the Determinants of International Relations

Before independence, Bourguiba and the Neo-Destour leadership saw their mission as one of educating the Tunisian masses in their own radical, modernising approach as much as one of convincing France to grant independence to Tunisia. This educational mission has continued to be a major concern of the regime after independence. The party and government leaders, Bourguiba foremost among them, have travelled the length and breadth of Tunisia to maintain direct contact with the people, to explain the regime's policies, and to preach the gospel of "radical economic and social change". The press and the mass media have spread the word, especially Bourguiba's speeches in which the President patiently explained his policies and exhorted his followers to a greater effort for the development of the country. A magnetic speaker, Bourguiba could use a vivid and earthy colloquial Arabic to hold the attention of his audience, as father, teacher, and spiritual leader. Bourguiba endeavoured to change the social mentality of his country through exhortation and example.[1] In this chapter, efforts have been made to analyse the challenges faced by the Tunisia for economic and social development of the people of country, because of the limited resources.

Bourguiba accurately sensed that this appeal would prove totally unsatisfactory to accomplish the concept of nationalism he envisioned. Although independence was certainly part of his plans, modernisation for Tunisia, rationalisation and action were equally important.

Bourguiba also sensed that his charismatic appeal was doomed to vanish, if it did not become identified with an ideology that would strengthen and preserve it. Also, whereas charisma could easily persuade the masses, a coherently formulated rational formula would be needed to attract the Tunisian elites. Ideology and charisma were meant to be mutually reinforcing with nationalism providing the element for better cohesion. This presupposed a "carefully thought out strategy of change, supported by an ideology that permits the insertion of innovation within a reassuring context of continuity and coherence.[2]

It also called for a leader who could organise the political system and transmit his political beliefs. Bourguiba's legitimacy had sufficiently been resolved before independence. What Bourguiba wanted in the future, however, was institutionalisation—a process that could only be achieved when the political structure is valued "not for what it does, but for what it is."[3] It is not surprising then that his early attempts were geared toward creating an ideology that would bring about his long-term objective. Characteristic of his nature, Bourguiba wanted an ideology that would reflect actual policy. He abhorred that peculiar type of rhetoric that becomes a ritual.

This pragmatic notion of ideology would prove to be an excellent device for effective social change. It also allowed Bourguiba to reinterpret events as they occurred in Tunisia, satisfying the divergent opinions of both masses and elites. Destourian ideology remained a method for political and social cohesion. Whereas, for example, Bourguiba had focussed almost exclusively on nationalism prior to the Bizerte crisis, he could easily shift his position and assert later that "the most urgent battle ... is the one we must wage against underdevelopment."[4] And although his appeals to the masses for independence were based on nationalism, he could assert to the Tunisian elites that the Tunisian struggle was "not led essentially in the name of nationalism, but in the name of an over powering desire for dignity."[5]

Bourguiba's ideology thus became an element of continuity. The combination of its three major elements—reason, human dignity and human solidarity—explains and justifies the dominant role pedagogy assumed in Tunisian life. His assumption was that since man is rational, education can lead towards modernity and good citizenship. The problem as the Supreme Commander perceived it was to try and raise the intellectual level until the masses equated general interest with their own interest.[6] He wanted to instill Tunisians with the notion that underdevelopment could be conquered through their own effort and intelligence. Mental structures needed to be changed before social or economic structures could be altered.[7]

The application of pedagogy for the purpose of obtaining consensus reached its apex at the time of the introduction of the Ten Year Plan in 1961. It constituted a systematic attempt to draw individuals and organisations into the consulting process, to explain the Plan and to elicit active support for the successful implementation of it. Bourguiba defended it against his critics—who regarded it as a aberration of the older Destour ideology, by pointing out that it did not signify a break with the past. On the contrary, it meant the rational pursuit of human dignity, the application of reason to society. As he was quick to point out, this "promotion of man" meant universal education, elimination of unemployment and equality of opportunity.

Foreign Policy and Politico-economic Agenda

Bourguiba's personal authority and the single-party system were able to elicit considerable popular support for Tunisia's foreign policy and to control what popular opposition existed. Bourguiba, thus, had a great deal of leeway to develop a policy of moderate goals and to apply it with tactical flexibility. Foreign policy was integrated with domestic policy, and both domestic and foreign objectives were compatible with the limited resources available to accomplish them.

The foreign policy of decolonisation and co-operation served the domestic objectives of the Neo-Destour regime: the consolidation of national independence, social unification and modernisation, and economic growth. The purpose of decolonisation was to force France to relinquish control of

Tunisian diplomacy, defense, financial and commercial institutions, the civil service, the judiciary, and the educational system.

Institutional autonomy was the precondition of economic and social reform. For example, economic planning was not possible as long as France controlled Tunisian monetary and commercial policy through the franc zone and the customs union. An additional advantage of the "battles" of decolonisation was the reinforcement of national solidarity in a period of rapid social change. However, Tunisia could not afford overindulgence in anti-colonialism because its plans for economic and social development as well as its independence and security depended on foreign assistance.

In the early years after independence, the regime carried out a series of bold social reforms: the elimination of the mammoth property, the emancipation of women, the unification and secularisation of the educational and judicial systems. French technical assistance was sought for the judiciary and particularly for education because rapid expansion of the modern school system was only made possible by the employment of French teachers. While attacking the traditional social structure, the regime accepted the existing economic system. It relied on private and foreign investment and tolerated the pattern of private ownership including foreign, primarily French, ownership of agricultural property, commercial and industrial enterprises.

When economic planning was adopted in 1960, Tunisian foreign policy reflected the new domestic policy. Priority was given to the search for sources of long-term public development assistance. At the same time, French domination of the commercial sector and French land ownership were no longer tolerable. Thus, economic decolonisation followed the completion of institutional decolonisation. The unilateral nationalisation of colon land in 1964 was primarily motivated by the requirements of economic planning rather than by domestic or regional political pressures.

Tunisian foreign policy was generally realistic in terms of Tunisian resources. The Tunisian leadership recognised Tunisian dependence on external assistance and tailored its policies to the requirements of French and Western foreign aid.

Towards New Society

Political independence from France did not precipitate immediate economic reform. Habib Bourguiba, promoted conservative strategies to permit a gradual adjustment to the loss of colonial skills and finance. The policy was moderately successful and decolonisation proceeded slowly with the departure of the majority of the large French and Italian populations over several years rather than months as had occurred in Algeria.

While no major attempt was made to reorganise the use of the country's natural resources or redirect the nation's economic orientation, major policies concerning the country's human resource base were introduced which had long-term consequences for the country's economy and particularly for the labour market. A Code of Personal Status was approved in 1956, which amongst other rights established a minimum legal age for marriage. Attempts were made to improve the status of women and an official family planning programme was launched. These changes combined with efforts to improve the distribution and quality of health and medical services resulted in a reduction in the rate of infant mortality, a lowering of the death rate and an increase in life expectancies.

The newly-established government also chose to allocate a large proportion of national resources (about one-fifth) of government spending to the improvement of education services hoping that this would lead in the long run to a more skilled and adaptable labour force. The impact of this decision was indeed substantial with enrollment in primary schools doubling and numbers in secondary schools quadrupling within a decade of Independence. While the benefits of increasing national literacy and importing other skills was undoubtedly very substantial the policy also stimulated problems for the future by raising the aspirations of the population and by creating a new demand for jobs in semi-skilled and skilled-professions which the nation would find hard to provide. Nevertheless, the overall result of these social and demographic policies must be accepted as beneficial to the Tunisian economy in leading to a vast improvement in the quality of the country's human resource base.

One crucial early decision determined the language of public instruction. Despite the status of Arabic as the official national language, government and party leaders recognised the importance of French as a bridge to the world beyond Tunisia and an essential tool for economic development. In any case, the country's reliance on a cadre of foreign instructors to supplement the 6,000 Tunisian teachers available at independence, and the disinclination to recruit educators from Arab countries with quite divergent political outlooks, made some instruction in French inevitable. Satisfied with the resulting bilingual system, the government made a commitment to eventual Arabization but took no significant steps in that direction. In primary schools the first two years were taught in Arabic, the remainder in French or a combination of the two languages. French was the norm at the secondary level, although the use of Arabic gradually became more common in subjects such as history, geography, and philosophy. This bilingual structure along with the paring down of religious instruction in the curriculum, left Zaituna graduates, many of whom traditionally pursued teaching careers, with few prospects in the post-independence education system.[9]

A second important decision concerned the method of promoting education. To fill the schools, government and party leaders preferred to utilise their considerable powers of persuasion rather than to make education compulsory. Enrollments at the primary level climbed steadily, eventually peaking at around 85 per cent of the boys and 70 per cent of the girls aged between six and eleven. A similar trend occurred in the secondary schools, except that attendance never exceeded 40 per cent of the twelve to seventeen-year-old population and only about a third of all students were women.[10]

To educate Tunisian women about the Personal Status Code, encourage them to venture beyond habitual limits, and offer them opportunities to improve their day-to-day lives, a number of women related to Neo-Destour leaders formed the *Union Nationale des Femmes Tunisiennes* (UNFT) in 1956. The party had some ties to the *Union Musulmane des Femmes de Tunisie,* an organisation founded in 1936 on the Salafiyya reform model, but had generally shown little interest in supporting such associations. In the 1930s most were too conservative for Neo-Destour tastes; in the post-war years, the most active groups were communist fronts. Beginning in the early 1950s, with more women taking more active roles in the nationalist campaign than ever before, they began creating networks of assistance for families whose men were in prison or had joined the *fellagha.* Some women also joined the guerrilia bands, while others provided information, served as scouts, or transported small arms, since French soldiers and policemen were unlikely to stop and search them. In 1955, a congress of three hundred women demanded civil and political equality with men, enfranchisement, the right to stand for elected office, and greater attention to female education, but the Ben Ammar government set the women's agenda aside while it focussed on bringing the protectorate to an end. The Neo-Destour, on the other hand, responded with the Personal Status Code and the UNFT. By 1960, the latter had almost 14,000 members in 115 branches.[11] In addition to promoting the Personal Status Code, particularly in rural areas where women and men alike had reservations about the reforms, the UNFT concentrated its initial efforts on urging women to exercise their right to vote, granted in 1957, on sponsoring literacy classes for the 96 per cent of the female population who could not read or write, and on developing health programmes, some of them devoted to family planning. In the decade between 1956 and 1965 women's literacy rose and their fertility fell, both quite dramatically. While by no means solely responsible for such reversals, UNFT members unquestionably contributed to them as the organisation's educational work benefitted tens of thousands of women in the early years of independence.

Hundreds of thousands of their daughters profited from party and government campaigns in favour of formal schooling for young women. Because a modern education had played so formative a role in the life of most of independent Tunisia's leaders,[12] they recognised the importance of expanding the state education system, aligning it with contemporary national needs, and drawing more students into it. In the past few girls had attended school, but Neo-Destour officials knew that providing girls with a modern education would influence the social values they would impart to their families when they became wives and mothers. In the mid-1950s, few women worked except in their homes and fields, but efficient economic development necessitated an increase in the number of women in the workforce and the opening of new sectors to their employment, thereby creating additional impulses to educate more females.[13]

Progress Toward Economic Autonomy

Tunisia, like other newly-independent non-industrial countries, could choose between two opposing economic strategies. On the one hand, it could continue to rely on French help to stabilise the economy and to finance economic development. This strategy of externally-supported development would entail the preservation of the colonial economic relationships, respect for French interests in Tunisia, and reliance on private capital and on foreign aid, primarily from the former metropole, to cover the balance of payments deficit and finance investment. On the other hand, Tunisia could aim for autonomous development through reliance on domestic resources, total or partial socialisation, authoritarian planning, diversification of the economy, mobilisation of the population for development programmes, and use of all fiscal and monetary tools to promote growth.[14]

The first strategy of externally-supported development was realistic in terms of Tunisia's scarce economic resources, its dependence on foreign skills, capital, resources and markets, and the French control of Tunisian commerce and finances. It was the safe approach because it did not call for the disruption of the existing economic pattern. However, the existing arrangement was the economic expression of colonialism, and its continuation went counter to the nationalist pressures for economic as well as political decolonisation.

Furthermore, the colonial economic relationship appeared to favour French interests over Tunisian ones. It held out little hope for rapid economic development or a more equitable distribution of resources and benefits among the population as a whole. Therefore, it is not surprising that the radical nationalist elite of Tunisia should be attracted to the strategy of autonomous development.

The Unsolved Problems

Although Tunisia had gained the right to have its own diplomacy carried out by its own diplomatic machinery, to organise its own police force to guarantee internal order of the country, Franco-Tunisian relationship was characterised by many unsolved problems.

At the wake of independence, Tunisia was still very much dependent on France culturally and economically. Its secondary and primary schools were heavily staffed by French instructors, and its higher education was completely French. The internal aspect of Tunisian economy was dominated by Frenchmen: they owned 750,000 hectares of the most productive lands and controlled the extraction of minerals, notably phosphates, zinc, iron, and lead the value of which amounted, in 1954, to 135 billion francs, or about one-third of the total value of Tunisian export. As Lovna Hahn describes this situation as follows:

> "of an approximately total of 4,700,000 hectares of cultivated or cultivable land in Tunisia, 1,300,000 hectares belonged to about 10,000 people, most of them Europeans. Forty-six per cent of the annual Tunisian wheat production, for example, was in the hands of some 3,000 colours. The situation regarding ownership

was considerably better with regard to Tunisia's major crop-lives-with ninety per cent of the trees being owned by Tunisians, rather than colons. However, a great difference in productivity between trees cultivated by Tunisians and those owned by Europeans existed here also. On the large European estates centred around Sfax, less than 2,000 families enjoyed an annual yield of approximately 2,532,000 bushels of olives, while smaller holdings of natives, centered around Sousse, produced some 2,800,000 bushels which were shared by some 100,595 families. European olive trees produced usually 2.8 bushels of olives per tree; the haphazardly raised Tunisian-owned trees yielded only 42 bushels each.

The other important aspect of the Tunisian economy, particularly from the standpoint of exports, is the extraction of minerals, notably phosphates (in which Tunisia ranks fourth in world production after Morocco), iron, lead and zinc. In 1954, for instance, the value of these four minerals totalled 135 billion francs, or about one-third of the total value of Tunisian exports. Control of these industries, however, was exclusively in colon hands, mostly the powerful Sfax-Gafsa and Djerissa companies. The sole benefit to Tunisians from their minerals on the eve of independence was approximately 4 billion francs a year, representing the total amount paid in wages to mineral workers; the rest of the nine billion francs went directly into colon pockets. Transformation industries, which could have provided both additional jobs and some income for the Tunisian budget, were never started by the French, the mine owners finding it more profitable to export crude ores, which were then refined in France. Because of such practices, Tunisia suffered perennially from an unfavourable trade balance, the value of her imports being worth approximately one-third more than that of exports.[15]

However, Tunisia at the time of independence lacked not only the resources but even the instruments of economic independence. The modern sector of the economy lay beyond the reach of the Tunisian government. French nationals owned 20 per cent of the cultivated land, and French companies controlled mining, large-scale industry, finance, transportation and power, and the export-import sector. French economic rights were guaranteed by the Conventions on Internal Autonomy, and French property was protected against expropriation. French dominance of Tunisian foreign trade was guaranteed by the customs union. By the pooling of all foreign exchange resources, by her acceptance of the French franc as her currency, and French foreign exchange regulations. In return, France promised to "facilitate the economic development of Tunisia by loans to the Tunisian Treasury or to Tunisian autonomous bodies, local authorities, and private enterprises" (Article 9, Economic and Financial convention).

The agreement of June 1955 was the "result of reciprocal concessions which allow the Tunisians to free their sovereignty from, the bonds which were paralysing it, and France to safeguard her higher interests and to guarantee the material and moral interests of the French in Tunisia", but in the words of the then Tunisian Premier, Tahar ben Ammar, it did not give "entire satisfaction to either side."[16]

As for Bourguiba, Tunisia's supreme combattant, he considered the final agreement as by no means representing Tunisia's ultimate goal, it nevertheless constituted a step forward. Again, at the first Congress of the Neo-Destour Party, as Sfax, he urged cooperation with France and acceptance of Mendes-France' s "revolution".[17]

Tunisian monetary policy was determined by its membership in the franc zone, the linkage of the Tunisian currency to the franc, and the role of a nationalised French bank, the Bank of Algeria and Tunisia, as the Central Bank of Tunisia. In the post-war period, the Tunisian budget was constantly in deficit. In exchange for its economic privileges, France promised in the Conventions to continue its policy of budgetary subsidies and loans for economic and social development.

A policy of autonomous development could not be carried out until the Tunisian government reacquired the means of making monetary and commercial policy and could exercise its authority over crucial sectors of the economy. However, a premature, unilateral abrogation of the Economic and Financial Conventions with France would have deprived the Tunisian economy of essential markets and capital. It would have alienated not only the French colons, who made a major contribution to the modern sector of the economy, but the Tunisian bourgeoisie as well, whose political support and economic contribution was important to the regime.

Faced again with the dilemma of the competing claims of independence and security, the Neo-Destour regime elected to accept gradual economic decolonisation while emphasising military decolonisation and political and social modernisation. The Algerian conflict did not fail to undermine Franco-Tunisian economic relations and accelerate the pace of decolonisation in this area. In addition, it became increasingly clear that externally-supported development would not stimulate rapid economic growth and significant improvement in the standard of living. Between 1956 and 1961, Tunisia retrieved the instruments of economic autonomy and in 1961 adopted a policy of economic planning. Economic planning and Destourian Socialism, in turn, required the completion of economic decolonisation, including the nationalisation of foreign-owned agricultural property. However, the first ten years of economic planning marked only the first steps toward self-sustaining growth, to say nothing of self-sufficiency, which was impossible for a country as poor in economic resources as Tunisia except at an unacceptably low standard of living.

Bourguiba's economic policy in the first years of independence reflected the strategy of externally-supported development. Bourguiba defended capitalism and private enterprise as the best means of attaining the investment necessary for economic growth. A policy of financial stability and balanced budgets was to attract private foreign investment. Tunisia also wanted public foreign aid, and French aid was considered the cornerstone of Franco-

Tunisian co-operation. Bourguiba hoped to diversify the sources of aid to include both Eastern and Western donors, thus lessening Tunisian dependence on France alone, the only qualification being the absence of political conditions. The conventions of 1955 were accepted, for the time being as the basis of economic and financial cooperation with France although Tunisian spokesmen indicated an interest in certain revisions. French property and investment were welcomed with the proviso that they conform to Tunisian national interests.[18]

Even within the Neo-Destour, there was opposition to the policy described above. The most opposition came from the UGTT, the national trade union programme for greater economic independence.[19]

The programme, presented at the UGTT Sixth Congress of September 1956, advocated global economic planning in a mixed economy with the aim of doubling the national income in ten years and structural reform including industrialisation and the creation of agricultural co-operatives. The UGTT proposed abrogation of the Economic and Financial Convention, the redistribution of large land holdings, specifically including colon land, the nationalisation of key industries, revision of Tunisia's relations with the franc zone, and the creation of a central bank and national currency. Although the UGTT spokesmen recognised that foreign aid, preferably multilateral, was necessary, they hoped that domestic resources would bear the principal burden of development.[20] For a while, there was talk of the formation of a second party, based on this platform and under the leadership of the UGTT Secretary-General, Ahmed Ben Salah. A series of manoeuvers led to Ben Salah's replacement by a more acquiescent union leader, who emphasised the professional rather than the political goals of the UGTT. However, both Ben Salah and the UGTT programme survived until at a more opportune moment, they were adopted by the government.[21]

The End of Decolonisation: Land Nationalisation

Tunisification, for the most part, was carried out gradually without any great difficulty. France accepted

Tunisia's need to control its own economy. Rather than resisting economic decolonisation, the French government sought guarantees for French property under Tunisian's sovereignty. Until 1964, agricultural decolonisation followed this pattern with inter-governmental agreements providing for the transfer of land to Tunisian ownership with compensation for the European owners. However, in 1964, the principle of decolonisation in co-operation with France came into conflict with the objectives of economic planning, and the latter took precedence. The Tunisian unilateral nationalisation of colon land completed the process of decolonisation but at the price of a severe disruption of Franco-Tunisian co-operation.

The colon farm was the very symbol of French colonialism in North Africa. Foreign ownership of 20 per cent of the best agricultural land was an affront to nationalist and egalitarian sentiments in a land in which tens of thousands of landless peasants flocked to the cities, and most of the rural population barely eked out a living on tiny plots of infertile land. Agriculture was the foundation of the Tunisian economy and land redistribution, the modernisation of agricultural methods, and the conversion of production to more profitable or essential crops were among the priorities of Tunisian economic planners, to which European land ownership was an obstacle.

One of the primary purposes of the 1955 Conventions was "to guarantee the rights and interests of the French residents in Tunisia..." The economic and financial convention exempted the landed property of French individuals and corporations and Tunisian corporations from any land reform.[22] Nevertheless, the recovery of colon land began soon after independence in response to political conditions rather than part of a coherent economic policy. The insecurity near the Algerian border led to the abandonment of some farms. Emigrating Europeans sold their property to Tunisians or entrusted it to the French embassy. In May, 1957, the two governments negotiated the first land agreement, providing for the transferral, at the expense of the French government of 127,000 hectares

(314,000 acres) in the border area to the Tunisian government for use in a programme for the development of the centre and southern regions of the country. The agreement was later extended to other areas of insecurity and to confiscated after the Sakiet crisis.

With these exceptions, the Tunisian government concentrated on the reorganisation of the archaic traditional land holding system rather than on the colon land and large Tunisian estates" which were both productive and politically sensitive. In March, 1956, public habus[23] (the revenues of which went directly to pious foundations) were abolished; in July, 1957, private habus were also abolished and the lands distributed among the heirs and occupants. In September, 1957, distribution of arable tribal land to individual ownership was made law. A true agrarian reform was implemented in the rich, irrigated Medjerda River valley under which land ownership was limited to less than 50 hectares. On May 7, 1959, law provided for the confiscation of insufficiently-exploited land and its distribution to landless individuals or small landholders. Both of these laws affected some European.[24]

It was not until late 1958, in a period of renewed co-operation with France, that Bourguiba raised the issue of a general recuperation of colon land. Political and economic reasons for the policy were evoked. Recuperation would reverse the Protectorate pattern of expropriation of land for the profit of France at the expense of the Tunisian peasantry. Just as France used land colonisation to guarantee its political influence in Tunisia, the Tunisian government wanted to recuperate the land to consolidate its sovereignty. Finally, all available uncultivated land had been redistributed, and the Tunisian people could no longer be deprived of the use of the rich colon land. Recuperation in co-operation with the French government and with indemnification of the owners would be spared over a three-to-five-year period in accordance with Tunisia's ability to exploit the land. Bourguiba exerted himself to reassure the colon population:

> The idea would never occur to us to deprive a "proprietor of his livelihood and throw him in the sea.... We intend on the contrary to respect the acquired rights of the French in this country. We do not intend to plunder them, but that does not mean that we are for maintaining them until the end of time. We envisage their transfer by legal means which exclude force, injustice or nationalisation... We shall only recover the properties ceded willingly and by means of a fair price.[25]

Nevertheless, the slow pace of negotiations provoked Bourguiba, in May, 1960, to threaten unilateral action on the land question, "in case agreement [with the French government] will prove impossible, the Tunisian State will assume its responsibilities: legislative measures would then be taken... which would guarantee the transfer of the 'colonial lands' by ways and means in effect in all countries.[26] On October 13, 1960, agreement between the two governments provided for the recuperation with compensation of 100,000 hectares (250,000 acres) by September 1, 1961. Additional blocks of 100,000 hectares were to be transferred annually.[27] At this rate, the approximately 300,000 hectares of French-owned land would have all been transferred to Tunisian ownership by the end of 1964. However, the Bizerte crisis sabotaged the 1960 Land agreement. In the aftermath of the battle, the Tunisian government confiscated 100,000 hectares of French land without French consent. Further negotiations on the land question were postponed until late 1962, when the Bizerte affair was officially closed.

Therefore, it was not until March, 1963, that the process of land recuperation was put in motion. A new Franco-Tunisian agreement provided for the recovery in 1963 of 150,000 hectares (including those selected in 1960-61 and 50,000 hectares confiscated after Bizerte).

The Tunisian government paid 10 dinars per hectare plus the costs of harvests and equipment, but the French government assumed responsibility for the greater share of financial compensation. The agreement provided for the recuperation of another 50,000 hectares in 1964. Those owners not affected by the agreement were guaranteed peaceful possession for a minimum of five years from the signing of the agreement.[28] In this and the earlier agreement, the French government recognised the necessity of land recuperation but protected the rights of French nationals by insisting on compensation and regular procedures.

The Tunisian government was apparently satisfied with this arrangement although it conflicted with the goal of total recuperation by the end of the pre-plan in 1964. Bourguiba stressed the economic reasons for recuperation and condemned spectacular agrarian reforms, the main purpose of which is political:

> [The partisans of Arab Socialism] demand agrarian reform. But, in fact, what do they understand by such a reform? Is it a question of enacting a law by the terms of which lands would be confiscated and distributed, their proprietors thrown in prison: such a spectacle would naturally excite the disinherited masses always susceptible to the spectacle of the downfall of the great or the rich. If it is thus, I would tell you frankly that I am not ready to make such "revolutions" which I consider as diversions although they are everyday occurrences in other States...
>
> What is important above all, it is not to put a Tunisian in the place of a French colon; it is necessary yet to maintain and if possible augment the level of production and more justly distribute the national income.[29]

The era of confrontation had ended with the Bizerte evacuation, and the long-delayed co-operation was initiated. Three agreements were signed in August. 1963, defining the status of the French community and its non-agricultural investments in Tunisia, the status of Tunisian emigrant labour in France, and the modalities of renewed French financial assistance.

The first sign of future difficulties appeared in late December, 1963, when France, because of its EEC commitments, unilaterally discontinued its subsidised purchase of Tunisian wheat. Ahmed Ben Salah threatened a response in kind:

> The French government attitude encourages us to pursue our policy of decolonisation. Also we must intensify our agriculture and convert it in terms of products and production cost...
>
> France did not consult us before making its decisions. We are not required to do so when we decide on the measures appropriate for compensating our losses.[30]

The matter appeared to be settled with the February signing of a financial aid agreement for 1964. An import credit of 110,000,000 NF and a long-term development loan of 100,000,000 NF were both raised 10,000,000 NF over the 1963 totals to compensate for the loss of the special wheat market.[31]

In this outwardly happy atmosphere, President Bourguiba's April 28, 1964, speech demanding renegotiation of the 1963 land agreement to relieve Tunisia of its share of the compensation costs came as a surprise. The invitation to negotiation was reinforced by a threat of unilateral measures which might "poison the atmosphere of co-operation." According to the Tunisian version, the French ambassador to Tunisia had been informed of the Tunisian desire for negotiations and had met with Bourguiba on this subject early in 1964. The Tunisians had "begged for negotiations, "but the Ambassador, acting like a notary public, had insisted on the inviolability of the 1963 contract, and refused to inform his government. Therefore, the April 28 speech was a last warning before Tunisia acted unilaterally. By April 30, the Cabinet had raised the stakes of negotiation from modification of the 1963 agreement to the "definitive liquidation of agricultural colonialism." The French Ambassador was approached a final time on May 8. The next day, the Political Bureau met; and the day after, the Cabinet, the Governors, and regional party officials. On May 10, the French government categorically rejected negotiations, and on May 12, 1964, the Tunisian National

Assembly passed a law nationalising (or as Tunisian authorities prefer, recuperating) all foreign owned land.[32]

The May 12 law completed the physical decolonisation of Tunisia by limiting agricultural ownership to "physical persons of Tunisian nationality or to co-operative societies." All agricultural societies, foreign or national, were outlawed. The recuperated lands were to serve as the nuclei for state-directed cooperative units of production.

The law, thus, went beyond decolonisation to a partial socialisation of agriculture. Most of the land was recuperated by the end of June, 1964. It amounted to nine per cent of the cultivated land of Tunisia and affected nationals of four countries: 230,000-240,000 ha. owned by French individuals and corporations; 60,000 ha. owned by Italians; 8,000 ha. belonging to Maltese; and 1,000-1,500 ha owned by Swiss nationals. The total land recuperation since independence equalled approximately 670,000 ha, (1,666,000 acres). Indemnification, in amounts determined by a Tunisian government commission, was provided for by the law. However, it was predicted that the Tunisian indemnification would amount to less than its 10 per cent contribution under the 1963 agreement. Bourguiba indicated that compensation would at best be symbolic and would not extend to the beneficiaries of official colonisation who "have been sufficiently compensated by the very numerous harvests that they have been able to amass."[33]

The 1964 land recuperation broke precedent with the earlier land transferrals which had been based on negotiated agreements and the consent of the owners and had taken the form of repurchase, although at prices below the actual value of the land. The French government refused to accept the unilateral nationalisation, even with indemnification. The Tunisian action violated the 1963 agreement, which provided for the peaceful enjoyment of the land for five years, and the French government refused to associate itself 'in any way with this illegal act. French retaliation extended to the whole range of Franco-Tunisian cooperation. The 1964 development loan was nullified although the import credits, which benefitted French industry, were untouched. The contracts of 61 agricultural experts were not renewed, and the French government waited until September to agree to the return of the French teachers for the new academic year. In June, 1964, the French government' announced its decision not to renew the 1959 preferential tariff agreement or the special purchasing arrangements for Tunisian wine. Thus, Tunisia was deprived of any preferential treatment in its most important market. In 1965, its exports to France fell by 33 per cent while its imports increased, and the commercial deficit with France rose by 61 per cent. The effects of land nationalisation were long-term since French financial assistance was not renewed until 1967, and friendly relations were not fully restored until late 1968.[34]

The Tunisian authorities denied any regrets about the land nationalisation policy and claimed that the costs in terms of Franco-Tunisian co-operation were the foreseeable and necessary price of de-colonisation and economic progress.[35] There is no question that the complete eradication of this last physical remnant of colonisation was the ultimate goal of Tunisian policy. In his May 12 speech, Bourguiba claimed that "all our misfortunes began with the appropriation of Tunisian land by foreigners," Land colonisation was the foundation of French political power in Tunisia, and its elimination was, therefore, an act of "legitimate defense."[36]

The Suspension of French Financial Assistance

The first step toward economic decolonisation was the direct result of Franco-Tunisian differences over Algeria as Guy Mollet, on the verge of defeat, announced a temporary suspension of aid to Tunisia to pressure Tunisia to adopt a position of proper neutrality on the Algerian question and to terminate its aid to the rebels. The French government had defended aid to Tunisia in 1956-57 against the criticism of the center and the right. It was argued that financial aid was a means of protecting French interests in Tunisia, preventing foreign influence in the former Protectorate, and avoiding severe economic problems which would injure the

French community as well as the native population. The government also expected a minimum of political co-operation in return. After months of delay, a financial aid accord was finally signed on April 20, 1957, providing for 15.1 billion old franca or $43.1 million in loans to Tunisia, of which 12.1 billion or $34.6 million for the public sector. A month later, Mollet suspended the aid because of Tunisia's attitude towards the Algerian problem.[37] His successor, Bourges-Maunoury, promised to reinstate aid to Tunisia and some 4.1 billion francs were delivered in late 1957.[38] No further financial aid agreements were signed until 1963 although technical assistance continued throughout this period. Thus, in the long-run, Tunisia suffered a considerable financial loss; the immediate effect of the Mollet gesture was to undermine the whole structure of economic and financial co-operation.

Tunisian acceptance of limitations on its economic autonomy depended on its receiving financial aid from France. According to Bourguiba, "The aid that they have threatened us with suspending was neither charity, nor a gift, but, the counterpart of important advantages accorded to France." Bourguiba rejected any political conditions attached to financial aid, "I have not hesitated to say that we would prefer to renounce all external aid rather than alienate our independence and our sovereignty." Specifically, Bourguiba refused to abandon the Algerian cause in the interest of foreign aid, "We are indefectably united with the Algerian people. We shall not agree, either for a credit, or for any other concession, to abandon it in a life and death struggle.[39]

Bourguiba claimed that Mollet's suspension of financial aid was a violation of the 1955 Conventions and that, therefore, Tunisia was no longer bound by their provisions. The Tunisian government was willing to maintain its co-operation with France by renegotiating Franco-Tunisian monetary and commercial relations on a basis of equality, taking into consideration Tunisian national interests. Otherwise, Tunisia was prepared to rely on domestic resources and, in any case, wanted to diversify its economic ties and "cooperate with all other countries and... accord to them the advantages until now reserved to France alone".[40]

Thus, it appeared that Mollet had squandered the patient work of three years and three governments for short-term political advantage. In fact, the Tunisian government did not have the means in 1957 to exploit the opportunity presented by French suspension of aid. Only the preliminary steps toward economic autonomy were possible: a policy of bilateral commercial agreements outside the customs union was inaugurated; a study was made on the creation of a Tunisian Central Bank; and official authorisation was required for all land transfers, including land owned by Europeans. To make up for the loss of French aid, the government allocated domestic budgetary resources for development projects, granted additional privileges for foreign private investment, and sought new sources of public foreign aid. Simultaneously, Tunisia called for renewed co-operation with France.

The major effect of the French aid suspension was to make the United States the most important source of financial support for Tunisia. In 1956, the French aid, the government accepted the principle of American aid to Tunisia, and Bourguiba treated, American aid as a supplement to French assistance.[41]

The 1957 aid crisis demonstrated the limitations of Franco-Tunisian economic co-operation. French devaluations in 1957 and 1958 convinced the Tunisian authorities that Tunisia needed to establish autonomous financial institutions and modify its relations with the franc zone. Tunisian monetary policy was determined by the Bank of Algeria and Tunisia (BAT), and the franc zone rather than the Tunisian government. The BAT functioned as the Tunisian central bank, printing the Tunisian francs, making advances to the Tunisian government, supervising Tunisian credit policy, and controlling foreign exchange transactions. The Tunisian government had no control over the BAT, which tended to follow the lead of the Bank of France. Tunisia's external finances were determined by its membership in the franc zone which required parity of the Tunisian franc with the French franc, free capital transfers between Tunisia and the rest of the franc zone, participation in a common pool for foreign exchange holdings, and central management of foreign exchange transactions.

In theory, Tunisia's membership in the French monetary zone insured greater monetary stability, relieved the pressure on the balance of payments, and created a favourable climate for metropolitan investment. Unfortunately, in the mid-fifties, France, itself, was suffering from inflation and balance of payments difficulties. In August, 1957, the French government decided on a policy of subsidising exports and taxing all but essential imports in what amounted to a selective devaluation of 20 per cent. This was a unilateral French decision, made on the basis of French interests. The Tunisian government was informed the day before the public announcement, but because of its membership in the franc zone, it was expected to implement the same measures.

Tunisian officials were unhappy about the French policy, feeling that partial devaluation would lead to inflation in Tunisia because of the great dependence on imports and would prevent commercial diversification since goods from France, unaffected by the import tax, would become relatively cheaper than foreign goods while Tunisian agricultural and mineral exports would not benefit greatly from the export subsidies. Despite these disadvantages, Tunisia had little choice but to go along with the French measure since a refusal would have been the equivalent of breaking with the franc zone, a step, which Tunisia was not prepared to take in 1957. The Tunisian reaction was limited to a mild protest about the French policy and the unilateral nature of the decision. In addition, France agreed to a Tunisian demand that certain imports necessary for Tunisian mass consumption and industry be exempted from the 20 per cent tax.[42]

Most significantly, the Tunisian government required the creation of a Tunisian central bank and national currency as the price of its compliance with the selective devaluation. The reasons for Tunisian emphasis on the central bank question were "threefold". In the first place, a national central bank through its control of monetary and credit policy was an essential instrument for maintaining economic stability and encouraging economic growth. The BAT "was criticised for lack of faith in the Tunisian government, reflected in a credit policy which discouraged productive investment and facilitated the flight of capital to France. In the second place, the establishment of the Tunisian Central Bank and the dinar would facilitate the separation of the Tunisian currency from the French in case of a future devaluation. However, the November, 1958, opening of the Central Bank did not alter the fundamental ties between Tunisia and the franc zone or the parity of the two currencies. At the time of its establishment the Central Bank and the minting of the national currency were primarily an expression of Tunisia's sovereignty like the establishment of the Ministry of Foreign Affairs and the national army. According to Bourguiba:

> The teaching to be drawn from this ceremony is that Tunisia is re-established in the full exercise of its sovereignty and that it is, henceforth, alone in managing its economy in order to put it at the service of the nation.[43]

The negotiations over the establishment of the Central Bank were prolonged, lasting for most of a year. Although the technical preparations were complete, the agreement was repeatedly postponed. The Franco-Tunisian differences over Algeria and military evacuation and French internal difficulties no doubt contributed to the delay. The BAT and other French economic interests were concerned about the transferral of monetary authority to the Tunisian government. Finally, in July, 1958, the new de Gaulle government intervened to expedite the negotiations, which had been conducted by officials of the Ministries of Finance, the BAT, and the Bank of France.[44] The Central Bank was opened in November, 1958, with the assistance of the French banks, in an atmosphere of cordiality.

The December, 1958, French devaluation presented Tunisia with the opportunity for a complete revision of its financial and commercial relations with France. On December 27, the French government devalued the franc and made it freely convertible with other international currencies. Once again, Tunisia was faced with the choice of following the French lead or striking out on its own by refusing to devalue. The first course posed the threat of inflation and even greater commercial dependence on France. The second course invited French monetary and commercial retaliation. Both Tunisia and Morocco chose at this time not to follow French devaluation. (However, Morocco did not otherwise revise its relationship with the franc zone, and in October, 1959, the Moroccan *dirham* was devalued by 20.44 per cent). Simultaneously, the Tunisian government announced a series of complementary measures to protect the Tunisian economy. The policy of free capital transfers within the franc zone was repudiated, and the Central Bank of Tunisia instituted a policy of restricted financial transfers. Tunisia also requested that its foreign exchange holdings be isolated from the franc zone common pool and be 'placed in a separate account. Thus Tunisia would be responsible for its own foreign exchange operations. The government requested that its holdings in francs be revalued to compensate for the Trench devaluation, and measures were taken to protect Tunisian exports from the adverse effects of non-devaluation. These policies accounted to a violation of all four requirements of franc zone membership. In addition, the Tunisian government proposed renegotiation of franco-Tunisian commercial relations because of French participation in the newly-created European Common Market.[45]

The reasons for these radical Tunisian policies were both political and economic. The creation of the Central Bank and the dinar had been a matter of considerable pride for the Tunisian regime. A decision to follow French policy and devalue the dinar less than two months later would have been an acknowledgement that despite these symbols independence, Tunisia was still economically dependent on

France.[46] Fortunately, economic arguments reinforced this nationalist response.

Economic experts of the Tunisian economy in this period endorsed the Tunisian decision to reject devaluation and, especially, to assume control of capital transfers. They upheld the government's reasoning that devaluation was inadvisable because it could cause inflation and greater commercial dependence on France while not substantially increasing the markets for Tunisian exports. The risk of French retaliation against Tunisian agricultural export was recognised, but the government and economists agreed that the circumstances were favourable for the necessary break with France. Tunisia had enjoyed extraordinarily good harvests in 1958, while its Mediterranean competitors had suffered from a bad agricultural year. The result was that for the first time in several years, Tunisia came close to closing the gap between its imports and exports with exports covering 99 per cent of imports. The promising commercial situation plus general financial stability convinced Tunisian officials that the time had come to sever the ties with the perennially unstable French economy. They did not foresee that this seventh French post-war devaluation would be the last for ten years after which France would enjoy a decade of financial stability and prosperity. In any case, the ensemble of measures proposed in December, 1955, and January, 1959, were prerequisites for the development of an economy independent of France. Business groups in Tunisia, especially producers of agricultural products dependent on French markets, were disturbed by the decision to break the economic ties with France. The regime, however, reinforced the economic arguments with appeals to nationalist sentiments, equating the "battle of the dinar" with the "battle of evacuation".[47]

French compliance was a more difficult problem. Revision of Tunisian membership in the franc zone and the customs union required French approval. Negotiations began in January, 1959, and continued until the summer. The major obstacle to agreement was the question of the special arrangements for Tunisian agricultural products under which Tunisian wheat and a quota of Tunisian wine were purchased at the domestic French price, higher than the world price. These arrangements were due to expire in June, 1959, and France opposed their renewal since, after the suspension of financial aid, they were the major French financial obligation to Tunisia. When Tunisia challenged other aspects of the economic union, France responded by refusing to bear the costs of these commercial arrangements.

The negotiations dragged on until August 20, 1959, when the Tunisian government unilaterally denounced the custom union. An independent tariff was established suitable to the needs of Tunisia's developing economy rather than the industrialised French economy: relatively high tariffs were imposed on competing agricultural and industrial products and on non-essential consumer goods while essential raw materials and capital goods were taxed lightly or not at all. However, Bourguiba gave the French government until October 1 to negotiate a new preferential commercial regime with Tunisia. At the same time, Bourguiba threatened to break with the franc zone entirely if Tunisian demands for revision of its relationship with the zone were not honoured.

Politically, these unilateral Tunisian actions served as effective bargaining points in the negotiations with France. On September 5, 1959, agreement was reached on all points. A new preferential tariff arrangement replaced the customs union. Most Franco-Tunisian trade continued to be duty-free and unrestricted, but the Tunisian government had gained the authority to determine Tunisian trade relations on a bilateral basis; without consulting France in the case of third countries. The purchasing arrangements for wheat and wine were maintained although the quota on wine was lowered, and the agreements became annually renewable and thus more vulnerable. In relation to the franc zone, Tunisia was given a special position: its holdings were placed in two separate accounts under Tunisian management although consultation with France and the franc zone was required if the deficits exceeded a certain amount. France also created an account to compensate for Tunisian export losses because of the 1958 devaluation although it refused to revalue the Tunisian franc holdings. Tunisia, thus, acquired a large degree of monetary independence while remaining within the franc zone.[48]

The September, 1959, agreement was a compromise, but Tunisia gained most of what it had sought in the way of institutional reforms, and most of its concessions were on questions of financial detail. Because of American financial support, the creation of autonomous financial institutions, and bountiful harvests in 1958 and 1959, Tunisia could afford to risk its commercial and monetary ties with France and therefore improve its bargaining position. The French devaluation and monetary liberalisation of December, 1958, and the establishment of the European Common Market reduced French dependence on the closed economic circuit of the franc zone, and therefore, a relaxation of commercial and monetary ties with-Tunisia as acceptable to France. By acquiescing in Tunisian demands, France was also defending its economic interests-among them the interests of French landowners and merchants in Tunisia, dependent on trade with France, and its long-term political influence in the former Protectorate.[49]

In spite of the establishment of autonomous financial institutions and the revision of commercial and monetary ties with France, the Tunisian economy continued to be heavily dependent on foreign support, especially that of France. After the two good years of 1958-59, the commercial deficit soared. Tunisia continued to show a substantial deficit in trade with France. Although the French share of Tunisian trade fell, it still represented half of Tunisia's foreign commerce. The Tunisian monetary position improved in the first two years after the acquisition of monetary independence and then drastically deteriorated until the crisis year of 1964, when fundamental reform including devaluation was required.[50]

Social Security Law

Bourguiba withstood challenges on the left of the Neo-Destour. In 1955-56, Ahmed Ben Salah, the Secretary-

General of the powerful UGTT, advocated a programme of economic nationalism and socialism which would have required the violation of the Economic and Financial Conventions with France and the nationalisation of French property. This programme threatened Bourguiba's policy of co-operation with France, and the prospect of the politicisation of the UGTT, which claimed 150,000 members in 1956, challenged the supremacy of the Neo-Destour. Bourguiba manipulated trade union politics in order to bring about the ouster of Ben Salah and his replacement by a loyal party militant. Deprived of his political base, Ben Salah accepted the post of Secretary of State for Social Affairs in 1957, and combined it with his Public Health Department. He wished to extend social security to cover maternity, health, and life insurance benefits, and to include other wage workers, notably in agriculture, industry and commerce. The UGTT had long urged these reforms, and the Neo-Destour Sfax congress had made a resolution in this direction. Helped by ILO studies, Ben Salah in early 1959 presented draft proposals to the government. His idea, revolutionary for a country accustomed to French social legislation, was to limit family allowances to cover no more than four children. A Cabinet Council meeting presided over by Bourguiba and including the UGTT and UTICA leaders discussed Ben Salah's proposals, but tentatively shelved them for further study. In the absence of necessary statistics, Bourguiba rejected the inclusion of pensions and invalids' benefits in the scheme.

After two months of technical drafting sessions at the presidency, the legislative draft was forwarded to the UGTT, UTICA, the chambers of commerce, European business directors, and doctors. Then for more than a year the legislation was stalled. At the Cabinet Council of October 24, 1,960, the draft law was formally approved by the government and submitted to the National Assembly for ratification. A separate law set up a commission of government officials, employers, and workers representatives to study the problem of pension and invalids benefits, and Thili hoped that within year, a pension scheme could be included in the social security system.[51]

Before the social security, law reached the Assembly, UGTT representatives and an expert from Ben Salah's ministry agreed at informal meetings to a number of minor changes. Benefits of the families of ill and deceased workers were slightly increased. Ben Salah approved of the modifications after consultation with Bourguiba. The Bureau of the National Assembly submitted the Bill to the Financial, Economic, and Social Affairs Commission, where the points of view of UGTT and UTICA, were again presented through their deputies. In a sense the passage of the law was a triumph for the UGTT over UTICA, for the latter had argued that Tunisia could not afford the luxury of extensive social legislation, while the former had long advocated a generalised social security system. UTICA was concerned about the small shopkeepers and artisans who could hardly afford to apply modem social legislation to their employees.

The final Bill, however, represented a compromise that UTICA was generally willing to accept, for its terms were favourable to important business interests. The law provided for an across-the-board salary raise of five per cent for all workers and employees. This would automatically be contributed to the social security fund, and business firms would contribute an additional 15 per cent of their workers' salaries to the fund. In the past, however, the mining industry had paid out roughly 27 per cent of the salaries to its social security fund, while the building industry paid 22.5 per cent. Ben Salah estimated that the law would save these two key industries, respectively, $600,000 to $700,000 and $500,000 annually. Other industries less important to Tunisian economic growth were harder hit, but the total business contribution was estimated at $700,000 less than under the previous system.[52] Certain categories of small shopkeepers and artisans were exempted from the legislation. In over-all benefits most workers made significant gains, while the rise in wages, not going into the workers' pockets, did not threaten inflation and, as *Tribune du Progres* cynically pointed out,[53] could be used as an argument against further wage increases.

The framing and passing of the social security legislation typified the process of consultation and compromise that characterised Bourguiba's rule. The UGTT must have made it amply clear to Bourguiba that the workers, with salaries blocked since 1954, were in need of some major "victory" like the social security Bill. In June, 1960, UTICS had secured its "victory" the passage of a law facilitating the dismissal of incompetent workers. Burguiba, thus, seems to have carefully balanced the demands of workers and employees. When once he had decided upon the General principles of the new legislation, the national organisations were allowed to participate in its elaboration.

Neo-Destour Socialism: The Birth of the Economic Planning

In early 1959, Bourguiba established a National Planning Council that included representatives of the national organisations and interested government departments.[54] Despite great fanfare, the Council met rarely and accomplished little, but it perhaps served, in Bourguiba's words, as a "psychological shock" to stimulate greater awareness of Tunisia's economic problems. A year later, after the nation's attention had been diverted to the problems of Sakiet Sidi Youssef, and 'the evacuation of French troops,' the battle of the dinar against the French devaluation served again to focus attention upon economic problems. Then the Neo-Destour congress in Sousse, March 2-5, 1959, defined the party's new mission: "To mobilise all the conscious popular forces and resources for economic growth and prosperity," and called for clearing up the "sterile and anarchical factors of the economy by the rule of a national Plan.[55] The New "struggle against under-development" became the nation's propaganda theme.

The decisive "psychological shock" came, however, in January, 1961, when, after months of rumours, Bourguiba officially appointed Ben Salah to head a new planning ministry. Even so, many businessmen, landowners, and politicians who distrusted Ben Salah's economic doctrines expected to be able to undermine his reforms. They privately argued that Bourguiba was showing himself to be progressive by using Ben Salah, but would then discredit and discard him, as in 1956. In response, Bourguiba publicly expressed his confidence in Ben Salah and articulated with increasing vigour a conception of planning and "Neo-Destour socialism."

At first, he simply defined planning, in Bourguibist fashion, as "an application of reason to action," to succeed "without recourse to constraint." He said:

> First, we should make an exact survey of our situation. Next, we should create the tools, the driving gear, the steering wheel... The people must follow every touch on the steering wheel, every change of direction, every instruction. Our goals should be clarified. Thus, what is required is a properly functioning machine which lights up our field of action with its headlights... It will still be necessary to ensure that the people sincerely and freely give their agreement and back-up their leaders.[56]

In June, he introduced the idea of "Neo-Destour socialism," defined as "the use of reason in the general interest." "If by bad management the farmer jeopardises his own affairs and the yield of his land, he will not be the sole loser. The whole nation will lose with him. We are all bound together. Thus, the concept of socialism takes on its full meaning." But Bourguiba added a note of rigor to the new idea by castigating wholesalers, who were dodging Ben Salah's price controls: "We will not hesitate to send these criminals to the gallows."[57]

Bourguiba tried to give his brand of socialism a religious coating by describing the Companions of the Prophet as "socialists before the invention of the word."[58] Put simply, national cohesion under Bourguiba was now to apply to economic as well as political matter. The Tunisian reaction was mixed. Price controls on basic food items, the first tangible impact of economic planning before the Plan was officially accepted, aroused much opposition. Wholesalers and shopkeepers often refused to sell commodities in scarce supply. During Ramadan (February-March), 1962, there was a severe shortage of eggs, nominally consumed in quantities during this month of evening feasts. The poor suffered because shopkeepers said they could no longer afford to extend the customary credit.

By 1962, however, Bourguiba had dashed the hopes of those who opposed Ben Salah by committing his own prestige to the latter's efforts. In March, he declared: "I personally claim responsibility for the Plan and control its application. Nothing in this field is done without my consent.[59]

In fact, however, even as Bourguiba tried to convince the people of the merits of his basic political decisions, he left open for discussion and consultation the practical reforms and economic decisions that the option for planning entailed. It was Ben Salah's task to draw up concrete proposals that everyone, including skeptical businessmen and landowners, could be persuaded to accept.

In the meantime, the Three-Year Plan was being drafted on the basis of the consultations. On March 17, 1962, the Cabinet Council approved the Plan and submitted it to the Neo-Destour National Council on March 20. After four days of discussion, mostly in commission, the sixty-five delegates gave the Plan and the seal of party approval. Modifications, if any, were minor, but the Plan was then sent to another consultative body before being submitted to the National Assembly.

On May 30, more than a year after Ben Salah undertook his first consultations, the Three-Year Plan reached plenary, Bourguiba's entire cabinet attended what amounted to a formal ceremony. The commission reports were read, and only one deputy made an intervention, asking Ben Salah a question about credit facilities. The Plan's three-year investment funds were unanimously voted.[60]

The Three Year Plan, envisaged an annual growth rate of six per cent, that would increase self-sufficiency, raise living standards, and begin to achieve an equitable distribution of income. Limited structural reforms anticipated state intervention in critical, but previously neglected, sectors of the economy, such as industry; bringing foreign-owned enterprises under Tunisian control (the last stage of decolonisation); and the establishment of a network of agricultural cooperatives. Carrying out so ambitious an agenda demanded greater investment in the economy than had previously materialised. From the early 1960s to the end of the decade, the proportion, of gross domstic product (GDP) represented by investment climbed from 10 per cent, to 23 per cent, but reliance on external loans and grants for more than a third of the financing of development projects during those same years created great difficulties.[61]

Three-Year Plan, 1962-5, was followed by a four-year plan, 1965-68 (after which further four-year plans have been devised). The objectives of the plans have been set out in the humanitarian terms of Destourian socialism: the aim of development is the welfare of man, for the benefit of all social classes in proportion to their efforts and also their needs. The first plans also set four broad objectives of economic and social development: decolonisation; reform of economic structures, including industrialisation; human development, including education, the training of cadres, and the fight against illiteracy and unemployment; and self-development, so that investment can come from internal resources and not be dependent on foreign assistance.[62]

The relative success or failure of the economy over the early years, difficult to calculate with precision, since much of the investment of the period was long-term and its impact was interrupted by the upheaval of 1969-71. But Bourguiba discribed the outcome of these plans in following words.

> Our achievements since independence are encouraging. In 1956 our G.N.P. was not above 265 million dinars ("$508,800,000); in 1965 it reached 435 million ($835,200,000). Before independence its annual rate of growth was only 2.5 per cent, just matching population growth. From 1960 to 1964, it rose at the rate of 5.5 per cent yearly and last year at 6.5 per cent, in conformance with the Four Year Plan of 1965-68. In

the last few years domestic savings have grown considerably. Between 1960 and 1964 they grew 86 per cent. Although capital formation represented only 10 per cent of G.N.P. in 1956, it is now 23 per cent, a rate generally observed in rapidly developing nations. Substantial growth has been accompanied by far-reaching structural reforms.[63]

The Co-operative Experiment

Immediately after the country achieved its full independence in 1956, the socialist path was adopted by the Neo-Destour Party[64] for economic and social development. But this socialism was considered to be authentically Tunisian as it was based on co-operatives that would be generalised to embrace all sectors of the economy excepting the heavy industries and public utilities. Out-right state ownership of the means of production was ruled out as alien to Tunisian heritage and mentality. From the official point of view, the essential was not the ownership of the means of production, but their utilisation in order to optimise output in a manner that would be more effective in serving the interests of the nation and in improving the lot of the lower income groups.

It was intended that co-operatives should play an important political and social role in the development of the country. It was also expected that the system would provide the key to a range of economic problems and would bring about a far more efficient mobilisation of the country's resources.

The first co-operatives were officially set up in 1960. These included production co-operatives in fishing, handicrafts and building industries, and service co-operatives in trade and agriculture. The creation of the first production co-operatives in agriculture occurred in 1962, the year the first development plan of 1962-1964 was inaugurated. The production co-operatives created in the agricultural sector between 1962 and 1968 were established wholly or partly on government-owned land.[65]

They were contemporaneous with the first Three Year Plan and with the beginning of the ten-year perspective of 1962-71 and were seen by Ben Salah as a means to achieve the objectives of these plans—an increase in the real rate of growth of NGP, self-sufficiency in cereals and other foods, a higher domestic saving ratio,[66] a surplus in the foreign trade balance, and a higher level of employment.

By the late 1960s, co-operatives accounted or more than one-third of Tunisia's cultivable land and employed almost one-third of the rural population.[67] The co-operative system seemed particularly appropriate to agriculture, where, it was hoped, it would both replace the private enterprise of the departed French fanners and provide the framework for the development of underdeveloped lands in the south. By 1965, the government had become a major land-holder. The land acquired by purchase or nationalisation from the French was added to habus land which had been brought into the public domain immediately after independence. None of this land had been disposed of permanently, although some was rented and some had been allotted to impecunious small purchasers on an installment plan (which the government could terminate).[68]

Consequently, these large farms became the nuclei of the agricultural production co-operatives. They were nuclei in the sense that the co-operatives included also the surrounding small plots owned by Tunisian peasants. These plots were either considered as forming part of the co-operatives with their owners being included in the membership, or that they wore simply rented from non-participating members.

The most favourable circumstances for the development of the co-operatives appeared to be in the north, where a fonner French estate could for the nucleus, to which smaller Tunisian holdings would be attached.[69] The members of the co-operative would then be the former small owners whose land was attached, and the workers who had previously been employed on the estate (who rarely felt that any change had, in fact, occurred). In practice the problem of welding

Table 5.1: Number of Agricultural Co-operatives Created Annually and their Area in Hectares

	Production Co-operatives		*Polyculture Co-operative*		*Commula-tive Total*
Year	*Number*	*Area*	*Number*	*Area*	*Hectares*
Dec. 1962	15	10,211	—	—	10,211
Dec. 1963	81	64,249	—	—	74,560
Dec. 1964	51	39,560	14	45,310	159,430
Dec. 1965	66	72,000	26	108,100	339,530
Dec. 1966	88	1,18,120	33	99,900	557,550

Source: John L. Simmone, "Agricultural Co-operatives and Tunisian Development", *The Middle East Journal,* Vol. 24. No. 1. 1970.

together small holdings and a large estate was greater than anticipated. There was no legal compulsion to join co-operatives at the same time, the movement had no roots in Tunisian popular culture and had never been the object of any spontaneous demand from the people. The creation of the co-operatives, and adherence to them, followed from government decision implemented by the administration, intermingled with the Neo-Destour Party. This constituted a formidable apparatus of bureaucratic direction and pressure which obviously weighed on small rather than large farmers. Many small farmers, no doubt, joined in a spirit of compliance or belief in Bourguiba's leadership. But they were often apathetic, or when hard-pressed resorted to the peasant's natural resistance to authority is non-cooperation.[70]

Large landowners either remained outside the co-operatives or received rent for the portion of their land which was incorporated.[71] Much bureaucratic energy was employed and no co·operative could be started outside the government's framework or without the proper planning and technical study. But the men who formed the bureaucracy, whether of party or state, lacked agricultural skill and sensitivity to the experience and wishes of those they administered. Even they lack the ability and the will to enlist the support of peasants in a scheme so incomprehensible to them, when their real wages were no better than under the colonists, and there was no freedom to cultivate private allotments.

Government credit policy gave priority to loans to the co-operatives. But to the extent that this policy was successful it immobilised funds instead of using them creatively. The Agricultural Bank was the main instrument of this policy, although it was independent of the ministry of finance. Traditionally, an important part of its loans were made at seed time and recovered with the harvest. But the co-operatives ran at a loss, although this fact was never publicly admitted, so that they accumulated an increasing debt. The total outstanding debt of the agricultural sector to the banking system doubled from 5.5 million dinars in 1960 to 11 million in 1966, and doubled again to 22 million in 1969.[72] Initially (until foreign aid was sought), these resources were inevitably diverted from elsewhere in the economy; notably loans to private farmers declined from 2.2 million dinars in 1964 to 1.6 million in 1968—whether through shortage of credit, or the disincentive to large farmers caused by the threat of the co-operative system.

Meanwhile, the co-operatives often used credit to pay a full labour force even when work was not available, and lacked funds when it was; or used credit for the wrong purpose and were denied further sources. If bad management was a major factor in the weakness of the co-operatives, the pernicious practice of pretending that all was well in spite of the widespread knowledge of failure aggravated the problem. It inhibited enquiry into the source of failure and made kow-towing to the requirements of a regional government authority, the most important criterion for survival in management.[73]

However, things became different after 1968. Here, it was a matter of imposing the co-operatives on individually owned and largely developed land. To its owners this land was not only a source of pride and income, but more so it represented most of their wealth and savings. As with all agrarian societies, land is the most important form in which the rural population tend to hold their wealth. Land would be bought, or sold, whenever they had an excess, or are in urgent need of cash. The imposition of co-operatives of the type created in Tunisia had the effect of making every land owner, big or small, feel that he became a pauper overnight.[74]

The attitude of the population towards the co-operative was very much reflected in a considerable destruction of the country's animal wealth. The farmers, expecting that their animals would be absorbed by the co-operatives, started a wave of selling immediate the generalisation move was put into effect. This selling in a heavily glutted market resulted in about 80 per cent fall in the prices of the animals that could be slaughtered for meat such as sheep and cattle, while in the case of horses and mules there were hardly any buyers. These low prices induced farmers and non-farmers alike to slaughter animals, particularly sheep and store their dried meats for future consumption. There was also a considerable smuggling of animals into Libya and Algeria.[75]

Many farmers concluded that, rather than improving their lot, the co-operatives left them worse off. To maximise state profits, the government paid artificially low prices for goods from the co-operative, resulting in a decline in their producers' real income. With reason, the peasants regarded the city-dwellers enjoying lower food prices as the primary beneficiaries of the system. The economic gap between rural and urban areas widened as the government continued to provide advantages to the restless, potentially more troublesome urbanites at the expense of rural interests.[76] To worsen the farmer's plight, the loss of their land and their animals left them with no other option than to sell their own labour in circumstances, they could not control the financial onus imposed on Tunisia by collectivisation contributed significantly to the experiment's ultimate collapse.

Ben Salah insisted on pursuing his policies despite mounting opposition and their obvious shortcomings. His decision to collectivise the rich olive groves owned mostly by middle-class Sahil farmers sent shock waves throughout the private agricultural sector. The Planning Ministry's 1969 announcement that it was taking steps to bring all cultivable land under state control raised a popular outcry that Tunisia's leaders could not ignore. The government backed away from the proposal and, more important, allowed farmers to withdraw from the co-operatives. Virtually all did. The decimated co-operative system was reduced almost overnight to the state-owned land of former colon farms.[77]

Bourguiba was anxious that blame for the problems associated with the co-operatives fall outside the presidential palace, charged Ben Salah with deliberately misleading him and subordinating the well-being of the rural population to his zeal to collectivise agriculture. Bourguiba claimed to have discovered that the co-operative, programme was really very unpopular with the people, and that Ben Salah had concealed the truth from him in order to build up his personal power.[78] Rumours that Ben Salah had condoned corrupt practices within the Planning Ministry further undermined his position. But perhaps Ben Salah's most serious offense in the eyes of the political leadership was his alienation of many long-time supporters of the Neo-Destour, especially workers, peasants, and small business people.

The Trade Union Movement and Bourguiba's System

Bourguiba's success derived in the first place from a sense of strategy and a clear vision of the future possibilities for Tunisia. In retrospect, it is easy to discern mistakes of strategy and judgement, of which his direction of the economy and his dealings with Ahmed Ben Salah are the most important. But he has had the talent of taking a long view and the stamina to move gradually towards the objective. He has combined forceful reasoned argument with rhetorical appeals to popular audiences (with a sense of theatre from which ham is not always absent), and has combined an authoritative presence with manipulative skill in the operation of the political system.

The first and hardest fought contest within the party started before independence, Salah Ben Youssef's opposition to Bourguiba stemmed from more than a tactical difference over the acceptability of the conventions of 1955. Although Ben Yousselfs regional support was strong, Bourguiba's overall command of the party was more powerful, the more so since the mass of the trade union movement, led by Ahmed Ben Salah, supported Bourguiba. In October 1955, the political bureau of the Neo-Destour Party expelled Ben Youssef from the party; the following month a party congress was called to meet in Sfax, where Jerbian (and therefore Youssefist) influence was weakest. The congress gave overwhelming support to Bourguiba.[79]

Tunisia was outstanding for the strength of its trade union movement at independence. Ferhat hached had shown organising skill in this area as Bourguiba had in the Neo-Destour Party, and had mobilised a membership of some 150,000. The vacuum in the leadership created by Ferhat Hached's assassination was filled in 1954 by Ahmed Ben Salah. A generation younger than Bourguiba.

The termination of the Youssefist split and the grant of independence quickly opened the way for the differences between Bourguiba and Ben Salah to emerge. Bourguiba's political objectives were to unify the party on the broadest possible base, to secure a virtual monopoly of power for it, and not to risk national unity or foreign investment by radical economic change. Ben Salah, in contrast, spoke of the nationalisation of all resources and proclaimed the need for a socialist plan for development and for the deployment of the UGTT as the 'national instrument of social and economic revolution', the disruption of the policy of gradualism, the possible danger to relations with France, and the bid for the union movement to direct social and economic policy were all unacceptable to Bourguiba, and the danger seemed the greater as the trade unions supported agricultural strikes.

However, Ben Salah's leadership of the UGTT was challenged within the movement by Habib Achour, who lacked Ben Salah's advanced education and distrusted his ambitions. Achour, who had been a colleague and friend of

Hached, led the Sfax section of the UGTT and played an important part in the UGTT strike of August 1947. His consequent imprisonment made possible Ben Salah's ascent in the movement, without his having participated in the heroic days of 1947.

Ben Salah's bid for position reached its peak at the sixth congress of the UGTT in October 1956. The economic report presented to the congress was an outline project for a planned socialist economy. The congress was showed by a secession from the UGTT led by Achour, who established the *Union des Travailleurs Tunisiens* (UTT). In December 1956, while Bell Salah was away in Casablanca discussing Maghrib trade union affairs, an unannounced meeting of the executive of the UGTT dismissed him and appointed Ahmed Tlili in his place. In September 1957 the break away UTT rejoined the UGTT.

In this way, the trade union movement was brought within the Bourguiba system, with a great economy of effort for Bourguiba, who had succeeded in exploiting rivalries within the movement. The victory thus achieved was demonstrated when the UGTT was forced, some years later to take an independent line on narrower issues; as the devaluation of the dinar cut real wages. In 1965, while Ben Salah was minister of national economy, Achour and Tlili were manoeuvred out of leadership of the UGTT and new statutes for the UGTT were devised, making clear the subordinate role which the organisation was to play in the state.

The relationship between the Tunisian government and the union leadership knows both periods of successful co-operation and strong opposition. Yet, it is yet too early to forget either Ahmed Ben Salah's efforts in the 1960s to make the UGTT give up its class-specific character and "put the organisation at the service of the nation"[80] or the bloody clashes between workers on strike and the police as well as the imprisonment of the UGTT Secretary General Habib Achour by President Bourguiba in the 1970s, when the government felt that the growing influence of the UGTT leaders and increased labour militancy represented a threat to its authority.

Politicisation, Co-operation and Development

The development programme for the countryside was built around the new co-operative system. Co-operatives were used in all sectors of economy, including marketing, credit, consumption, commerce, and agriculture. The rural activity will be emphasised here because it was in the provinces that the full organisational and political implications of the co-operatives became apparent, particularly in the northern provinces of Beja and Kef where large tracts of land formerly cultivated by the French were rapidly converted into production co-operatives. The initial strategy was to devise a regional plan for a valley or watershed area, often conforming to a sub-provincial area called a delegation, and establish a *Union Regionale de Developpement* (U.R.D.). The U.R.D. was to co-ordinate all co-operative activity at the regional level and obviously was well-suited to work alongside the party organisation in the same area. At the level of the province, a *Union Regionale de Co-operatives* supervised all co-operative activity and served as a co-ordinating body between government technicians and the local structure. The Governor was chairman of this group, as he was also of the party's Committee of Co-ordination.[81] As this structures took shape Tunisia acquired an organisational network reaching into the lives of ordinary citizens that probably had no equal in Africa.[82]

The critical programme in the extension of developmental activity to the general population was that of co-operatives. It is relevant to note here that although the party structure extended to the grassroots, it had never been a mass party. Indeed, had the party structure devised for the developmental push been in place before Ben Salah's programmes began to take effect, the party organisation might have immediately resisted the co-operatives and similar efforts to build more complex organisational links. As it worked out, and as appears in other developing countries energetically engaged in development, the new provincial Committees of Co-ordination were part of a reorganisation from the top downward, which, though begun before the plan was drawn up and Ben Salah installed, were implemented while his ministry was implanting the new institutions for development. The urban population was well-organised for developmental purposes, but the rural population for the most part had only emotional links with government.

The co-operative programme can be viewed as an effort to link these patriotic ties to the political system, and to convert them into working relationships with definite organisational significance to the participant. In turn, the citizen was expected to contribute more effectively to the solution of the problems confronting the country. In any event, the leadership may have been propelled more quickly into building rural co-operatives than anticipated, and the co-operative sector of the development plan was rapidly expanded to maintain agricultural production.

Despite the pressures on the Tunisian elite to resolve their differences in the higher councils of the party and government, development at the rate envisaged and with the structural changes advocated, generated severe strain for the political system. Mestiri preserved the dignity of the party by concealing his objections to the growing influence of Ben Salah, but it was widely reported that he felt that the new commercial code was issued by the President without being properly discussed and reviewed by the Political Bureau.

The unfolding of the crisis at the higher levels of the party is difficult to trace, but several unusual events took place over the period. Both the National Council of the Plan and the Central Committee of the party met many times. Both these organisations are essentially second echelon groups for the communication of new proposals and plans to party regulars in direct contact with the top elite of the country. The Central Committee was established in the 1964 Congress as an interim-representative body between full party congresses, and very likely continued to include a number of provincial and regional party militants, who are critical of Ben Salah's reforms.

In typical Bourguibist style the President recalled Ben Salah's early deviance from the party line in 1955 and spoke of Ben Salah's departure from the approved forms of Destourian socialism, with paternal disappointment. The attack mounted when Ladgham addressed the Assembly to accuse Ben Salah of 'hiding his actions, diluting national options, and abusing his power' in a way that endangered the entire nation. For the first time, the co-operative scheme was clearly identified as the root of official discontent.

In sum, in many respects Tunisia may be considered a special case among developing countries, but it may nevertheless be useful to examine her experience over the past several years for the more general conflicts that may recur in the development of African and Asian countries. The intensive programmes to establish new institutions or increase productivity inescapably have political effects, though these repercussions are most often conveniently omitted from both, the national elite's designs and also the elaborate justifications produced by international and foreign sponsors of change. The omission is by no means explained away by methodological difficulties even though it is much easier to calculate the rate of return on the investment in a new factory than its effects on the labour movement, the community, and an endless number of additional stresses and strains created, for the social and political system. For different motives officials tend to agree on neglecting the political dimension, the national elite because it is awkward, if not uncomfortable, to raise problems of leadership recruitment and evaluation in a strong hierarchy, and the foreign elite because international etiquette makes this delicate ground.

The problem is also complicated by the necessity to reverse the usual order or priorities in our analysis if we wish to anticipate the effects of widespread social and economic challenge on the political system. As individuals are affected by the benefits of change, their political expectations and interests will in many respects be diversified and articulated much like the material products of their labour. Political activity will become differentiated and the psychological, distance between ruler and ruled will be diminished. The role of leadership is inescapably affected, particularly where the elite is accustomed to the many precautions that preserve unanimity and restrict open criticism, like those found in Tunisia. The demise of the co-operative programme, which may well have been an economic failure, must also be seen as a leadership crisis for the country, a crisis that may have a number of explanations.

The first and most simple, of these is that Ben Salah managed to deceive and mislead the entire nation, which is ridiculous. If the elite was indeed so thoroughly, subjected to the President's decision to back Ben Salah that they could not ask questions and examine the results of development, the decision-making structure of Tunisia was lacking and the responsibility for errors must be shared. At the worst, Ben Salah's misdeed was to use the old Destourian pattern for making decisions while building new grassroots institutions, whose participatory structure contradicted the elitist structure of the centre. Because his manoeuver coincided with increasing concern among the elite over the succession of power in Tunisia, the entire developmental effort of Tunisia was momentarily called into question and its implications were more carefully examined. But it is absurd to censor Ben Salah for doing what any leading politician in Tunisia would surely do himself, build a platform to acquire the Presidency.

The second explanation might be at the organisational level, and it is here, the delicate relationship between the party and development may be introduced. There should be no illusions that if Ben Salah felt capable of seizing the party from within by using the positions under his control, he would very likely have done so. The scope of the co-operative programme was such that this was indeed imaginable and some of the most bitter attacks from the old elite were based on these grounds. But the Socialist Destourian Party, and quite possibly similarly dominant parties in other states, are continually faced with the challenge of specialised institutions increasing their influence as social change takes place. The rationale for a single party state is not demolished by raising the question of how new political norms are to be reconciled with party solidarity. But the co-operative programme did threaten the essentially middle-class base of the party, and it is significant that it was only when energetic reforms were begun in the historic strongholds of the party, Jabeul and Sousse, that the organisation rallied to destroy Ben Salah. The pitfall of the Destour, and very likely of similar regimes, was that the leaders' attention was heavily concentrated on the central hierarchy and the intense jockeying for favour in the succession process. The result may be that new forms of participation and new kinds of involvement in the party were resisted in order to preserve the familiar, collegial pattern of control from the center. If political relationships can only be regulated through a single organisation, the ability of the country to make decisions in an ever-expanding field of social and economic complexity will be gravely impaired.

The third explanation joins the problems of party control and developmental management. The process of social and economic change means individual change in the final analysis and the effective political system must devise ways of acquiring accurate and prompt feedback as its policies are implemented.

Granting that the elite was successfully isolated by Ben Salah and also that their action to preserve party dominance was justified, there remains the problem of how to know what is happening at the grassroots of society. The fact that thousands of Tunisians could be driven to desperate acts by an official policy without the system responding to these strains stands as an indictment against the entire machinery of the government and the party. Better accountability and statistical reporting are no doubt needed, but these issues may be a convenient subterfuge to avoid the larger issue of how the party organisation and developmental activities will be sensitised to the socio-economic effects of development programmes. The engineering of agreement prior to major decisions is naturally easier in a smaller and relatively homogeneous country, but will it suffice for activities that bring the people directly into the process of change?

In this context, succession problem becomes most acute for the Socialist Destour and for other single-party states. If feedback needs to be explicitly aggregated and weighed, the facade of spontaneous and acclamatory solidarity, so essential to the preservation of party dominance, must be sacrificed, or at least modified.

References

1. Clement Henry Moore, *Politics in North Africa: Algeria, Morocco and Tunisia,* (Boston, Little, Braun and Co. 1970), p. 96.
2. Charles A. Micaud, Leadership and Development: The Case of Tunisia *Comparative Politics,* Vol. 1, No. 4, 1969, pp. 468-84.
3. Charles A, Micaud, Politics in North-Africa, *Africa Today,* Vol. 18, No. 4, Oct. 1971, p. 61.
4. Jean Lacouture, *Quatre Hommes et Leurs Peupes: Sur-Pouvoir et Sous-Developpment,* (Paris: Editions du Seuil, 1969), as quoted in Dirk Vandewalle, Bourguiba, Charismatic leadership and Tunisian one Party System, *Middle East Journal,* Vol. 34, No. 3, Summer 1980, pp. 149-59.
5. *Ibid.*
6. Charles A. Micaud, *Leadership and Development, op.cit.,* n. 2, p. 471.
7. Therefore, the reluctance in the 1956-1962 period to introduce new economic and social structures. Not only were the masses unable to absorb these changes mentally; the institutionalisation of Bourguiba's ideology and charisma was not yet strong enough to risk upsetting the temporary unity that had been attained in the struggle for independence.
8. Kenneth J. Perkins, *A History of Modern Tunisia* (Cambridge : Cambridge University press, 2004), p. 139.
9. *Ibid.*
10. Kenneth J. Perkins, *Tunisia: Crossroads of the Islamic and European World,* (Boulder, Co: Westview Press 1986), p. 120.
11. Kenneth J. Perkins, *A History of Modern Tunisia, op.cit.,* 8, p. 138.

12. Between 1955 and 1969, 63 per cent of them were graduates of the Sadiki College, while 14 per cent studied at the Lycee Carnot and 15 per cent more at other Lyce'es and colleges offering a European education.
13. For more details of education programme see Tunisia', in Coleman (ed.), *Education and Political Development (Princeton,* Princeton University Press, 1965), pp. 144-68.
14. Charles, A. Micaud, Leon Carld Brown, Clement Henry Moore, *Tunisia: The Politics of Modernisation,* (New York, Frederick A., Praeger 1964) pp. 131-39.
15. Lorna Hahn, *North Africa: Nationalism to Nationhood.* (Washington, Public Affairs Press, I960), pp. 215-16.
16. *Keesing's Contemporary Archives,* July 2-9, 1955, p. 14290.
17. *The New York Times,* November 16, 1955.
18. Kenneth J. Perkins, *A History of Modern Tunisia, op. cit.,* n. 8, pp. 126-29.
19. Charles A. Micaurd etc *op.cit.,* n. 14, p. 100.
20. *Le Petit Matin,* October 17, 1956, as quoted in Clement Henry Moore, *Tunisia since Independence: The Dynamics of one Party Government* (Los Angeles, University of California Press, 1995), p. 87.
21. Charles A, Micaud etc. *op.cit.,* n. 14, p. 132.
22. "Tunisia Faces the Future", *Le Monde Economique* (June, 1956), pp. 172, 203.
23. The "habits" is essentially a system of land or real estate endowment made under moslem law on person and their descendants, or public institutions, such as mosque, schools, and hospitals. The person making the endowment determines the beneficiaries and the manner of benefit, but the hobous itself can neither be sold nor transferred except when the named beneficiaries disappear altogether, in which case the hobous reverts to the state to do with it as it sees fit.
24. Charles A. Micaud. ed. *The Politics of Modernisation op.cit.,* n. 14, pp. 9-63.
25. *Le Petit Matin,* December 12, 1958.
26. *Ibid.,* May 26, 1960.

27. *Ibid.*, October 14, 1963.
28. *Jeune Afrique,* March 11, 1963, p. 24.
29. Bourguiba, *Vers unsocialism authentique* (Tunis: March 2, 1963), pp. 16-17.
30. *Le Petit Matin,* December 28, 1963.
31. Les accords Franco-Tunisiens du 25 fevrier 1964", *Maghreb,* No. 2, (March-April, 1964, p. 10.
32. Interview with Habib Bourguiba, Jr. Tunis, May 22, 1969; *L'Action* (Daily), April 29; May 1, 10, 11, 12, 1964.
33. Habib Bourguiba, *Liberation of the soil: an essential element of our national sovereignty and pre-requisite of our development,* (Tunis: May 12, 1964), pp. 23-24.
34. *Maghrib,* No. 4 July-August, 1964, p. 8.
35. Interview with Habib Bourguiba, Jr., Tunis, May 22, 1969; *L'Action* (daily), March 26, 1966.
36. Bourguiba, *Liberation of the Soil, op.cit.,* n. 33, pp. 8, 17.
37. Claire Sterling, Habib Bourguiba: Revolution and Responsibility, *The Reporter,* September 5, 1957, p. 22.
38. *Keesing's Contemporary Archives,* Vol. 11, November 30 - December 7, 1957, p. 15885.
39. Bourguiba's speech delivered to the Constituent Assembly, May 27, 1957. *The New York Times,* May 29, 1957.
40. *Keesing's Contemporary Archives,* November 30-December 7, 1957, p. 15885.
41. American Aid to Tunisia has been discussed in chapter 4.
42. Mansour Moalia, "Quelges aspects de l'experience Monetaries Tunisienne, *Aspects of Perspectives,* New Series, No. 5, March 1961, pp. 8-11.
43. Government Tunisien. *La Gataille economique: Propos du President Habib Bourguiba* (Tunis, 1960), pp. 63-64.
44. *L'Action* (weekly), July 28, 1958, p. 6.
45. Government Tunisien, *"La bataille eeconomique", op.cit.,* no. 43, p. 39.
46. *Ibid.*
47. *Le Petit Matin,* December 31, 1958; January 9; February 5, 1959, *Ibid.,* pp. 35, 38-39.

48. *Ibid.*, pp. 91-92, *see also L'Action* (Weekly), June 3, 1957, p. 8. *Le Petit Matin,* August 11, 22; September 16, 1959.

49. *Le Petit Matin,* August 21, 1959; Ayari.

50. Moalla, *Aspects et perspectives, op.cit.*, n. 42, p. 17.

51. *La Presse* October 26, 1960 as quoted in Clement Henry Moore. *Tunisia Since Independence: The Dynamics of One Party-Government, op.cit.*, n. 20, p. 192.

52. *Ibid.*, p. 194.

53. *Ibid.*

54. Charles A. Micaud etc. *op.cit.*, n. 8, p. 134.

55. Neo-Destour Covenant, Passed at the 1959 Congress, as quoted in Clement Henry Moore, *Tunisia Since Independence op.cit.*, n. 20, p. 196.

56. *Ibid.*

57. *Ibid.*

58. Some modernist Tunisian intellectuals have tried to draw connections, while others have argued that the modern socialist's tie to Islam is sentimental at best. 'Solidarity and equality are values common to both ideologies, and each might be reinterpreted in the intellectual, context of Tunisia. As yet, however, "Islamic socialism" is not an articulated ideology. Perhaps it summarises aspirations that remain confused.

59. Habib Bourguiba, Speech of March 12, 1962 on the occasion of cabinet change *Keesing's Contemporary Archives* March 31-April 7, 1962, p.18681. Bourguiba implied another reason-behind his option for 'socialism'— the experience of Egypt before the 1952 military coup: "With our rapidly growing population, the rising generations are exerting pressure on us. If we are not careful now, in ten or twenty years time there will be a marked disproportion between the national income and the number of people we have to feed. A race against the clock is going on between our economic development and the demographic increase. Unless we take, as of today, the necessary measures, the country in a few decades will experience serious convulsions. The disinherited will find leaders to express their grudges. Their children, brought up in hatred, will infiltrate the ranks of the army. Then one day at dawn, they will try to seize power and

arrest the Head of State, Sovereign or President of the Republic with his ministers. They will want to put all end to corruption. The national resources will have become too small for a vastly increased population. The new masters, once faced with the difficulties of power, will look for diversions. The whole thing will become nothing but an adventure." *See also* Kenneth J. Perkins, *A History of Modern Tunisia, op.cit.,* n. 8, p. 146.

60. *The International Herald Tribune* (Paris) May 31, 1962.

61. Kenneth J. Perkins. *A History of Modern Tunisia op.cit.,* n. 8, pp. 147-48. *The Plan Decennale* gives a description of the development of the Tunisian economy from 1950 to 1960, outlines the general goals to be achieved by 1972, and then indicates the necessary 'structural reforms' for details see also *Perspective Decennales de Developpment, 1962-1971,* Republic of Tunisia, Secretary of Planning and Finance (n.d.), pp. 69-110. Also *Plan de Developpment Economique et Social 1969-72,* Republic of Tunisia, Secretary of State for Planning and Finance, pp. 14-17.

62. Wilfrid Knapp, *North West Africa: A Political and Economic Survey,* 3rd Ed. (London, Oxford University Press, 1977), p. 381.

63. Habib Bourguiba, The Tunisian Way, *Foreign Affairs,* Vol. 44, No. 3, April 1966, pp. 483.

64. The name of the Party was subsequently changed in the 1964 congress to Socialist Destourian (PSD).

65. Abdessatar Grissa regards this as one or the most important, though least publicised objectives of the co-operative policy, and reports: "There have been profitable co-operatives, particularly in wholesale and retail trade but they rarely distributed any dividends to their members. These profits were often invested in other enterprises, such as hotels, without the co-operative members being even informed, Abdessatar Grissa, *Agricultural Policies and Employment: Case Study of Tunisia* (OECD, 1973,) pp. 69-96.

66. Wilfred Knapp, *North West Africa: A Political and Economic Survey, op.cit.,* n. 62, p. 382.

67. Kenneth J- Perkins *Tunisia: Crossroad of the Islamic and European World op.cit.,* n. 10, p. 134.

68. The early phase of the co-operative programme is analysed in Douglas E. Ashford, 'Organisation of Co-operatives and the Structure of Power in Tunisia', *Journal of Developing Areas,* Vol. 1, 1967, pp. 317-32.

    On the eve of independence the total agricultural area classed as hobous covered some 1,150,000 hectares, of which about 150,000 hectares were public hobous, and the rest were either for the benefit of private individuals, or mixed of public and private.

    However, the hobous land was either badly utilised or neglected altogether, and this especially in the case of public hobous. With the abolition of the hobous the government assumed the maintenance of those institutions that are considered on social and historical grounds, worth maintaining.

69. Abdessatar Grissa, *op.cit.,* n. 65, p. 74.
70. Wilfered Knapp, *North West Africa, op.cit.,* n. 62, p. 383.
71. Kenneth J. Perkins, *Tunisia op.cit.,* n. 8, p. 134.
72. Addessatar Grissa *op.cit.,* n. 65, p. 82.
73. Wilfered Knapp. *North West Africa, op.cit.,* n. 62, p. 384.
74. Abdessatar Grissa *op.cit.,* n. 65, p. 86.
75. *Ibid.,* p. 87.
76. Kenneth J. Perkins, *A History of Modern Tunisia op.cit.,* n. 8, p. 151.
77. *Ibid.*
78. Edward Mortimer, Tunisia: Why The Socialist Experiment has failed *The Times* (London), September 28, 1978.
79. *The New York Times,* November 16, 1955.
80. Eva Bellin *Civil Society Emergent? State and Social Classes in Tunisia* (Princeton, Princeton, University p. 267). (Ph.D. Dissertation).
81. Lars Rudeleck. *Party and People:. A Study of Political Change in Tunisia* (Stockholm, Almnquist and Wiksell, 1967), pp. 103-04 *see also* Bourglas E. Ashford *National Development and Local Reform: Political participation in Morocco, Tunisia and Pakistan* (Princeton, Princeton University Press, 1967), pp. 6093.

82. The major exception might be Algeria where the farmers seized the land at independence. One of the curiosities of the Tunisian experience is that they could embark on so ambitious a scheme without learning from the Algerian precedent.

6 Conclusion

Like many other the protection of national objectives of Tunisian foreign policy have been the preservation of sovereignty, the promotion of national progress, and the preservation of human dignity. The distinct characteristics of Tunisian foreign policy have to be found in the specific problems she has had to confront and in the method she adopted to achieve her ultimate goals of foreign policy.

History, geography, and culture have been chiefly responsible for the existence of the specific problems of Tunisian "foreign policy in regard to France, the United States, the Maghrib, the Middle East, and Africa. The problems of Franco-Tunisian relations, for example, were deeply rooted in history, while cultural orientation has been the main basis for Tunisian relations with the United States, and geography was principally responsible for the existence of African problems in Tunisian foreign policy.

In tackling these problems, the predominant characteristics of Tunisian foreign policy have been moderation and pragmatism. Undoubtedly, the frequent resort to negotiations as opposed to the use of force to achieve the goals of Tunisian foreign policy may be attributed to the fact that Tunisia is a small country with insignificant military power, yet one should not lose sight of the deep-seated preference of the Tunisian leaders for negotiated settlement to military solution, their willingness to make concessions and to accept compromises, and their success in solving the outstanding problems of external relations by peaceful methods.

The pragmatic aspect of Tunisian foreign policy has been amply demonstrated by its adjustments to African awakening, to the problems of the cold war (the adoption of non-alignment), and to the outcome of the leadership conflict in Algeria, etc. Yet, these adjustments have been dictated by logic; therefore, Tunisian foreign policy has been conspicuously devoid of emotionalism, xenophobia, and opportunism. Tunisia adopted non-alignment but did not buy its anti-Western aspect. On the contrary, she remained courageously faithful to Tunisian-American friendship when anti-Americanism had become a vogue elsewhere. And Tunisia's sophisticated, restrained and impartial approach to the Suez crisis, the Hungarian affair, the Goa incident, and the Cuban conflict in the midst of emotional agitation in other small and developing nations has clearly established the political and diplomatic maturity of Tunisia and her unwavering adherence to principled convictions.

Pragmatic adjustment to new conditions of international politics and unwavering adherence to high principles have become the hallmarks of Tunisia's foreign policy and distinguished it from that of many other small and developing nations. They also show how much the style of foreign policy of a small and developing nation, like Tunisia, is determined by her decision-makers.

As such, the foreign policy of Tunisia is identified with President Habib Bourguiba and he can be considered as the sole decision-maker of Tunisia's Foreign Policy. Bourguiba was a revolutionary, a noble one. He was a Muslim who believed in the modernisation of Islam in the tolerance of religion. Not only does Bourguiba wanted his country to be a religious cross-road, he also wanted it to be the meeting ground of East and West. Cross-cultural experience has motivated his favourable disposition towards a French-led community (wherein all states are independent; linked, together only by freely entered economic and cultural conventions), a Franco-Maghrib Federation which would maintain for "white Africa its Western vocation, its Euro-African orientation and which would be-for Black-Africans a relay point of Western values."[1]

Although Bourguiba always holds a prejudge favourable for his opponent, and compromising in tactics, he is absolutely firm on principles. The essential characteristics of Bourguiba's strategy is the constancy of objective and flexibility of means of achieving it. In the struggle against France, he had never hidden his aim which was the independence of his country. He candidly admitted that independence would not be absolute and it should reconcile with interdependence, but he wanted to get for Tunisia gradually and persistently all the sovereign attributes of independence. In working toward his uncompromising aim, Bourguiba prefers negotiation, tactical compromise, to fighting. He used to say:

> We prefer to abandon war and accept what France offered stage by stage. If I accepted, it was because one is unable to predict the results of war. Many know how to enter a war, but few know how to end one.[2]

In effect, Bourguibist strategy was an "art of seizing the opportunity, and to make the best use of it" a "combination of pressure and concession". It emphasises on tactical concession and insists on gradual pressure to use each little gain as a stepping stone for getting another until final victory. The French colons label it "ask-for-an-inch-and-take-an-ell" tactic; Gallagher calls it:

> that political art of stepping stones, which makes each one gained the jump-off for another, and whose mixture of insistent optimism, compromise, a realism often end(s) by hypnotising or wearing down the listener into agreement that Bourguiba solution is the least bad of all solution.[3]

Bourguibism excludes hasty, unthought-out actions. It presupposes cool analysis, the use of logic, the consideration of the "laws of psychology".

To foreign policy analyst, Bourguiba was a perspicacious decision-maker who had the strong backing of his internal community, a tough negotiator who knows what he wants and was ready to fight for it, a loyal partner who was dedicated to high ideals, a convincing debator known for his clear and realistic analysis, and a skillful strategist who was flexible in means but persistent in aims.

In International politics, Bourguiba is known for his intellectual attachment to France and the Western world, his dislike of repressive political doctrines, his paternalistic attitude towards the African states, his suspicion of Egyptian ambition, his pride in his people and his country, and his desire to serve as a link between the West and the African world. Reflecting his own personal preferences and experiences, foreign policy under his rule was unmistakably secularist, modernising, westward looking, and realist.

For Bourguiba, the French legacy was almost as much a part of the Tunisian identity as was Arabness. Bourguiba also viewed Tunisia as having a unique identity among the Arab states. While others in the region were expressing their nationalism through a specifically Arab prism. Tunisia, according to Bourguiba was unable to separate this identity from the many others that had been absorbed from the various conquering forces. According to him, these had given Tunisia a greater propensity for openness to the outside world. The country had less difficulty in accommodating itself to relations with the West, and was generally less constrained in its external relations. Unlike many of his Arab-nationalist allies, Bourguiba thus had no problem in developing his relations with the United States. He had personally recognised the importance of the United States early on in his efforts to win independence from France. During the occupation by Axis powers, he had called on Tunisians to unreservedly support the Allies and in 1946 he had embarked on a "hand-shaking" visit to New York and Washington, much to the opposition of France and the embarrassment of the United States, but nonetheless staking his claim to U.S. friendship. The rewards came quickly. When France suspended financial and material assistance to Tunisia during the Bizerte crisis, an Anglo-U.S. alliance filled the gap. In 1961, Bourguiba embarked on a tour of English-speaking countries that included making an address to the U.S. Congress, where he was warmly welcomed by

President Kennedy. This friendship with Washington was ultimately to come under pressure from Arab quarters. Tunisians were themselves uncomfortable with U.S. support for Israel (especially when Israel invaded Lebanon in 1978 and 1982) and with its war in Vietnam, and outraged by the U.S. raid on Libya in 1986. Nonetheless, the incentive of U.S. military aid to help buttress Tunisia against possible Algerian or Libyan territorial ambitions proved sufficient to keep the regime closely aligned to Washington.

Bourguiba's Tunisia also had an ambiguous relationship with the wider Arab world. Prior to independence, the country was under the spell of Nasser's Egypt and Bourguiba was eager that he should be seen as a committed and competent Arab nationalist. He was unable to reconcile himself, however, to Nasser's geo-political visions for the region, especially when it came to Arab policies toward Israel and Nasserist conceptions of Pan-Arab unity. In February 1965, he proclaimed that, whole Israel was a danger, even a catastrophe for the Arabs, "the negative attitude of the Arab leaders has no effect but that of strengthening the status quo.[4] He criticised Nasser's aggressive rhetoric, arguing that negotiating with Israel would be more productive for the Arabs, managing thereby to endear himself to the West while engendering hostility toward his government in the Arab world. What he argued was his realism was also reflected in his attitude toward Arab unity. Again he rejected Nasser's grandiose visions.

He was to come similarly into conflict with Nasser over their respective positions in Africa. Tunisia's priority was to support African struggles for independence (for example, intervening in the Congo, and cutting off diplomatic relations with Southern Rhodesia in 1965). With pragmatism again in mind, Bourguiba initiated efforts to develop franco-phonic African co-operation through an economic organisation. His efforts to develop hinterland markets for Tunisian goods would in theory unite black and white Africa. Nasser was meanwhile making his own bid for leadership through the Afro-Asian Peoples' Solidarity Conferencc, which first met in Cairo in 1957. The organisation was fiercely anti-Western, was sponsored by the Soviet Union, and was viewed by Bourguiba as an attempt by Nasser to turn the Maghrib into little more than a political appendage to the Arab East. Bourguiba found some sympathy among sub-Saharan Africans, who were willing to go along with the pro-independence rhetoric, but who found the violent denunciations of Israel and the United States less relevant to their own, Pan-African, positions. The rivalry between Bourguiba and Nasser, led the former to boycott sessions of the Arab League and the latter to denounce him for it as a lackey of the West.

One of the principal reasons for Bourguiba's reluctance to be drawn into Nasser's orbit was his conviction that Tunisia's best interests lay in developing globally good relations, dealing as comfortably with the developed world as with the underdeveloped. Since military and political alliances would, in the Cold War epoch, reduce a nation's capacity for making friends, they were to be avoided and pragmatic neutrality pursued as often as possible. International organisations such as the United Nations were, therefore, viewed as a positive force, providing small states with voice and some degree of protection in international affairs.

Arab states often found Bourguiba's diplomacy disconcerting. While politics dominated their international agendas from early in their independent lives, Bourguiba quickly determined that political economy should guide Tunisia's policies. Realism and enlightened self-interest predominated over any ideological persuasion and the Ministry of National Economy frequently had as much input into foreign affairs as the ministry directly responsible. For that reason above all, Tunisia opted to politically align itself with the West rather than the East during the Cold War. The still vigorous pursuit of co-operation with Eastern-bloc countries was never on the basis of ideological affinity but rather on the coat-tails of mutual advantage. Agreements with Yugoslavia, Poland, Bulgaria, Rumania, Czechoslovakia, and the Soviet Union were intended to improve trading possibilities and enlarge Tunisian options, not to indicate a political preference.

Business had also dominated Tunisia's post-independence dealings with other Western European states, although none of those nations has approached France in terms of the magnitude or intensity of its contacts with Tunisia. In addition to attracting Western European investors, Tunisia, has benefitted from economic aid contributed especially by West German and the Scandinavian countries, as well as from the stream of European tourists. Tunisia has also cultivated European markets for its products and its excess major force. Italy has been the major continental consumer of Tunisian goods, but during the 1980s, EEC Import restrictions and the entry into the Common Market of southern European countries producing goods similar to Tunisia's have reduced the volume of exports across the Mediterranean.

Thus, Bourguiba sought not to balance East and West but rather to extract the maximum possible from both, thereby reducing Tunisia's dependency on either. Even the pro-Western political alignment was as much about the latter's ability to contribute to Tunisia's modernisation as it was about any congruence of values or aspirations.

Even so, Bourguiba could not escape entirely his regional obligations nor did he wish to. Tunisian diplomacy worked on the basis that the country lay at the centre of four concentric circles: the Maghrib, the Arab World, Africa, and the underdeveloped world. He viewed greater Maghrib unity as a moral vision, although he believed it should be established through economic collaboration rather than political or ideological means: "If we succeed in rationalising and organising our production, our outlets and our development in a coherent way, we shall have taken a great step towards Maghrib unity.[5]

For three decades Tunisia's "supreme combatant," Habib Bourguiba, guided his country along a path of social and economic progress that remains practically unequalled in the region. Staunchly pro-Western, Tunisia was once considered a brilliant showcase of development, able to pursue economic progress without the debilitating social upheavals that marked several post-independence African countries.

If one increasingly worrisome aspect detracted from this success, it was Bourguiba's growing authoritarian rule and his continued stranglehold on Tunisian political life. This dominance raised longstanding worries about his succession, concerns heightened by the fact that Tunisia's economic development showed signs of faltering. Even before this relative decline, number of events had indicated the toll exacted by a lingering political and economic malaise.

Despite these signs of unrest and of indications that several groups within Tunisian society would no longer abide by the enforced accommodation that had been imposed upon them, the Bourguiba government showed little inclination to implement political reforms.

Although foreign policy under Bourguiba was very much a reflection of Bourguiba himself, it nonetheless found a deep resonance in a Tunisian identity that saw itself as pragmatic, adaptable, moderate, and modernising. It was not set off course by popular Arab-nationalist sentiments, but rather incorporated the latter into a more profound Tunisian nationalist whole. The brief experiment with socialism did not include any ideological commitments to the Eastern bloc and moves such as the agreement for unity with Libya were aberrations. Bourguiba's own self-belief and his desire for personal greatness were generally pursued through realism rather than rhetoric, and his personal charisma enabled him to lead his country down a non-aligned path that was frequently unpopular with his neighbours but equally did not enslave Tunisia to the agendas of others. Through his control over the party and his popular appeal; he managed to constantly tone down the demands of party leftists, internationalists, and Arab nationalists and sustain a continuity in Tunisian diplomacy that won him respect from both East and West.

In summation, we can see elements of both alteration and continuity in Tunisian foreign policy and policy-making during the decades since independence. Continuity has been evident in the generally pragmatic and non-ideological thrust of policy in the prioritising of development and modernisation friendly international relations, and in the primacy of the presidential figure in determining the specifics of policy.

Change at the international level has coincided with efforts to resolve the domestic economic crisis of the form of Tunisian participation in the process of globalisation. Efforts to increase Tunisian economic independence under Bourguiba have necessarily been replaced by a clear choice in favour of global integration. Foreign policy now serves the search for ever wider markets, for foreign investment, and for connectedness to international communication systems that standardise rather than recognise cultural alternatives. Inevitably, this comes into conflict with domestic public fears of new forms of cultural and economic imperialism. The United States and Europe are seen as both the source of career-enhancing education and employment, and the producers of the most desirable consumer goods, while at the same time representing colonialism in both old and new forms. The regime has clearly made its choice in favour of globalisation, but in order to preserve its own stability and legitimacy it has simultaneously sought to reassure the population with a rhetoric that speaks of a Tunisian way of achieving economic growth.

As with Bourguiba, Tunisia's policy has been principally a balancing act between two poles of interest. On the one hand, strong relations with the West with the United States and the EU in particular are considered essential for economic and military security. On the other, the Arab Maghribi dimension to Tunisia's geographic and social identity draws it into commitments that might at times run counter to the pro-Western alignment. Bourguiba have attempted to reconcile these poles rather than choose between them. Bourguiba perhaps seemed more often to forfeit Arab and Islamic identities for economic development strategies.

President Habib Bourguiba is surely one of the most remarkable figures in African politics, and the history of an entire generation in Tunisia will be written in his biography. It is probably easier for the observer to imagine Tunisia without Bourguiba than for the ordinary Tunisian. His acts of boldness and courage are the history of modern Tunisia: the negotiations for autonomy in 1954; the rejection of Beng Yousef and Arab socialism in 1955; the nationalisation of French land in 1964. But as Moore has pointed out, his action do not represent an ideology as much as a tactic.[6] Bourguiba is unrivaled in making contact with the masses, but his most important skill has been to do this while steering a successful course among the undercurrents of the Tunisian elite. The fact that Tunisian leadership is a relatively homogeneous middle-class group makes his success more remarkable.

References

1. Interview with Jean Daniel in *L'Express,* September 1, 1900 as quoted in Vera Michelee Dean, Builders of Emerging Nations, (New York: Holt, Rinehart and WinSton, 1961), pp. 148-149.
2. Habib Bourguiba, *Electoral Campaign Speeches, October 26 November 5, 1959,* (Tunis : Secretariat of State for Information Publications, 1959), p. 24.
3. C.F. Gallagher, "North African Crossroads, Part III: The Tunisian Hour," *American University Field Staff Reports, (AUFS)* Vol. VII, No. 4, April, 1961, p. 10.
4. Pierre Rossi, *Bourguiba's Tunisia* (Tunis, Editors Kaha, 1967), p. 185.
5. *Ibid.,* p. 180.
6. Cement Henry Moore, *Tunisia Since Independence: The Dynamics of One-Party Government* (Berkeley and Los Angeles, University of California Press, 1965), p. 43. Also Douglas E. Ashford, 'Neo-Destour Leadership and the "Confiscated Revolution", *World Politics,* Vol. XVII January 1965, pp. 215-31.

Bibliography

Primary Sources

Conference of Head of State or Government of Non-Aligned Countries, (1961) Belgrade September, 1-6, 1961, Belgrade, The Publishing House, Jugoslavija.

Conference of Uncommitted Countries (1961) Belgrade, The Publishing House, Jugoslavija.

Foreign Affairs Record (New York) (1969): 15(6): June: 129-133.

League of Arab States Council: Minutes of League.

Nehru, J.L. (1952) *Press Conference,* Delhi, India Information Service.

Nehru, J.L. (1954) *Speeches,* Vol. II, August 1949- February 1953, Delhi Publication Division.

US Congress, House Committee on Foreign Affairs (1961), *Activities of Private US Organisations in Africa. Hearings before the Sub-committee on Africa,* 87th Congress, 1st Session, Washington: Government Printing Office.

US Congress, House of Representatives (1958), *Report of the Special Study Mission to the Near East and North Africa,* Sub-committee on the Near East and Africa, 85th Congress, 2nd Session, Washington: Government Printing Office.

US Congress, Senate (1958), *Committee on Foreign Relations, North Africa and the Mediterranean, Report of Senator Mike Mansfield,* 85th Congress, 2nd Session, Washington: Government Printing Office.

US Department of State Bulletin, 1957-61. Ambassador of Tunisia in India—Embassy of Tunisia, Vasant Vihar, New Delhi.

Books

Abun-Nasr, J.Y.M. (1975) *History of Magbrib* 2nd ed. Cambridge: Cambridge University Press.

Adelson, R. (1995) *London and the Invention of the Middle East:*

Money, Power, and War, 1902-1922, London : Yale University Press.

Al-Fasi, Alal (1970) *The Independence Movements in Arab North Africa,* New York, Octogon Books.

Alnasrawi, A., (1991) *Arab Nationalism, Oil, and the Political Economy of Dependency.* London: Greenwood.

Amin, S. (1970) *The Maghrib in the Modern World,* Harmondswoth, Penguin.

Amin, S. (1978) *The Arab Nation: Nationalism and Class Struggles,* London: Zed Press.

Appadorai, A (1985) *Select Documents on India's Foreign Policy 1947-72.* New-York, Oxford University Press.

Aroial, L.A. and Richard, P. Mitchell (1984) *The Modern Middle East and North Africa.* New York, Macmillan.

Ashford, Dourglas E. (1967a) *National Development and Local Reform: Political participation in Morocco, Tunisia and Pakistan,* Princeton, Princeton University Press.

Ayubi, N., (1995) *Overstating the Arab State: Politics and Society in the Middle East,* London: I.B. Tauris.

Balhaonan, A. (n.d.) *Revolutionary Tunisia* (in Arabic), Tunis, pp. 142-143, quoted in Hassan Sayet Suliman (1987).

Baraket, H. (1985) *Contemporary West Africa.* London, Croomhelm.

Barnett, M, (1999) *Dialogues in Arab Politics: Negotiations in Regional Order:* New York: Columbia University Press.

Bill, James and Robert Spingborg (1990) *Politics in the Middle East.* Glenville, IL: Little Brown.

Blyden, F.W. III, (1964) "The Idea of African 'Neutralism' and 'Non-alignment'; An exploratory Survey", in Kurt London, ed., *New Nations in a Divided World,* New York: Praeger.

Bourguiba, H. (n.d.) *The Independence of Ghana, The Advancement of Africa.* Tunis: Secretariat of State for Information.

Bourguiba, H. (1954) *La Tunisie et la France,* Paris, quoted in H.S. Suliman (1987).

Bourguiba, H. (1956) Speech delivered at the plenary meeting of the UN General Assembly, November 22, 1956. Publication

No. 2, New York: Tunisian Permanent Mission to the United Nations.

Bourguiba, H. (1957) "Nationalism: Antidote to Communism", *Foreign Affairs,* 36(4), July: 657-58.

Bourguiba, H., Jr. (1963) The Foreign Policy of Tunisia in Joseph E,, Black and K.W. Thompson eds., *Foreign Policies in a World of Change,* New York, Harper and Row.

Bourguiba, H (1963a) *Bizerte Has Served the Cause of the Nation and Brought the Arab People Together,* Tunis: Secretariat of State for Cultural Affairs and Orientation.

Bourguiba, H. (1963b) *Vers un socialism authentique,* Tunis.

Boutros-Chali (1964). The Addis Ababa Charter. *Internation Conciliation* 546: January: 7.

Bourguiba, H. (1964) *Liberation of the Soil: an essential element of national sovereignty and pre-requisite of our development* Tunis.

Brown, S.E. (1976) *The Young Tunisians* (Unpublished Ph.D. Dissertation, Institute of Islamic Studies, Montreal, Quebee, McGill University, cited in Norma Salem (1984),) Habib Bourguiba Islam and The Creation of Tunisia, London, Croom Helm.

Bourguiba, H. (1978) Hayati Ara Jihadi (My life, My opinion, My Struggle) Tunis, Ministers Del' information. The French translation of the Arabic text of Bourguiba's speech as published in *Al Nahadah* (10-15 March, 1934} is to be found histories II, pp. 26-32, quoted in Norma Salem (1984), 96.

Brown, L.C. and Micaud, c. (1964). *Tunisia: The Politics of Modernisation,* New York, Praeger.

Brown, L.C. (1984) *International Politics and the Middle East: Old Rules, Dangerous Game,* Princeton, NJ: Princeton University Press.

Cantori, Louis J. and Steven L. Spiegel (1970) *The International Politics of Regions: A Comparative Approach,* Englewood Cliffs, NJ: Prentice Hall.

Cofeman (ed.) (1965), *Education and Political Development,* Princeton, Princeton University Press.

David, L. (1996) *The Middle East and the United States,* Boulder, CO: Westive Press.

David, L Long and Bernard Raich, ed. Government *and Politics of Middle East and North Africa,* Colarado. (1980).

Dawiasha, A. and I,W. Zertman (1988) *Beyond Coercion: The Durability of the Arab State,* London: Croom Helm.

Dessouki, Ati E. Hilal (1993) Dilemma of Security and the Development in the Arab World: Aspects of Linkage", in Koarany, Baghat (1993) *et. al.,* eds. (1993) *The Many Faces of National Security in the Middle East,* New York: MacMillan 76-90.

EI-Ayouty, Y. (1975) *The Organisation of African Unity After Ten Years,* New York. Praeger.

Embasssy of Tunisia, Bulletin (Washington), 23, November 21. Speech at Sayda, 13 November.

Entelis, J.P. and M.A. Tessler, (1986) Republic of Tunisia In David E. Long and Bernard Reich (Ed.) *The Government and Politics of the Middle East and North Africa* Boulder, Westview Press.

Entelis, J.P. and M.A. Tessler, (1986) The Maghrib: An Overview, in David E. Long and Bernard Reich (Ed.) *The Government and Politics of the Middle East and North Africa* Boulder, Westview Press.

Evron, P.Y. (1973), *Nations, Superpowers and Wars,* London: Etek Books.

Gallagher, C.F. (1962) "Tunisia", in G.M. Carter *edd., African Que-party States,* Ithaca, New York: Cornell University Press.

Gallagher, C.F. (1963a) *The United States and Africa,* Cambridge, Mass.: Harvard University Press.

Garas, F. (1956) *Bourguiba et la Naissance d'une nation,* Paris quoted in Hassan Sayet Suliman, (1987): 22.

Gelvin J., (1996) "The Ironic Legacy of the King-Crane Commission", in David W. Lesch, ed., *Te Middle East and the United States: A Historical and Political Reassessment,* Boulder, CO: Westview Press.

Gerges, F., (1994) *The Superpowers and the Middle East: Regional and International Politics,* Boulder, CO: Westview Press.

Gibb, H.A.R. (1953) "The Future of Arab Unity", in Philip W. Ireland, ed., *The Near East,* Chicago: The University of Chicago Press.

Goode, Robert (1962) "State Building as a Determinant of Foreign Policies in the New States", in Laurence W. Martin, ed., *Neutralism and Non-Alignment,* New York: Praeger.

Gopal K., and Kokila, K. Gopal (1981) *West Asia and North Africa —A Documentary Study of Major Crises, 1947-48,* New Delhi: V. I. Pub. 354-55.

Government of Tunisa (1959) *Constitution of the Tunisian Republic,* Tunis: Secretariat of State for Information.

Government Tunisien (1960) *La Gataille economique: Propos du President Habib Bourguiba,* Tunis.

Grissa, A. (1973) Agricultural Policies and Employment: Case. *Study of Tunisia.* OECD.

Guazzone, L., (1997) *The Middle East in Global Change: The Politics and Economics of Interdependence Versus Fragmentation,* London: Macmillan Press.

Hahn, Lorna (1960) *North Africa: Nationalism to Nationhood,* (Washington : Public Affairs Press.

Harik, I. (1987) "The Origins of the Arab State System", in Ghassan Salome, ed., *The Foundations of the Arab State,* London: Groom Helm.

Harold and S. Margaret (1962), *Foundations of International Politics,* New York: D. Van Nostrand Co.

Hasou, T.Y. (1985) *The Struggle for the Arab World,* London, KPI Ltd.

Hassouna, Hussein, A. (1975) *The League of Arab States, and Regional Disputes,* New York, Oceana Publications.

Hey, A.K. (1995) "Foreign Policy in Dependent Staes," in L. Neack, J. Hey, and P. Haney, eds., *Foreign Policy Analysis: Continuity and Change in Its Second Generation,* Englewood Cliffs, NJ: Prentice Hall.

Hopwood, Derek (1992) *Habib Bourguiba of Tunisia: The Tragedy of Longevity,* Hampshire, England: MacMillan.

Hovet, T. Jr. (1963), *Africa in the United Nations.* Evanston, Northwestern University Press.

Hudson, M. (1990) *Arab-Politics: The Search for Legitimacy,* New Haven, CT: Yale University Press.

Ismael, Tareq Y. (1974) *International Relations of the Contemporary Middle East: A Study in World Politics,* Syracuse, NY: Syracuse University Press.

Jabri, M.A. (1985) Evolution of the Maghrib Concept: Facts and Perspectives in H. Barakat, *Contemporary West Africa,* London, Croomhelm.

Jansen, G.H. (1966) *Afro-Asia and Non-alignment* London, Faber and Fabor.

Jean and Simone Lacouture (1958) Le Maroc a l'epreuve, Paris, Editions du Seuil, 358, as quoted in H. Barakat (1985).

Jones, S.B.C. (1945) *Africa and American Security.* New Haven, Yale Institute of International Studies.

Julien, Charles-Andre (1952) *L'Afrique du Mord in Marche,* Paris, Julliard, quoted in H. Baraket (1985): 66.

Karunakaran, K.P. (n.d.) *India in World Affairs 1950-1953: Review of India's Foreign Relation,* Calcutta, Oxford University Press.

Kerekes, Tibor (ed) (1961) The Arab Middle East and Muslim Africa. New York, Frederick A. Paraeger.

Kerr, M., (1971), *The Arab Cold War : Gamal Abd-al-Nasir and His Rivals, 1958-1970,* London: Oxford University Press.

Khalidi R., *et al.,* eds., (1991) *The Origins of Arab Nationalism,* New York: Columbia University Press.

Kienle, E., (1990) *Ba'th Versus Ba'th: The Conflict Between Syria and Iraq,* London: I.B. Tauris.

Knapp, W. (1970) *Tunisia,* London, Thomes and Hudson.

Knapp, W. (1977) *North West Africa: A Political and Economic Survey,* Oxford, Oxford University Press.

Korany, B., (1987) "Alien and Besieged Yet Here to Stay: The Contradictions of the Arab Territorial State", in Ghassan Salame, ed. (1987) *The Foundations of the Arab State,* London: Croom Helm.

Korany, B. (1986) *How Foreign Policy Decisions Are Made in the Third World,* Boulder, CO: Westview Press.

Korany, B. (1988) "The Dialectics of Inter-Arab Relations, 1967-1987", in Abdullah Battah and Yehuda Lukas, eds. (1988) *The Arab-Israeli Conflict: Two Decades of Change,* Boulder, CO: Westview Press.

Korany, B. and et al (eds.) (1993) The Many Faces of National Security in the Middle East, New York: MacMillan: 76-90.

Lacouture, J. (1969) *Quatre Homimes et Leurs Peupes: Sttr-Pouvoir et Sous-Developpment,* Paris: Editions du Seuil, quoted in Dirk Vandewalle, Bourguiba, Charismatic leadership and Tunisian one Party System, *Middle East Journal,* 34(3), Summer.

Ling, Dwight L. (1967) *Tunisia: From Protectorate to Republic,* Bloomigton, Indiana University Press.

Long, D. and Reich, B., (1986) *The Government and Politics of the Middle East and North Africa,* Boulder, Co:Westview Press.

Merlin, Samuel, *The Search for Peace in Middle East* (London, Thomas Yoseloff, 1968).

Micaud, Charles, A. *et al.,* (1964) *Tunisia: The Politics of Modernisation,* New York, Frederick A., Praeger.

Modelski, G.A. (1962) *Theory of Foreign Policy;* New York: Frederick A. Praeger.

Moon, B., (1995B) The State in Foreign and Domestic Policy", in L. Neack, J. Hey and P. Haney, eds., *Foreign Policy Analysis: Continuity and Change in its Second Generation,* Englewood Cliffs, JN: Prentice Hall.

Moore, C.H. (1965) *Tunisia Since-Independence: The Dynamics of one-Party Government,* Los Angeles, University of California Press : 28-29.

Moore, C.H. (1970) *Politics in North Africa: Algeria, Morocco and Tunisia,* Boston, Little, Braun and Co.

Morsy, Magali (1984) *North Africa 1800-1900,* London, Longman.

Mufti, Malik (1996) *Sovereignty Creations: Pan-Arabism and Political Order in Syria and Iraq,* Ithaca and London: Cornell University Press.

Murphy, E.C (2002) The Foreign Policy of Tunisia, in Raymond Hinnebusch and Anoushiravan Ehteshami ed. (2002) *The Foreign Policies of Middle East States,* Boulder, Lynne Rienner.

Noble, P. (1991) "The Arab System: Pressures, Constraints, and Opportunities", in Bahgat Korany and Ali E. Hillal Dessouki, *The Foreign Policies of Arab States: The Challenge of Change,* Boulder, CO: Westview Press.

Owen, R., (1981) *The Middle East in the World Economy, 1800-1945.* London: Methuen.

Owen, R., (1992) "Arab Nationalism, Arab Unity and the Practice of Intra-Arab State Relations", in Roger Owen, ed., *State, Power and Politics in the Making of the Modern Middle East,* London: Routledge, chapter 4, 81-107.

Parker, Richard B. (1984) *West Africa: Regional Tensions and Strategic Concerns,* New York, Praeger.

Parks, N.A. and Husayn, M.T. (1955) *The Crescent in Crisis,* Lawrence: University of Kansas Press.

Perkins, K.J. (1986) *Tunisia: Crossroads of the Islamic and European Worlds,* Boulder, Westview Press.

Perkins, K.J. (2004) *A History of Modern Tunisia,* Cambridge : Cambridge University.

Peter, Calvert (1986) *The Foreign Policies of New States,* Sussex: Wheatsheaf Books.

Pye, L.W. (1961) "The Non-Western Political Process", in James N. Rosenau, ed. (1961) *International Politics and Foreign Policy,* New York: The Free Press of Glencoe.

Ramazani, R.K. (1976) The European Community and the Middle East-in Collin Leagum, *Middle East Contemporary Surveys.* New York, Homes and Meier.

Roberson B.A., (1988) "The Superpowers and the Middle East", *in Global Politics.* Milton Keynes: Open University.

Roberson B.A., ed., (1988) *The Middle East and Europe: The Power Deficit.* London: Routledge.

Rossi, P. (1967) *Bourguiba's Tunisia,* Tunis Editions Katha.

Rudeleck, L. (1967) *Party and People: A Study of Political Change in Tunisia,* Stockholm, Almnquist and Wiksell.

Ruedy, J. (1985) *Historical Influences on Intra-Regional Relations in the Maghrib* in H. Barakat, (1985).

Salem, N., (1984) *Habib Bourguiha, Islam and the Creation of Tunisia,* London, Croom Helm.

Sayigh, Yezid and A. Shlaim (1997), *The Cold War and the Middle East,* Oxford : Claredon.

Secretariat of State for Information (1959), *Tunisian-American Relations,* Tunis: Tunisian Documentation Service.

Sela, Avraham (1998) *The End of the Arab-Israeli Conflict: Middle East Politics and the Quest for Regional Order,* Albany: State University of New York Press.

Special Mission for Economic and Technical Co-operation (1963) *US Aid Programme to Tunisia,* Tunis, Secretariat of State for Cultural Affairs and Orientation, 1963.

Suliman, H.S. (1987) *The Nationalist Movements in the Maghrib,* Upsala, Scandinavian Institute of African Studies.

Sylvester, Anthony (1969) *Tunisia,* London, The Bodley Head.

Taylor, A. (1991), *The Superpowers and the Middle East;* Syracuse, NY : Syracuse University Press.

Tibi, B., (1990) *Arab Nationalism, A Critial Enquiry,* edited and translated by Marion Farouk-Sluglett and Peter Sluglett. London: MacMillan.

Toumeau, R. Le. (1962) *Evolution Politiqite de l'Afrique du Word Musulmane* 1920-1961 2nd ed. Paris, A Colin, quoted in Hassan Sayet Suliman (1987): 22.

Walterstein I. (1974b) *The Modern World System,* New York: Academic Press.

Wendt, A. (1999) *Social Theory of International Politics,* Cambridge: Cambridge University Press.

Wilcox, Francis O. (1962) UN and the Non-aligned Nations. *Headlines Series,* (155) New York: Foreign Policy Association: 28-29.

Yaniv, A. (1987) "Alliance Politics in the Middle East: A Security Dilemma Perspective", in Auriel Braun, ed., *The Middle East in Global Strategy* Boulder, CO: Westview Press.

Zeine, N. Zeine, (1976) *The Emergence of Arab Nationalism, with a Background? Study of Arab-Turkish Relations in the Arab Nationalism, with a Background Study of Arab-Turkish Relations in the Near East,* 3rd ed. Delmar, NY: Caravan Books.

Articles

Aarts, P. (1999) "The Middle East: A Region Without Regionalism or the End of Exceptionalism?" *Third World Quarterly,* 20(5), October : 911-925.

Akhund, H. (1958) The Maghrib in Search of a Union. *Pakistan Horijon,* 11(2) June : 79.

Armstrong, A. (1981) "The Political Consequences of Economic Dependence," *Journal of Conflict Resolution,* 25: 401-428.

Ashford, Douglas D. (1978) Organisation of Co-operatives and Structure of Power in *Tunisia. Journal of Developing Areas,* 1: 317-32.

Ashford, Douglas E. (1965) "Neo-Destour Leadership and the "Confiscated Revolution", *World Politics,* 17, January : 215-31.

Barbour, Nevill (1963) "The Maghrib Liberated, II, *The World Today,* 19(9), September.

Barnett, Michael N. (1993) "Institutions, Roles and Disorder : The Case of the Arab States System" *International Studies Quarterly,* 37(3) September.

Barnett, Machael N. (1995) "Soverignty, Nationalism, and Regional Order in the Arab States System", *International Organisation* 19(3) Summer.

Bourguiba, H. (1958) "We choose the west," *Orbis,* 12(4) Fall: 316.

Bourguiba, H. (1959) *Electoral Campaign Speeches, 26 October - 5 November, 1959,* Tunis : Secretariat of State for Information Publications.

Bourguiba, H. (1961) *Explanations and Clarifications, Tunis:* Secretariat of State for Cultural Affairs and Information.

Bourguiba, H. (1961a) *Signs of an Improvement in International Relations,* Tunis: Secretariat of State for Information and Tourism.

Bourguiba, H. (1961b) "Building a New Tunisia", *American Universities Field Staff Reports,* 2(1), 30 January: 9.

Bourguiba, H (1961c) speech to Joint Meeting of US Congress, 4 May, *Vital Speeches,* 1 June : 487-489.

Bourguiba, H. (1966) The Tunisian Way, *Foreign Affairs,* 44(3), April : 483.

Boutros, Chali (1964) "The Addis Ababa Charter", *International Conciliation,* (546), January : 7.

Brown, L.C. (2001) Bourguiba and Bourguibism Revised: Reflections and Interpretation, *Middle East Journal,* 55(1), Winter :54.

Buzan, B., (1991) "New Patterns of Global Security in the Twenty-First Century", *International Affairs,* 67(3) July : 246-47.

Chattopadhya, K. (1952) Nationalism in Tunisia. *Foreign Affairs Report,* 1 (1 and 2), July-August.

Crutcher, J. (1963) "Pan Africanism: African Odyssey," *Current History,* 44(257), January: 5.

Damis, J. (1985) United States Relations with North Africa, *Current History,* 84(502) May: 193-196.

Daniel, J. (1960) Interview with Bourguiba. *L'Express,* 1st September, 1960 quoted in Vera Michelee Dean (1961), *Builders of Emerging Nations,* New York: Holt, Rinehart and Winston, 148-149.

Foster, B. (1957) "Tunisian Problems", *Contemporary Review,* 192, September : 141.

Frankel, J., (1963) *The Making of Foreign Policy,* London: Oxford University Press.

Gallagher, C.F. (1960) "Ramadan in Tunisia: Aspects and Tunisian Republic," *American Universities Field Staff Reports,* 6(1) 15 April: 13-14.

Gallagher, C.F. (1961) "North African Crossroads-part III: The Tunisian Hour, *American Universities Field Staff Reports,* (7(4), May.

Gallagher, C.F. (1963b) "The Tunisian Way: Moderation and Progress in the Maghrib," *American Universities Field Staff Reports,* 9 (11) November.

Gallagher, C.F. (1964). "A Note on Northern Africa," *American Universities Field Staff Reports,* 10(4), June :14.

Gallard, K., (1960 "The Republic of Bourguiba" *International Journal* 16 Winter: 35.

Galtung, J., (1971) "A Structural Theory of Imperialism", *Journal of Peace Research* 8 (2)81-98.

Gause, G. (1999) "Systematic Approaches to Middle East International Relations", *International Studies Review,* 1 (1) Spring: 11-31.

Hahn, Lorna (1954) "Tunisia: A Challenge to American Foreign Policy, *The Middle Eastern Affairs,* May: 165.

Hahn, Lorna (1964) "North Africa: A New Pragmatism", *Orbis,* 8(1), spring: 139.

Hapttulla, N. (1991) Indo West Asian Relations: The Nehru Era. New Delhi: Allied.

Harber, Charles C. (1973) Tunisian Land Tenure in the Early French Protectorate. *Muslim World* 63(4) October: 307-15.

Hoskyns, Catherine (1964) "The African States and the United Nations, 1958-1964, *International Affairs,* 40, July: 466-467.

Indian and Tunisia: Perspective and Trade and Economic Co-operation (1967) *Indo African Trade Journal,* 3(3), March: 14-15

Kenny, L.M. (1963) "The Goal of Arab Unification, "*International Journal,* 19(1), winter: 50.

Keith Callard (996-61) "The Republic of Bourguiba", *International Journal,* Vol. 16 No. l.

Lacouture, J., (1961) "Dilemma of the Two Bourguibas", *New York Times,* Magazine, August 20:13.

Less Accords Franco-Tunisians du 25 fevrier 1964", *Maghrib,* (2), March-April, 1964.10.

Mansfield, E. and Jack, Snyder (1995) "The Dangers of Democratisation", *International security,* 20(1) Summer: 5-38.

Micaud, Charles A. (1969) Leadership and development: The case of Tunisia *Comparative Politics,* 1 (4): 468-484.

Micaus, Charles A. (1971) Politics in Middle East and North Africa, Africa Today, 18 (4) October.

Moalla, M. (1961) "quelges Aspects del' Experience Monetaries Tunisiennes, Aspects *of Perspectives,* New Series, (5) March: 8-17.

Moon, B.(1995) "Consensus or Compliance? Foreign-Policy Change and External Dependence", *International Organisation,* 39(2) spring: 297-330.

Moore, C.H. (1963) "Bourgibism in Tunisia," *Current History:* 44(257), January: 40.

Moore, C.H. (1962) "The Neo Destour Party of Tunisia: A Structure for Democracy", *World Politics,* Vol. 14, No. 3.

Mortimer, E. (1978) Tunisia: Why the Socialist Experiment has Failed *The Times,* (London), 28 September.

Ramazani, R.K. (1964) "Cultural Change and Intellectual Response in Algeria, Tunisia, and Iran", *Comparative Studies in Society and History, (2),* January, 225-226.

Rivlin B *"Tunisian Nationalist Movement:* Four *Decades of Evolution,* Rees, G. (1959) "The Green", *The Encounter,* September. 39.

Ruf, W.K. (1971) The Bizerte Crisis, A Bourguibist Attempt to Resolve Tunisia's Border Problems, *The Middle East Journal*', 25(2): 2010-11.

Schissel, Howard (1984) Tunisia Facing a Future Without Bourguiba, *Africa Report,* 20 (6), Novemeber-December.

Schwarzenbach, E.G. (1963) "A report on the Africans' Addis Ababa Conference", *Swiss Review of World Affairs,* July: 10.

Shepherd, G.W. (1959) "Tunisia and Arab Nationalism," *Current History,* 35(212), 16, Winter: 49-52.

Seigman, H. (1962) "Arab Unity and Disunity", *The Middle East Journal,* 16, Winter: 49-52.

Sterling, Claire (1957) "Habib Bourguiba: Revolution and Responsibility, *The Reporter,* 5 September: 27.

Thompson William R., (1970) "The Arab Sub-System and Feudal Pattern of Interaction: 1965", *Journal of Peace Research,* (7): 172-203.

Tunisia Faces and Future ", *Le Monde Economique,* (1956) June : 172-203.

Walterstein, I., (1974a) "The Rise and Future Demise of the World Capitalist System: Concepts for Comparative Analysis", *Comparative Studies in History and Society,* 6(4), 387-415.

White, F. (1958) "Dilemma of a leader who wanted to be our Friend," *Life,* 24 February.

Young K.T., (1961) New Politics in New States. *Foreign Affairs,* 39(3), April: 503.

Young, O., (1968) "Political Discontinuities in the International System", *World Politics,* 20(3) April.

Ziadeh Nicol. A., *Whither North Africa.* Aligarh Institute of Islamic Affairs,1957.

Newspapers

Afriques Action (New York)

Jeune Afrique (Paris)

La Petit Matin (Tunis)

L'Action (Daily, Tunis)

L'Action (Weekly, Tunis)

Le Monde (Paris)

Le Presse (Tunis)

The International Herald Tribune (Paris)

The New York Times (New York)

The Times (London)

The Times of India (New Delhi)

Washington Post (Washington)

Foreign Affairs Record,

Ambassador of Tunisia in India—Embassy of Tunisia, Vasant Vihar, New Delhi.

Index

F

N

Bibliography

Primary Sources

Books